The Provocation of the Senses in Contemporary Theatre

Routledge Advances in
Theatre and Performance Studies

The Provocation of
the Senses in
Contemporary Theatre

Stephen Di Benedetto

Routledge
Taylor & Francis Group
New York   London

First published 2010
by Routledge
711 Third Avenue, New York, NY 10017

Simultaneously published in the UK
by Routledge
2 Park Square, Milton Park, Abingdon, Oxon OX14 4RN

Routledge is an imprint of the Taylor & Francis Group, an informa business

First issued in paperback 2011

© 2010 Taylor & Francis

Typeset in Sabon by IBT Global.

Library of Congress Cataloging-in-Publication Data
Di Benedetto, Stephen.
    The provocation of the senses in contemporary theatre / by Stephen DiBenedetto.
        p. cm. — (Routledge advances in theatre and performance studies)
    Includes bibliographical references and index.
    1. Performing arts.   2. Senses and sensation.   3. Human information processing.
4. Performing arts—Philosophy.   I. Title.
    PN1584.D5 2010
    792.01'3—dc22
    2009045097

ISBN13: 978-0-415-50699-1 (pbk)
ISBN13: 978-0-415-87267-6 (hbk)
ISBN13: 978-0-203-85209-5 (ebk)

To Anthony and RoseMarie—
the perfect blend of art and science

Contents

Preface
Why Contemporary Performance
Can Provoke the Senses

Theatrical practice can benefit greatly from an understanding of contemporary neuroscientific discoveries. This study lays the foundation for considering the physiological basis of the power of theatre practice to affect human behavior. What do these theories enable us to see about the ways in which the theatrical event is created? I present a general summary of the ways that the senses function in relation to cognitive science and physiology, and then offer an overview of dominant trends of discussion of the realm of the senses in performance. Following on, I offer examples of how those ideas are illustrated in recent theatrical presentations, and how the different senses form the structure of a theatrical event. Finally, I suggest the possible implications that these sensorial ideas have upon our understanding of theatrical composition, audience response, and the generation of meaning. A corollary of this project suggests what theatre artists can do with recent research on the nature of the senses.

In many ways, artists have intuitively been using concepts that science is only now beginning to explain. It is knowledge of the world as expressed through material art objects. By its nature, the success of a theatrical performance relies on the subjective responses of its attendants. In what may be referred to as a "traditional" perceptual experience, the interactions between spectator and performers are modulated by our conscious reception of everyday experience that creates a personal understanding of the characters and the situations in which they are involved. As a result, the attendant can utilize well-practiced analytical strategies to make rational judgments about the intent and success of the theatrical work. However, when performances are operating in a sphere outside the modes of conventional representation, the attendant may not be able to judge the work by utilizing the experiences that have modulated his or her sensorial perceptions. This latter situation is a common phenomenon in modern and contemporary artistic endeavor. Attendants find that their responses have become deranged and confusing. For example, in the field of dance, the choreography of classical ballet was developed around well-defined sets of conventional poses and steps. Appreciation of the quality of the performance was strongly dependent on the ability of the dancers to execute these steps.

Contemporary dance, pioneered by Martha Graham in the early 1920s and 1930s, added the concept of movement designed to express emotional content of the performance that was unique to the work. Attendant appreciation of this contemporary work required the development of a new set of sensorial understandings, which did not come easily to many attendees. Recent neuroscientific discovers have proved that the brain is plastic and all sensations it experiences continually modify how it perceives the world. Theatrical performance has the potential to change our experience of the world and therefore, the potential to change our ability to perceive the world in a new way. This book explores how being aware of and marshaling one's senses can enrich the viewing of a contemporary theatrical presentation. By tracing the transformational power of the senses and the ways in which performance affects and influences attendant understandings of artistic expression we can begin to consider how sensorial perception is intrinsic to the power of theatrical representation to transform the human experience.

As humans, our biological composition dictates that our knowledge and exploration of the world take place through the visual, aural, tactile, and aromatic. Our senses guide us and confirm for us our perceptual awareness. Most often, in our interpretations and analyses of artistic composition we have focused on hearing and sight; however, proximity to the performers and their bodily exertions adds to the level of information that we pick up while observing the performance. Sensorial analysis examines the reception by attendants of proximate odors, sounds, and textures. How these sensations originate, and are intended to activate sensorial interpretation, is illustrated in works by Franko B, a performance artist who deliberately stimulates visceral responses within attendants with the formation of his live compositions. He wants his performance work to be like the active experience of going to a museum to see a beautiful painting. However, he wants more than an image—he wants attendants to be able to smell it and touch it too. Franko B employs a range of non-traditional media, such as bodily effluvia, to insure that his attendants will have a range of sensorial experiences. In addition, the configuration of his intimate live art performances encourages the active participation of attendants in the event. While images generated during the performance may fade from memory, a semblance of the experience will remain within the memory of the attendant. The goal is common to all theatrical performance, but the method is unconventional, indeed often disturbing. Whereas the distinctive method of presentation may not by itself provide a rational understanding of what is occurring on stage, the unexpected visceral experience is intended to offer the attendants a pathway for participating in the performance. I choose examples that stretch the notion of performance to suggest potential applications of the concepts introduced here, and thereby expand our understanding of the role that the senses play in our interpretation of the theatrical event.

The Provocation of the Senses describes the reception and analysis of sensorial theatrical events as seen through the lens of neurology, cognitive science, and phenomenology. Its introductory chapter sets up an explanation of the ways in which human physiology is attendant to both sensory stimulation within an artistically mediated event and to the direction of non-verbal thinking and analysis. Description of a range of performative events connect the ways in which stimuli trigger events that lead to the subjective monitoring of sensory stimulation, and then potentially serve as data to support theoretical analysis. Each subsequent chapter explores, in particular, how each of the five senses are processed, considers how they are used in performance, and what this suggests about the power and function of theatre. Examples are drawn from a variety of international performance modes and traditions that blur the traditional definitions of performance and visual art, including performance art, dance, visual art, and theatre. Case studies demonstrate the ways in which the senses come together during the duration of an event to create a visceral experience for the attendant.

Chapter 1 introduces the physiology and neurology of the human body as a receiver of outside stimuli. First the brain and its processing mechanisms are described (what parts of the brain do what), and then current notions of perception, consciousness, and sensorial interpretation are outlined. Case studies explore the ways in which theatrical and other live artistic creations capture the attention of the neural networks of the body and make real experiences that might not be accessible in our everyday interactions. Chapter 2 considers the role light and movement play upon our physiological perception and the ways in which theatre practitioners have manipulated physiological traits to keep us stimulated and interested in what is happening on stage. After an introduction to the physiology of sight, I describe how visual stimulation entices our brains to pay attention to what is going on in the theatrical event. Case studies describe movement and illusion, spatial organization, setting, and light and dark to demonstrate the potentials of stimulating the attendant through visual effects. Chapter 3 considers art experiences where touch is more actively sought as a means for attendants to experience the art work in a more direct fashion; cutting out the middle-ground of haptics or synesthethia. After describing what is touch and what are the ways in which our body processes stimuli, I present case studies that explore the implication of touch on performance and the most commonly thought of manifestations of touch within our conventional assumptions of the interaction between the performer and the audience. Chapter 4 considers how gustation and olfaction factor in performance, and the ways in which harnessing these alert sensations intrinsically defines theatre as a live event that connects the attendant to the artistically mediated environment. Case studies trace technological experimentation and olfactory activation, historical forays into olfactory stimulation, and feasting as a theatrical event. Chapter 5 discusses how noises, vibrations, and other stimulators of cochlear perception demonstrate the intimate nature of aural stimulation and the use of sound to create atmosphere and the generation of a visceral mood in the context of performance. After an overview of the anatomy and physiology of the auditory system, I consider how sound captures our brain's attention and triggers visceral reactions that can be analyzed. Case studies suggest the potential of sound composition and demonstrate the importance of cultivating listening to a wide array of sounds in the context of performance. Chapter 6 explores the ways in which being attentive to the performance allows us to hone our abilities to identify what is causing our bodies to respond and, in turn, identify how our bodies are being stimulated. Awareness enriches our ability to interpret the form and function of the theatrical event. A result of the artist arranging the components of composition to provoke the attendant's experience is that each new experience creates neuronal pathways that forever change the brain. Theatre has the ability to keep our brains flexible. Case studies describe somatic adventures for the percipient attendant to explore the ways in which the theatrical event uses the social experience of theatre to keep alive the events of the past, making real the imaginary, or making present the past.

This study presents an overview of the ways in which the brain, the mind, and the senses function; an exploration of the effects of taste, touch, smell, hearing, and vision have when activated in performance; and an interrogation of the ways in which an understanding of how taste, touch, smell, hearing, and vision affect perception and the ways in which sensorial techniques may affect future theatrical performances. As a result, we can understand why contemporary performance makes use of sensorial stimuli to provoke an attendant's experience of theatre.

Acknowledgments

This project would not have been completed without the help of so many. In particular, I need to thank Maria Gali-Stampino for her encouragement, feedback, and counsel, Bruce McConachie for his advice on strengthening my argument, and Erica Wetter and Talia Rogers for their help getting this project to press. Also, this project would have never been completed without the support provided by the University of Miami and the 2008 and 2009 Max Orovitz Summer Award in the Arts & Humanities. Grateful acknowledgment is made for permission to reprint the material extracted from: Coco Fusco, "The Other History of Intercultural Performance." *TDR* 38, no. 1 (1994): 143–167; Jim Drobnick, ed., *Aural Cultures*, Toronto & Banff: YYZBOOKS & Walter Phillips Gallery Editions, 2004); Max Keller, *Light Fantastic*. Munich: Prestel, 1999; Claudia Castellucci, Romeo Castellucci, Chiara Guidi, Joe Kelleher, and Nicholas Ridout. *The Theatre of Sociètas Raffaello Sanzio*. Abingdon and New York: Routledge, 2007; Molly Steenson, "What is Burning Man?" http://www.burningman.com; Alison Croggon, Theatre Notes blog, theatrenotes.blogspot.com; Sarah Cowan, "MIT's 'Sensorium' Brings Sixth Dimension to Five Senses." *Tufts Daily*, November 2, 2006. Finally, I must thank Juliet Di Benedetto for her patience, love, and solace, which enabled me to complete this project.

1 Our Sensing Bodies

A Multidisciplinary Approach to Understanding Live Theatrical Experience

Theatrical form is an expression of contemporary thought processes; the world changes, and so too do our ways of representing it. Virtual technology has transformed modes of creating and viewing art, thrusting the art world into a state of flux where live art events often occur in unfamiliar environments and where the attendant may not be able to judge the work by utilizing conventional analytical modes. An understanding of physiology and neurology of the human body as a receiver of outside stimuli can assist the artist in using sensorial stimuli to compose a live theatrical event and create an in-between state of experience and awareness. Likewise, the attendant can be aided in the process of restructuring those stimuli through cognitive thought processes for a visceral analysis of the event. I will explore how application of theories drawn from cognitive science and physiology affect live art practice and the attendant's experience of the performance. To be an "attendant" of a live theatrical performance does not necessarily imply conscious awareness of sensorial stimulation. Whereas our bodies are constantly attendant to the world around us, they note change and decide whether or not to respond. Mimesis, then, stimulates our brains. As Michael Gazzanga argues, to stimulate the brain is to constantly remodel its neural pathways to accommodate and store new information.[1]

Theatre Studies has a long tradition of speaking about the visual in relation to art practice that takes into consideration physiology as well as perception and psychology. As advances in neurobiology and neuro-psychology continue to elucidate for us many of our assumptions about theatrical and visual representation, it is important that we look to these scientific hypotheses as we investigate contemporary live performance. Many of the ideas and concepts outlined here from neuroscience, cognitive science, and psychology are generalized and basic from a scientific standpoint; however, they serve to instigate a series of questions about the relationship between sensorial perception and performance. Scientific discoveries are rapidly changing our understanding of the human brain and the ways in which we experience and understand the world. Those from whose work I draw have extrapolated the conclusions of published scientific experiments to explain in layman's terms the status of brain science today. It is not my intent to add to that body of knowledge, but rather to consider what implications these scientific explanations of the senses can suggest to theatre and performance scholars and to practitioners. There are already a number of theatre scholars working on various approaches that articulate systematically the content of seminal cognitive science researches.[2] Taken together, all of these studies provide the foundation for understanding the ways in which cognitive neuroscience can provide a new framework for understanding theatrical expression. To understand the ways in which stimulation of human brain processes can be used in the creation and interpretation of theatrical and performance practice, we need to consider how our perception and processing systems function. Physiology and cognitive science provide a framework for theatre studies to consider and apply our understanding of mimesis and its significance. The usefulness of vision, hearing, touch, taste, and smell lies in how they each aid cognition, and for our purposes, it is how they aid the creation, reception, and interpretation of mimetic representation.

The brain is what it is because of the structural and functional properties of neurons. It contains between one billion and one trillion neurons that signal by transmitting electrical impulses along their axons. It is through these impulses that we perceive, monitor, and interpret the data that our senses collect. The fragments of sensations that sight, touch, hearing, taste, and smell present to the nervous system are the means by which we create the world around us. Typical neurons are made up of three parts: its dendrites, the cell body, and the axon. Dendrites branch out to obtain information from other neurons and bring it to the cell body. The cell body contains the nucleus of the cell and DNA. Finally, the axon brings information away from the cell body to other neurons. It is a cable of sorts that can reach the extremities. A synapse is the point of communication between one neuron and another. They transmit electrical impulses towards the dendrites of the neighboring neurons. The process is like a relay race, passing messages from the senses to each neuron until the message reaches the brain for processing. All of the senses are sending fragments of information that the brain puts together into a percept. A neuron receives either an excitatory signal that triggers it to fire off and send a message to the next neuron or an inhibitory signal that tries to prevent the firing. Neuronal messages can be turned on and shut off depending on how much stimuli fuel them. Because neurons do not touch, they depend on chemical massagers to bridge the gap of the synapse to excite or inhibit action. It is like a giant stadium wave cresting and falling into a frenzy of activity. When fewer people participate, the wave dies out. All we sense and perceive relies on this chemical process, whose goal is cognition.[3]

To understand how cognition works, we first must familiarize ourselves with the basic mechanics of the brain and the senses, because they provide the input that cognition uses to create thought. The brain is one of the largest of adult organs, consisting of over one hundred billion neurons and weighing about three pounds. It is typically divided into four parts: the cerebrum; the cerebellum; the diencephalon (thalamus and hypothalamus); and the brain stem (medulla oblongata, pons, midbrain), which is an extension of the spinal cord.

The most important part for our purposes is the cerebrum because it is most closely related to the receiving and processing of the senses. We are what we are because within the human cortex lies our sensory capacities and sensitivities to the external world, our motor skills, our aptitudes for reasoning and imagining, and our unique language abilities. The cerebrum is made up of two sides, the right and left cerebral hemispheres, which are interconnected by the corpus callosum. Though asymmetrical, the two hemispheres are mirrored, each with centers for receiving sensory (afferent) information and for initiating motor (efferent) responses. The cerebral cortex is the outermost layer of the cerebral hemispheres, which is composed of gray matter. It also is divided into two hemispheres, both of which are able to analyze sensory data, perform memory functions, learn new information, form thoughts, and make decisions. The cortex is divided into four lobes: frontal, parietal, temporal, and occipital (named after the cranial bones under which they are situated). The frontal lobe is involved in planning, organizing, problem solving, the ability to concentrate and to attend, personality, and a variety of higher cognitive functions including behavior and emotions. The parietal lobes contain the primary sensory cortex, which controls sensation (touch, pressure). Behind the primary sensory cortex is a large association area that controls fine sensation (judgment of texture, weight, size, shape). The temporal lobes allow us to tell the smell of grease paint from the smell of bacon grease and a hooting owl from a car horn. They also help in sorting new information and are believed to be responsible for short-term memory, as well as being responsible for visual reception and processing. It also contains association areas that help in the visual recognition of shapes and colors. In summary, the cerebrum gives us awareness of one's self and one's environment, thought, reasoning and memory, vision, hearing, touch, speech, language, motor control, and emotions. It controls our responses to the theatrical events that we are attendant to.

The cerebellum is the second largest brain structure. It sits below the cerebrum. Like the cerebrum, the cerebellum has an outer cortex of gray matter and two hemispheres. It receives and relays information by way of the brain stem. Its major functions have to do with skeletal–muscle control: balance and equilibrium of the trunk; muscle tension, spinal nerve reflexes, posture, and balance of the limbs; and fine motor control and eye movement. This is the system that enables us to walk into the theatre, watch the movements of the actors, and turn our heads to better see a lighting effect that might occur in the periphery of our vision.

The diencephalon is located between the cerebrum and the midbrain. It is made up of the thalamus and hypothalamus. The thalamus is a bilateral mass of gray matter serving as the main synaptic relay center that receives and relays sensory information to and from the cerebral cortex. The hypothalamus is a collection of ganglia and is associated with the pituitary gland. It has a variety of functions, including sensing changes in body temperature, controlling autonomic activities, controlling the pituitary gland, regulating appetite, functioning as part of the arousal or alerting mechanism, and linking the mind (emotions) to the body. It allows us to notice when the air conditioning clicks on and reminds us to have a snack at intermission. In summary, it controls voluntary movement and motor integration, perception, sensory, and mind–body integration, temperature, and appetite.

The brain stem controls our most basic life functions: breathing; heart rate; blood pressure; reflex centers for pupillary reflexes and eye movements; and vomiting, coughing, sneezing, swallowing, and hiccupping. All functions of the brain stem are associated with cranial nerves. There are twelve pairs of cranial nerves: ofactory (smell), optic (vision), oculomotor (eyelid and eyeball movement), trochlear (turns eye downward and laterally), trigeminal (chewing, face and mouth, touch and pain), abducens (turns eye laterally), facial (controls most facial expressions, secretion of tears and saliva, taste), vestibulocochlear (hearing, equilibrium sensation), glossopharyngeal (taste, senses carotid blood pressure), vagus (senses aortic blood pressure, slows heart rate, stimulates digestive organs, taste), spinal accessory (controls swallowing movements), and hypoglossal (controls tongue movements).[4] These are the basic tools the actor uses to move across the stage, speak lines, and create a character. Although a thorough understanding of this biology is not necessary for theatre practitioners, becoming aware of the basic biology of brain function that we share with humankind can remind us that despite culture, race, and identity we all share the most basic elements that define our experience of the world as a human.

How and what the senses perceive are important to developing an understanding of the potential interpretive strategies that are available as we become attendant to sensory perception. Our senses are any of the physical processes by which stimuli are received, transduced (converted from one form to another), and conducted as impulses to be interpreted in the brain. The spinal cord is the main nerve trunk, bringing all the sensory data of the body up to the brain and carrying the control signals back to the organs of the body. The nervous system is the body's information gatherer, storage center, and control system. Its overall functions are to collect information about the body's external/internal states and transfer this information to the brain to analyze and send impulses out to initiate appropriate motor responses to meet the body's needs. All information transfer in the brain and in the nervous system is mediated by neurons. They trigger any cerebral process, ranging from the higher functions (learning and language) to the simplest spinal reflex. Neurons bring sensory data from both internal and external sensors about the state of the organs, the working of muscles, the perception of sound vision, taste, touch and smell, which are all handled by way of bundles of nerves known as the "afferent nerves" traveling into the brain. Efferent nerve bundles traveling out of the brain control our muscles and our general response to incoming stimuli. All the various inputs are channeled into the nervous system.

The nervous system is divided into the central nervous system (CNS) and the peripheral nervous system (PNS). They function together, with nerves from the periphery entering and becoming part of the CNS, and nerves from the central entering and becoming part of the PNS. In the PNS, collections of neurons are called ganglia; in the CNS, collections of neurons are called nuclei. The CNS is made up of the spinal cord and the brain. The spinal cord conducts sensory information from the PNS (both somatic and autonomic), and the brain conducts motor information from the brain to our various effectors. The somatic nervous system consists of peripheral nerve fibers that send sensory information to the CNS and motor nerve fibers that project to skeletal muscle. The autonomic nervous system is divided into three parts: the sympathetic nervous system, the parasympathetic nervous system, and the enteric nervous system. Together they control smooth muscle of the internal organs and glands.

Somatosensory receptors are our input to the nervous system in the form of our five senses. Pain, temperature, and pressure are known as somatic senses. Sensory receptors are classified according to the type of energy the receptor can detect and respond to. These include the mechanoreceptors, which detect and respond to energy related to hearing and balance; stretching; photoreceptors, which detect and respond to light; chemoreceptors, which detect and respond to energy related to smell and taste, as well as internal sensors in the digestive and circulatory systems; thermoreceptors, which respond to and detect changes in temperature; and electroreceptors, which detect electrical currents in the surrounding environment.[5]

PERCEPTION, CONSCIOUSNESS, ATTENTION, AND EMOTIONAL RESPONSE

Perception, consciousness, and attention are the component means by which we understand and interpret stimuli. There are a number of conflicting theories being explored by researchers offering multiple perspectives of the ways in which the brain processes and interprets data. The different disciplines of evolutionary biology, neuropsychology, and memory studies all offer differing interpretations of new discoveries in brain science. Although these fields lack definitive answers of why we respond to the world in the way that we do, they suggest that the senses shape our consciousness. The aim of considering these concepts in relation to performance is to suggest that they also will determine how a theatre of the future may be willfully created, and how its experience may be understood more readily through conscious analytical methodologies. Arlette Steri offers one perspective:

> Perception is a process by means of which the organism becomes aware
> of its environment on the basis of information taken in by its senses
> . . . from the cognitive standpoint, one of the functions of perception
> is to interpret sensory data, and hence to process information . . . This
> function is assumed to involve two types of processing: data drive . . .
> and concept-or-representation-driven. . . . the part played by each type
> depends on whether the processing bears primarily on the sensory in-
> formation drawn directly from stimuli, or on the subject's knowledge,
> expectations, motivations and so on.[6]

Our perception is influenced by both conscious and unconscious mechanisms. We both assess sensory data that streams into our neuro-pro-
cessing center, as well as assess sensory data according to experience.
Whereas we are aware of make-believe, there is little difference between
our reception of mimesis or reality, because they share the stimulations
of neurons that fire within the different regions of the brain. As the brain
fires and experiences the sensations that stimulation and context provide, the triggers become a part of our experience. The attendant's body
is pivotal to the theatrical event because the body is both the means by
which the attendant's brain receives stimulus and the means by which the
brain interprets the event.

Norman Doidge describes our continuous active engagement with the
world around us:

> The perceiving brain is active and always adjusting itself. Seeing is as
> active as touching, when we run our fingers over an object to discover
> its texture and shape. Indeed, the stationary eye is virtually incapable
> of perceiving a complex object. Both our sensory *and* our motor corti-
> ces are always involved in perceiving.[7]

Before we make conscious sense of a stimulus:

> Information taken in by the sensory systems provokes a sensation.
> Each system detects only information that is specific to it, and for this
> reason, it remains incomplete and fragmented. At this level, process-
> ing is automatic, pre-wired, [and] essentially inaccessible to conscious-
> ness . . . before the stimulus is identified, various grouping together
> and breaking down processes are performed on the sensory flow ac-
> cording to the perceiver's knowledge. This knowledge is what drives
> the perceptual structuring process and enables object identification . . .
> Attentional processes also play a major role by determining what in-
> formation gets selected . . . The identification of an object generates a
> series of multimodal representations (visual, auditory, somesthetic and
> possibly gustatory and olfactory), as well as motor, lexical, and seman-
> tic representations.[8]

Once this process has occurred we become conscious of some of the information generated, and we can begin to make sense of our emotions and our feelings. This is a biological process; "[c]onsciousness as we commonly think of it, from its basic levels to its most complex, is the unified mental pattern that brings together the object and the self."[9] As we respond to a theatrical event, consciousness leads us to make personal associations with the material that is being performed in front of and around us. By recognizing patterns, we pay closer attention to the details of the event and begin to make conscious our understanding of the objects. We are designed to respond to sensory stimulation.

Sensory stimulation is tied to our survival, and as a result we use our experience to make judgments about different types of stimulation. Antonio Damasio explains:

> Although the precise composition and dynamics of the emotional responses are shaped in each individual by a unique development and environment, the evidence suggests that most, if not all, emotional responses are the result of a long history of evolutionary fine-tuning. Emotions are part of the bioregulatory devices with which we come equipped to survive.[10]

Therefore, the senses utilized in the composition of a theatrical event create an in-between state of experience and awareness. It is this constant monitoring over time that allows us to make sense of the sensations we experience. Whereas I might enjoy watching Stellarc hang from meat hooks piercing his skin on points of his back, others may recoil in horror or discomfort. This does not mean that we are not experiencing the same stimulation, merely that we are modifying the input differently according to our own cultural or environmental conditioning. Those of us familiar with Stellarc's practice will have a more intense neuronal response capable of analyzing his performance than those unfamiliar with the performance traditions that he is using.

Still, because we share a basic biology, artists can be certain that they can use some strategies to insure a biological reaction to their work. Damasio's finding states, "[t]his is why in spite of the infinite variations to be found across cultures among individuals and over the course of a life span we can predict with some success that certain stimuli will produce certain emotions,"[11] and therefore they can be made use of in the creation of artistic stimulation. However, consciousness may not be as important as we like to think. A majority of the most complex levels of understanding and thinking is preconscious. Our intellect is the last step in a series of sensations that inform the brain, which then decides whether to, and how to, respond. It is only later that we can put our embodied experience into words or actions. Bernard Baars asserts:

> Sensory perception is the input mode of the nervous system, and we are exquisitely conscious of the details of each sense impression. But

thinking seems to be devoid of conscious qualities, except where it involves inner speech; but inner speech seems to be a simulation of ordinary outer speech input. Likewise, if we look at speech and action
we seem to have much less conscious appreciation of details than in
sensation, except where actions create sensory feedback, which is of
course nothing but sensory input again! In sum, it seems as if we get
our most detailed conscious information from sensations, or simulated
inner sensations: qualitative, percept-like events.[12]

Sensations are triggered before thought and the intellect, though our senses
are already interpreted by embodiment, so this pre-consciousness does not
tell the whole story. Our neural pathways have preferences based on our
own personal experiences of the world, and therefore, have already pre-
determined the eventual interpretation of sensory data. The brain's processing center is never objective. Plato may have preferred the calmness of
rationality to the imprecise qualities of feelings and emotions, but he did
not account for the skewed data that had already been shaped to fit the
whims of the brain. Sensations are not to be trusted because they cannot
be controlled; however, the brain has done its thinking earlier. It is this
process of triggering uncontrollable involuntary responses that is of most
interest to any discussion of how we can account for the role of sensation
in communication, perception, and theatrical expression. If we understand
how this happens, then we can understand its power and how we can harness it to create a powerful theatrical experience. Theatre practice can help
train neural preferences.

According to Baars, whose views are contentious among researchers,
all current unified theories of cognition involve theatrical metaphors. He
describes consciousness as a brightly lit spotlight of attention onstage,
whereas the rest of the stage corresponds to immediate working memory.
The director and the production team are those who seamlessly construct
and shape conscious experience unseen by the audience. Simultaneously
the audience operates as an array of unconscious mechanisms, such as
automatic routines (impulses that guide speaking or eye, hand, and finger
movements), autobiographical, declarative, and implicit memories. These
routines maintain consistent attitudes, beliefs, facts, and decorum, rather
like the functions of the chorus in Ancient Greek tragedy. Other functions
occur outside of awareness, such as the working memory. Onstage an actor
may inhabit the spotlight center stage, but there is a whole production team
working backstage.[13] Despite our reliance on consciousness to make us
aware of what we think about the world, there is far more going on. We
never are aware of all the factors that influence our understanding of what
we experience. Our working memory is that inner domain in which we talk
to ourselves. It is usually thought to include "inner speech" (what you hear
yourself saying while silently reading this passage) and "visual imagery"
(the mind's eye, where you imagine your wife coming home from work

and interrupting your reading). It is only when the spotlight of attention focuses on an element in the working memory that the conscious contents reveal themselves. We are also cursorily attentive to actions that occur in the fringe of the focus:

> We have feelings of knowing about items in working memory that are not currently conscious. Moreover, we seem to have feelings of knowing about things that are readily available to consciousness, though they are not conscious at the moment—our ability to find known words, our mood, our ability to act and control some mental functions, our basic knowledge about friends, relatives, and ourselves, and much more.[14]

It is in this hazy area where some action may grab our attention and attract our automatic functioning, and we will shift our gaze to that spot. We even, at times, have control of whether to redirect the current stream into consciousness when something more urgent happens. This is not to say that it is impossible to track our responses to sensory stimulation; merely it demonstrates the importance of becoming cognizant of the potential meaning generated by stimulation from sensory input. We need to work to bring to consciousness our visceral perception of mediated events.

It is also important to note that we cannot release ourselves from the constraints of our physical states. Our organism monitors events outside of consciousness even when we are attentive to a task at hand. Consciousness allows us to focus on one experience until a change in circumstances demands out attention.[15] Our individual brain connections color all our perceptions, and the moment-to-moment complexities of living can interfere with our monitoring of events. Our brains prioritize on the basis of survival and will filter out unnecessary data. If we have ever attended a play after stepping off a trans-Atlantic flight, while sitting in the dark, our bodies may have succumbed to sleep no matter how intriguing the play.

We are constantly bombarded by stimulators. If our brains did not limit our attention, we would be overwhelmed by input. Imagine constantly feeling our clothes against our skin, our arm hair resting on it, and the humming of the electric light. It would be as if we were at a party and everyone was speaking to us at the same time demanding an immediate and simultaneous response to millions of questions. It is impossible to be conscious of all that we sense. Conscious ideas occur one after another, are highly structured, and internally consistent. Each idea competes for access to consciousness. While we watch a play, it is difficult to solve an abstract problem. However, we are able to juggle both conceptual qualities as well as sensory qualities of an experience. For example, as we see the visual qualities of printed text while we read, hearing it in our heads evokes an aural quality that also allows us to grasp its meaning. These experiences also trigger emotions and thoughts. Consciousness is competitive, and it is necessary for our organism to prioritize conscious content. It does not mean that the stimulation was not received, incorporated, and made a part of the conscious thought, but rather that we can only be conscious of a limited amount of the thoughts that we process.

Our bodies are good at keeping tabs on bits of information and guessing based on stored memory. Prediction is going on all the time in everything that we do. Each time we go into the living room to watch television, our brains guess the location of the couch and the weight of the remote control based on past experience. It is when these predictions fail that we take notice. Gazzaniga terms this as a "what-the-heck alert."[16] It is that moment when we plop down where the couch's cushion should be and fall an extra four inches. Where did it go? Our expectations did not match predicted pattern. Once the alert reaches our attention we begin to monitor and identify change to determine if action is necessary. From the perspective of performance when a new element is introduced into the action or the composition of the blocking, such as a new color or a new character, then the attendants begin to take notice and determine how the introduced element contributes to their overall prediction of what will happen during the course of the scene.

Temporality is essential in the possessing and identification of stimuli. Regardless of the sense used as we examine an object, we make comparisons moment to moment in aiding its identification. As Doidge explains, all stimuli are examined by way of multiple sensory receptors:

> An operator is a processor in the brain that, instead of processing input from a single sense, such as vision, touch, or hearing, processes more abstract information. Our operator processes information about *spatial relationships*, another *movement*, and another *shapes*. Spatial relationships, movement, and shapes are information that is processed by several of our senses. We can both feel and see movement and shapes. A few operators may be good for only a single sense (e.g. the color operator), but spatial, movement, and shape operators process signals from more than one . . . An operator is selected by competition . . . the ablest group of neurons is selected to do the task.[17]

As a result, multiple data streams are compared and selected according to the quality of information that it provides to the brain. Our brains are flexible; whereas different portions of the brain may have different tasks assigned to them, they are able to take on other functions and operations when necessary. Even when a sense receptor is damaged, it is still possible to perceive that sense. Other brain cells and regions can take over tasks if trained to do so. There are numerous studies describing brain mapping, proving that sound can be perceived through vision receptors, or how vision can be rewired to touch receptors. We make use of whatever resources our bodies have at hand to function.

As a result, all sensations have a potential to stimulate us regardless of the health of the sense receptors. Whereas we perceive a stable and unchanging conception, such as a steady temperature, the brain searches for patterns and pattern violation. How a stimulus reaches our brain over time is important in determining what it is. If the temperature changes by a couple of degrees in a few minutes, our bodies will note the change. Thus, when artists make use of patterns, they can attract the brain's attention by violating that pattern. For example, when we played duck-duck-goose as children, the word "goose" accompanied by a pat on the head would trigger the physical response of jumping up and chasing the old goose around the circle.

Regardless of what sense's input is being processed, its spatial and temporal patterns are processes. When we hear "duck," it is not only the duration between sounds, but also the actual spatial position of where the sound hits our receptor cells that is important. It is evident that there are spatial patterns with vision, but what we do not recognize is that, with every image of the running goose that we perceive, the eye is actually moving about to fixate on different points. What we perceive as a stable picture is fragmentary. Our visual system compensates and presents them as stable.[18] Our senses act as a web, catching various bits of stimuli through the different sense receptors and making sense of them as a whole. Doidge points out that touch is also spatial, but one single sensation is not enough; an object has to be touched in more than one spot to be identified, which adds a temporal aspect. While discussing each individual sense, it is important to remember that the senses are intimately entangled, and what may seem like touch perception could be augmented by smell and vision.

As we know, the brain is unable to consciously do two things at once. Baars speculates that this is why we are able to willingly suspend our disbelief when watching performance. While we are absorbed watching a performance, we are able to accept mimesis as real. Our absorption while watching *Peter Pan* or any other fantastic creation is a result of the suspension of skeptical questioning. Baars explains this by way of the brain's ability to filter out unnecessary noise:

> If other conscious contents have higher priority than disbelief, it must logically fall by the wayside. By soaking up the entire limited capacity of consciousness and working memory, *absorption may make it momentarily impossible to disbelieve.* It allows us for a while to live in wishful fantasy.[19]

Our brains respond as if stimuli, whether real, imagined, or remembered, are occurring now.[20] Our brains will register pain hearing about a knee to the groin that an athlete experiences during a foul, or from the slap the actor receives on stage.

An example of our ability to accept fiction as fact is an experiment that V.S. Ramachandran describes. Subjects felt a touch sensation when an experimenter made contact with a fake rubber hand in the place where a real hand ought to have been.[21] Subjects are instructed to sit with one hand on their legs below the table with the other hand placed on the table next to a fake hand. Ramachandran stroked the subject's hand under the table while stroking the fake hand on the table. The subjects' brains were tricked into incorporating a piece of rubber into a part of their body schema. They describe that, within moments, the feeling of their own hand being stroked disappeared and the feeling of the rubber hand being stroked took over. This illusion is the same as perceiving that a cartoon or ventriloquist's dummy is speaking because their lips are in sync with the sound that we are hearing. It makes sense to our brains that the dummy is alive because our brain predicts plausibility. We do not have to be conscious or even see everything within our field of vision; it is more efficient for the brain to predict what it believes should be there. Only if a change captures its attention does it register. The snapshot that picks out key elements is filled in automatically.

Even more amazingly, we can see violence committed to a table as violence to our own body, responding as if our physical body has been damaged. Instead of using a dummy hand, Ramachandran simply stroked the table and generated the same illusion of touch. He described an experiment measuring galvanic skin response (GSR):

> If I hit you with a hammer or hold a heavy rock over your foot and threaten to drop it, your brain's visual areas will dispatch messages to your limbic system (the emotional center) to prepare your body to take emergency measures (basically telling you to run from danger). Your heart starts pumping more blood and you begin sweating to dissipate heat. This alarm response can be monitored by measuring the changes in skin resistance—the so-called GSR—caused by the sweat. If you look at a pig, a newspaper or a pen there is no GSR, but if you look at something evocative—a Mapplethorpe photo, a *Playboy* centerfold or a heavy rock teetering above your foot—you will register a huge GSR.[22]

When he bashed the table with a hammer, the GSR registered the same activity as if the subject's hands had been smashed. It was as if the table had been incorporated into the subject's body schema. Our brains respond to the illusion as a generator of pain. This goes a long way in explaining why the use of puppets and prosthetics can cause us to cringe when in Scott McPherson's *Lieutenant of Innishmore*, bodies are blown apart and a stuffed cat is painted. Whether we see real or constructed actions, our bodies respond to the results of that action. Doidge argues that:

> What these "imaginary" experiments show is how truly integrated imagination and action are, despite the fact that we tend to think of imagination and action as completely different and subject to different rules. But consider this: in some cases, the faster you can imagine something, the faster you can do it.[23]

MIRROR RESPONSES AND BRAIN ACTIVITY

An actor performs an action that an attendant either witnesses or is a part of, and then the attendant has an embodied response. Typically, our premotor areas are on alert while we watch an actor, or if we preparing to act ourselves. Thus we are cued to respond. If we were not in control of our mirror responses we would be in an endless game of follow-the-leader. Gazzaniga believes this control is partly what makes us uniquely human:

> There is a system of inhibition to prevent observers of an action from emitting a motor behavior that mimics it . . . . However, sometimes if the observed action is particularly interesting, there can be a brief lapse of inhibition and an involuntary response from the observer. . . . The individual performing the action (the actor) will recognize a response in the observer, and the observer will see that his reaction caused a reaction in the actor. If the observer can control his mirror neuron system, then he can send a voluntary signal and thus begin a rudimentary dialogue of sorts.[24]

Others actions have such an effect on us that we can have involuntary responses to them. Because we are mostly in control of our responses, we have control of what our overt responses to stimulation are, even if our brains are on high alert. This control is in part distinct to humans. Therefore, if artists make use of stimuli, they can trigger involuntary responses within attendants or, at least trigger mental reactions.

Communication is more complex than monkey-see–monkey-do. We have many ways to detect and understand behavior and actions that we see, such as when we scan faces and other bodily signs to determine whether something is worth believing. Gazzaniga explains that we are highly skilled at face perception, and it is critical in our social interactions. Scientists have determined that identity systems are different from movement and expression systems.[25] The multiple pathways that are available through theatrical representation affect different parts of the brain and are perceived differently. It does not matter what the stimuli are, we can perceive vision with sound or smell and receive similar information. The senses are a web of fragmentary information that we piece together to form a conception of the world. We use different neural pathways to distinguish different sets of information, but the conscious processing does not detect the redundant information taken in by the other senses. It is only when the senses work in concert with each other that we really start to perceive the world. Smell can trigger a range of sensations, touch another, but when understood together, they create an entirely different conception of the world.

One of the most fascinating elements in understanding why we learn visually is that our electrical system is able to respond as if what we have seen has been done by our bodies. Specialized mirror neurons enable us to empathize and communicate with others from a distance without direct contact. Gazzaniga explains:

> at least for disgust, there is a common area in the brain that is activated for visually seeing the facial expression of the emotion in someone else, for one's own visceral response, and for feeling the wife's face when she sniffs the sour milk activates your own disgust emotion. . . . Now you don't have to test it.[26]

This has immediate implications in watching performances. We can watch Gertrude drink from the poisoned chalice and see her contorted disgust reaction and our brains will have the same visceromotor response. Our empathy and understanding of what others are experiencing is a result of our brain activity.

Likewise, when you see the poison-tipped sword scratch Hamlet, you are aware of the sensation of being cut and anticipate the pain the effects the poison will have. Science shows us:

> whether you anticipate the pain for yourself or another, the same area in the brain is used. Looking at pictures of humans in painful situations also activates brain activity in the area that is active in the emotional appraisal of pain, but not the area that is active with the actual sensation of pain. There is evidence the same neurons mediate the emotional appraisal of both personal and vicarious pain.[27]

The effect that looking at Goya's *Disasters of War* provokes shows that our brains are active to the sensations of pain and disgust, thereby producing empathetic feelings and emotions. It is not simply an intellectual argument against war, but a visceral trigger that manipulates our mental and emotional states for an effect. Mimetic representation of life is offered for perception to enable the attendant to experience the sensations offered by the performance. Obviously, the more a performance evokes sensation, the more able it is to create a sympathetic response within the attendant. There are complex numbers of emotions available. For example: "When you feel a negative emotion, such as fear, anger, or pain, you also get a physiological response. . . . Your heart races and you may sweat or get the shiver up your back, and so forth. In fact, you get a different set of physiological responses with each different emotion."[28] Our responses are specific to the emotions that are generated by the stimuli. If I am riding a rollercoaster, then my body will have automatic responses, such as nausea from the rapid displacement of inner-ear fluid, as well as emotional responses dependent on whether I am fearful of sensations produced as a result of the altitude drops. When we see another person riding the roller coaster, depending on whether they display joy or fear, our brains will respond in kind. Likewise, our own experience of the sensation may further color our response to witnessing others riding the roller coaster.

Our bodies go even further than empathy. As we feel emotions, specific physiological responses are triggered automatically. When we perceive that Hamlet is exhibiting a morose mood or is emotionally turbulent, "we automatically mimic it, both physiologically and physically, and psychologically to some extent. . . . We have a mirror system that understands actions and the indications of actions, and it is also involved with learning through imitation and emotion recognition."[29] We simulate the expressions and the emotions of the people around us. Therefore, we are primed to make the emotional journey presented within theatrical expression and its effects are greater than we can possibly imagine. We are inherently social beings and our own physiological states are tied to those we perceive around us. The more we are in contact with others, the more we are tied into the social mood. As live theatre is a shared experience, simply our proximity to others during the event affects our response; therefore, the unconscious affect of sensorial stimulation is intrinsic to the theatrical event. The crowd's response has the potential to modulate our responses and vice versa in a feedback loop.

Despite our ability to activate the same neural areas in our own brains when we observe actions and emotions in others, we are aware of the differences between ourselves and others. I am both able to perceive another's experience as well as know that it is not happening to me. Gazzaniga explains the most common challenge to this conception, if mirror neurons are put into motion when we see our spouse's disgust, then how can I tell if I am disgusted or if he or she is?[30] We imagine that we walk in on Gertrude while her lover hides behind the tapestry; we can simulate Hamlet's anger and feel it ourselves, but we know it is Hamlet's anger we imagine, not our own. Gazzaniga concludes, therefore, that we have mechanisms to distinguish between ourselves and others. Also, our conception of the self is both physical and mental.[31] This is an ability that no other creature shares. It gives us the ability to learn without having to physically feel the effects of encountering a given stimulus. The greater our exposure to certain situations and contexts, the more deeply we will be affected. Knowing triggers a greater number of neurons to fire. More importantly, it gives us the tools to become engaged in theatrical mimesis.

The more familiar an experience, the more likely we will respond to it. If we trained as a dancer when we were young, we are more likely to have a dynamic response to seeing a dancer fall and twist an ankle, because we are more precisely familiar with how that injury feels. George Mandler describes the judgment of familiarity and the recall of information, which are the two stages involved in the recognition process:

> The judgment of familiarity is an automatic process, requiring no conscious effort and occurring as an immediate response to the event. However, the familiarity of information available of the event may be inadequate to make a confident judgment of prior occurrence. In that

case, a search process queries long-term memory system whether the event in question is in fact retrievable. If such an attempt is successful then the event is considered to be "old" i.e. having been previously encountered. Thus, recognition involves a judgment of familiarity which is supplemented by a retrieval attempt.[32]

The more often we encounter or experience a sensation, emotion, or situation, the more familiar it becomes and thereby creates a more distinct pathway within our brain. There are a number of steps that need to take place to recognize something and make sense of it consciously. Gazzaniga explains:

> It seems that we have gone beyond a world of emotional contagion, where simulation is a reflexive automatic response to facial expressions or other emotional stimuli, and entered into the world where the conscious brain plays a role. Here you are able to use your memory, the knowledge you have gained from past experiences, and what you know about the other person as part of your input. This leads us to one more simulation ability we have, one that is most probably unique. We can simulate an emotion with only abstract input.[33]

Therefore, we use our past experience and knowledge to understand the journey on which stimulation takes us. We have automatic responses, followed by recognition, which, in turn, begins to make the experience conscious. Through abstract means we are able to live through performance experiences that are unimaginable or inaccessible. It is a training ground to give us experience before we need the skill set to deal with it when we encounter it at a later date. The more familiar an experience, the more invigorating it is for our brain. Gazzaniga relates that we have the ability to shape our own perspectives and change those perspectives:

> We can manipulate what emotions we are simulating by imagination alone. Different perspectives can lead to simulating different emotions. This can be done without the presence of any immediately available physical stimulus. We can transfer emotional knowledge with abstract tools, such as language or music, through books, songs, e-mails, and conversations.[34]

We can feel sadness as we see Cordelia mourn for Lear; we can feel mirthful as we watch Chaplin make a dinner out of a shoe; and we can feel triumphant as we listen to Beethoven's Ninth Symphony. We do not always have to learn things by having to experience them firsthand. Likewise, others can learn from our experiences without necessarily experiencing the same duration of hardship. Gazzaniga explains that "these abilities to simulate emotions from language and imagination, to alter our simulations by using perspective, and to project ourselves into the future and past enrich our social world."[35]

In the same manner, we cling to that which we know because

> We find familiar types of stimulation pleasurable; we seek out like-minded individuals to associate with, and research shows we tend to ignore or forget, or attempt to discredit, information that does not match our beliefs, or perception of the world, because it is very distressing and difficult to think and perceive in unfamiliar ways.[36]

However, we are not trapped in a static state. As our brains have the capacity to be flexible, we can, through repeated exposure, change our perception of the world. Mandler indicates that "Repetition affects the process of integrating the representation of an event; it establishes its familiarity independent of its context or its relations to other mental contents."[37] Where once audiences found rock music's rhythms threatening to the fabric of the American nation, presidential candidates now use rock anthems to connect to the populace. When exposed enough to a given context, we begin to accept it as normal. Through the stimulation of our senses, theatre allows us to become exposed to new perspectives and train our minds to be open to different types of experience.

Our memories of a theatrical event are determined by biological processes. We remember by arranging data within our brain according to taxonomy. The more frequently we use information, the more easily we can access that information. By repeatedly exposing ourselves to actions, we develop a consistent relationship to those actions. Mandler explains:

> A set of objects, events, or mental representations is said to be organized when consistent relations among the members of the set can be identified and specified. The result of such organization is called a structure. Structures may exist among events in the world as well as among mental events. A special kind of structure is the schema which is a mental structure, specifically an organized representation of a body of knowledge. Thus, schemata determine the expectations people have about events to be encountered, and about the spatial and temporal structure of those events.[38]

Once our expectations become predictable, we can more easily understand the familiar. It is from this context that we most often form our conceptions of the world and interpret stimuli in relation to that conception. Here is where conscious interpretation of events takes place. Our brain interprets the situation according to well-worn expectations. However, it is difficult to keep track of all that we experience that may be meaningful, because we are unable to keep elements in our working memory for very long. There are limits to our working memory. The reason that phone numbers are seven digits is because that is as many unrelated items that our verbal memory can keep at a time. Like a film frame, our working memories stream through our mind one event at a time, moving from one focal point to the next in rapid succession. To change expectations, stimuli must affect the brain before it makes conscious sense of the data. This gives the sensation of the experience an important role in pre-cognitive development of expression. Despite our working memory's limitations, we are able to shift our attention:

> Our capacity for conscious contents is radically small: essentially we can take in only one dense train of conscious contents at a time. Fortunately, we can pack a vast amount of information into that single flow of experience, and sometimes, as in talking to a friend while driving, we can jump back and forth between different streams.[39]

By calling attention to the ways that we experience the sensations of taste, smell, sound, sight, and hearing, we can begin to filter new data into our well-worn interpretive strategies. What follows are examples of artistically mediated events that affect the attendant through primarily sensorial means. Through these examples, we can begin to discuss how the senses act as a web of experience that our brains later struggle to ascribe meaning.

DERANGEMENT AND THE ATTENDANT

The Burning Man Festival is an example of the ways in which an attendant becomes aware of an artistic event through multi-modal sensorial stimulation. Burning Man is a yearly festival that draws tens of thousands of participants to Black Rock City in Nevada's Black Rock Desert. The participants are dedicated to community, art, self-expression, and self-reliance. Everything attendants see there is participant-generated, and any unifying meaning is fleeting. As its founder, Larry Harvey, says, the festival is not about meaning: "They [attendants] think they will find the germ of the meaning of the whole thing. I've come to understand that is really irrelevant. The real story is in the act itself, in the immediate experience, and of course that is what this is all about." [40] The events at Burning Man become meaningful in the immediate experience of the attendants present. They are constantly commenting on the sensations of being there, the smells of sweat, the heat of the desert and the fire, and blowing air going through tactile portals. It is about the sights and sounds and how they trigger in the attendants the feeling of being a part of an ancient ritual, as if they were living two thousand years ago. Burning Man organizers state that the premise of the event is that there are no spectators, only participants. Each person present is attendant to the world, both a part of it and a witness to it. For participants, it is liberating. They have created an aesthetic environment they can respond to and live within without following the social constraints they normally live by. Contributing to this experience is the fact that they must survive in desert conditions, as well as become a part of the event. It is about total immersion in the event physically, mentally, and metaphorically.

Many participants are reluctant to ascribe meaning to their experience. As it is a personal journey, they are reticent to speak about what it meant to them. Additionally, it is difficult to articulate the barrage of sensations they experienced over the event's duration. Most often the only way to make sense of the experience is to identify the moments and objects that got them excited. When participants choose to share their experiences, they describe its sensations, what they felt, smelled, looked at, and what the resulting emotions and feelings triggered within them. It is only later that they begin to build a larger metaphorical analysis of the meaning of the event, in such sweeping terms as to sound pseudo-academic. Burning Man is about having a good time and expressing oneself, and the resulting sensory overload goes beyond the normal boundaries of everyday life. What it may mean intellectually is less important to the participants than what it makes them feel as they experience the stimulation of a week-long survival art retreat in the Nevada desert.

To understand their sensory experience and how it relates to their understanding of the event, we must break down the different types of stimuli. On the first level there are the basic survival instincts and responses to the physical environment. Whereas they may seem incidental to an intellectual approach, they are essential from a sensorial standpoint. Each participant's body has to acclimate to the extreme desert conditions, cope with the heat and the dust and the sweat. Molly Steenson explains:

> You're here to survive. What happens to your brain and body when exposed to 107 degree heat, moisture wicking off your body and dehydrating you within minutes? You know and watch yourself. You drink water constantly and piss clear. You'll want to reconsider drinking that alcohol (or taking those other substances) you brought with you—the mind-altering experience of Burning Man is its own drug. You slather yourself in sunblock before the sun's rays turn up full blast. You bring enough food, water, and shelter because the elements of the new planet are harsh, and you will find no vending.[41]

Our bodies are forced to cope with the accumulated effects of lack of sleep, dehydration, sunburns, and other somatic trauma that ensue as we participate in the event. The second layer of reception is one's response to the aesthetic stimulation produced by the various artists and participants of the event. Our responses to art and performances that are happening all around us are colored by our physiology. Dehydrated and light-headed, the transvestite dressed in silver lamè on stilts with heat vapor rising off him/her can be hallucinatory. Violet Blue pokes fun of the effects, quoting a circulating email list that included many observations about the experience, like: Before eating any food, drop it in a sandbox and lick a battery; and stack all your fans in one corner of the living room. Put on your most fabulous outfit. Turn the fans on full blast. Dump a vacuum cleaner bag in front of them.[42]

How one copes in this extreme environment is just one of the levels of total immersive experience involved. Your basic afferent and efferent nerve systems might be haywire as they acclimate to the dust and heat of the desert in August.

Everyone at the festival is meant to be a participant; there are no spectators. Like a Kaprow Happening, each of us contributes to some part of the event. Whether we serve as "greeter," build one of its sculptures, or drive one of the art cars, we are participants. Though there is a permissive attitude, participants must abide by the rules of the community by bartering for goods, contributing to the greater whole, and by cooperating and collaborating with others. As a result, there is art everywhere at Burning Man. It is a temporary city laid out on the playa centered around the statue of the burning man, which is torched on the last night of the festival. The more salacious elements of the festival capture the attention of the press with its nudity, sex, and illicit drug use, but this is a grand social experiment where anything goes for a week in the desert. Participants wander around dressed in a kaleidoscope of weird outfits challenging everything you know about clothing, identity, or propriety. Goodwill and free thinking predominate at the festival, and there is social pressure to adhere to the participatory edicts. Everything that is brought to or built in this world must depart at the end of the event. There is always something to capture the attention of one's senses. At night, black light may illuminate your clothing in the Black Light district, vibrations from the rave area may be discernible to your feet, or flashes of light may grab your peripheral vision. The art one encounters can take on profound meaning as a result of the extreme conditions in which it is experienced. You may come across the "Thunderdome," a large geodesic scaffold dome where bungee jumping warriors battle each other in a scene reminiscent of *Mad Max in the Thunderdome*. Here, the impact of the foam clubs will bruise your sensitive skin. Or, you may come across lighting-bolt man zapping electricity around his cage, and feel its ambient charge. Encounters are not always so extreme. To run across a piano on its own is an ordinary experience accessible to most in a normal city. But in "Piano Panorama," this experience is de-familiarized:

> Here's another example of how context changes meaning. A piano by itself doesn't mean much. But a piano sitting in the middle of hundreds of square miles of nothing is something different. And imagine that you come across a piano in the middle of the desert while someone is playing it! To see a solitary human using a complex machine like a piano to make music in the midst of nothingness, with no audience, for no

purpose, that is truly a surreal experience. Each element of the scene, in this context, becomes concentrated and makes a lasting impression.[43]

It is the total experience of the artwork within its context that imbues the object with meaning. We must chart our sensations of our place in relation to the object or event that may or may not communicate directly to our conscious appraisal of the event.

A photographer related an extreme example of the ways in which his senses were excited and the ways in which his body responded:

> Among my adventures was nearly getting incinerated by an exploding pyramid. I was shooting a panorama of this wooden pyramid when the fireworks inside it exploded. It was the first time I experienced what a war zone must be like. People ran in every direction as fireworks exploded on the ground. I happened to have my back turned when this happened. Next thing I know I'm covered in sparks. I could smell my hair burning. So I grabbed my tripod and ran. It was all quite exciting.[44]

Sound, heat, contact, and smell triggered this participant to flee to safety away from the danger of the exploding pyramid. In this environment, we cannot rely on our sense of prediction. We simply cannot foresee when someone will blow something up, spray some water, or enter into our field of vision, or when a dust storm may blow up over the playa. We must be in a state of attention monitoring the world around us for the physical conditions of the area, as well as be aware and become interested in the aesthetic stimulation offered up by the other participants. We are simultaneously attendants and participants within the event because our senses are on a continuous state of alert.

The apogee of the event is the ritual of torching the Burning Man. It becomes a gigantic tribal spiritual event. In what way does the stimulation of the sights, sounds, smells, temperature, and taste of the event generate meaning for a participant? Michelle Bienias recounts:

> Like most art at Burning Man this structure is burned on the last day of the festival. I can honestly say that to stand among thousands of people in the middle of the desert to watch this structure go up in flames is one of the most beautiful things I've ever seen. It is a poetic experience not easily described. If you look into the crowd while the temple is burning you will see many faces filled with tears. There is just something so intensely aesthetic about the experience you cannot help but feel something. In part I think it's that the structure, which is so delicate and intricate, looks like some sacred shrine; to see it on fire pulls at your instincts to protect it. Yet the sight of it burning, the swirling flames and dancing shadows, is so fascinating you can't help but enjoy it. It's very exciting and the fire creates an incredible amount

of heat and light. At a certain point, when the structure is completely engulfed, the excitement changes to a kind of sadness or finality. It's as if this burning temple is a symbol all things. Every beautiful and intricate thing into which people have put so much hard work and planning eventually "burns up" in one way or another.[45]

The blood, sweat, and toil of traveling to, creating, participating in, and destroying the art objects of the event take on subjective meaning to each attendant. Much of the language used to describe the experiences at Burning Man match the tone of Damasio's descriptions of memory and the distinguishing of the self. This lived event imbued and shaped by art practice is a total body experience that incorporates all of the traditional sensory receptors, as well as those of pressure, pain, and temperature. It changes each participant's consciousness. In words similar to many accounts of the experience:

> you'll take the world you built with you. When you drive back down the dusty roads toward home, you slowly reintegrate to the world you came from. You feel in tune with the other dust-covered vehicles that shared the same community. Over time, vivid images still dance in your brain, floating back to you when the weather changes. The Burning Man community, whether your friends, your new acquaintances, or the Burning Man project, embraces you. At the end, though your journey to and from Burning Man are finished, you embark on a different journey—forever.[46]

Ultimately, if we accept that sensual stimulation changes the brain, then this is the aim of all artistic stimulation, and the potential effect that our plastic brains allow us. As we experience the world, our sensations shape and mold our brains and color our perceptions of the world. Art is pleasurable, and the brain is conducive to stimuli that are pleasurable, thereby art can deeply influence the way that the brain is structured. Recent brain studies have proven that our memories of events activate the same parts of the brain that the actual experience did—to remember is to relive, and therefore it is experience. How we interpret these experiences gives the experiences meaning.

What type of experience do all of these disparate events yield, and what sense can an attendant make of the Burning Man Festival? Much of what is experienced there is difficult to quantify, for there is little reason to be consciously aware of the amount of sweat that your body has secreted or how when sand got in your eye, fluid was secreted to protect your body from infection. Likewise, many of the sights and smells of the days, such as the port-o-potties or abject bodies writhing in drug-induced frenzies, are gladly repressed or blended in with general impressions of the event. Words and conscious interpretations are not important, "Many participants . . .

have been reluctant to discuss the event, cognizant of the inadequacy of words in articulating an event that can only be experienced."[47] Embodied memory and the transformations of the attendant over the course of the event are more important. These effects are produced as a result of the body's capacity to perceive and respond to the world. The artistic stimulation afforded by this event are the mediated creation of an unfamiliar alien experience that lets participants live in a world that is other than our twenty-first century society.

By mimicking ancient rituals a performance event makes use of our inherited modes of perception. Cognitive anthropologists suggest that the perception of the physical world may be our oldest form of consciousness, because sensory perception allowed the Paleolithic hunter–gathers to discriminate between leaves of nutrient-rich spinach leaves and poisonous Taro leaves. It was in the Stone Age, only ten thousand years ago, when we began to distinguish ourselves as being able to cope with a larger array of conscious decisions. Burning Man places us in a situation for which our brains are well suited. The event works because we are primed to be able to appreciate and respond to the stimulations that the event affords the brain. The power of Burning Man does not emerge because an anthropologist can trace the ritual of a Dionysian celebration to a human need to be released from the constraints of Apollonian civil society. Rather, it comes from an understanding that we need to exercise our biological senses in unfamiliar ways, and at Burning Man, the web of the senses—taste, touch smell, sound, and sight—intermingle in unfamiliar ways for the participants. We do not live today in the world to which our bodies adapted thousands of years ago; our bodies have not caught up. We crave physical stimulation. It is not always necessary to articulate what our experiences mean. We would rather do and understand rather than do and consciously ordain what something might mean within the inherited traditions of intellectual thought. A. Leo Nash sums up his memories of attending the festival:

> When I recall my visits to Burning Man, my mind fills with arcing lasers and multicolored blinking lights, hallucinatory sunrises, hordes of costumed revelers dancing in the dust, and the enormous bonfires that consume the hand-built sculptures and structures at the end of the week. Burning Man is over-stimulation and cacophonous saturation, where the rhythm of your pulse syncs with the electronic beats that pound 24/7, and sleep is an enemy to be conquered.[48]

To be saturated by sensation is a release from the Platonic anti-sensorial constructions of educated societies. Though we can still find meaning through sensation, becoming attendant to the ways in which our emotions and sensations were generated can offer us a rich palette of stimuli with which to create new performance events. If we pay attention to the sounds, sights, smells, touches, and tastes—to what triggers them, to what they make us feel—we will have a toolbox to stimulate attendants and create an evocative theatrical expression.

TRIGGERING THE BRAIN'S SPOTLIGHT OF ATTENTION

Whether we are attentive or not to multi-modal stimulation, our bodies are receiving and processing the stimuli generated at the theatrical events that we attend. As we begin to become attentive to those stimuli we can consciously consider those stimuli as meaningful. How do attentive spectators experience sensory stimulation? One evening in the early 1990s, I went to see the Dutch company DogTroep perform in an unfinished Chicago theatre. The event surprised me by not adhering to the structures that I had come to expect from theatrical performance. As I watched I kept trying to make sense of all of these images. Shacks flew from the ground transforming into outhouses and then into homes. Giant showers of earth and rock created mounds. Try as I might, each time I tried to create a narrative out of the experience some element would disrupt it. I would construct a metaphor about the global warming, and then a commentary on families. I was frustrated at every turn and my expectations were deranged. All those interpretations have since escaped from my memory—or seem so irrelevant they cannot be summoned to mind. What remains are the goose bumps from the chilly night air of a June summer on the waters of Lake Michigan, the memory of the friend who I went with, and a series of images and sounds that I experienced. I remember the equipment and refuse of the construction world of Chicago, the rain of rock and dirt, and the bodies that hung out of the outhouse that looked as if streams of their pee were flooding the stage. The only way that I could understand what was going on was to try and make rational all of the stimuli that were flooding my senses. I was filled with awe and wonder. The magic of the theatre was manifest. I was shocked and surprised. Up until that point I had always made an argument for well-made plays, realism, and classical tragedy, but that night a whole new world was opened to me. I had to adapt to a sensuous world where it was appropriate not to understand in a conscious way. It was years until I realized that I did understand, that I could unravel the knot of sense impressions, and that there were other means of organizing a performance beyond text that could guide its composition and analysis. That performance could be composed of sounds, smells, feelings, and images rather than words, characters, and sets. That is not to say that one is better than the other, or that the conventions that we have grown accustomed to are wrong. Rather, by making use of our innate attentiveness to our physical sensations we can begin to savor the stimuli that some arts make use of in their expression of the world. It can be a barrage of stimuli to bask in.

DogTroep created mediated live events using sculpture, shape, and color. Many of the strategies they used to structure their works can be described as sensory-rich. Rarely performing in a traditional theatre, they created assemblages of local elements to create site-specific theatrical events. There is no sense of traditional dramaturgical narrative, because visual and aural elements are incorporated to create ever-changing moving images over the course of each performance. Each time a semblance of a narrative started to coalesce out of the flow of images it was subverted by spatial, visual, or aural means. For example, in *Camel Gossip II* (1993), men in a house bring pails out of an interior as if they are working, and then the image is interrupted by long trumpets that stretch over the heads of the attendants from the back of the theatre. When a surprising transformation takes place in front of our eyes, or some significant siren rings out in the building, our nervous system goes into high alert, sending messages through our bodies. This is an orienting response triggered by the hippocampus, which spots events that are mismatched to our expectations. Our attention moves to understand the event and determine whether action is necessary. Three hundred milliseconds after a surprising stimulus, we become conscious of whether we ought to leave the burning building or ignore the fire alarm. Illogical shifts in imagery during the performance change the focus away from any understandable narrative, as well as capture our attention. DogTroep creates fantastical objects and uses bodies in inventive ways that confound theatrical convention. Instant shifts of images create humor. They use costume and change to shape human form, to create texture, and to color the performance environment. Human figures are overpowered by vast spaces filled with found objects. With the introduction of a new element, or the transformation of one object into another, our attention is drawn to that change. In *Assimil* (1995), clothing hung all around and a figure manipulated a rope that was highlighted by light. That light drew the eye in and we focused on the illuminated action and pushed the former experience to the periphery of our vision. The company often will transform objects from one thing to another. For example, a kitchen transforms into an outhouse, or dirt falls from the sky as rain. The stage environment was created in a surreal expression of changing visual arrangements of figure, objects, and materials. The form of the presentation confounds any conscious attempt to understand or interpret. What we are left with is a series of images, which revolve around a range of themes. What we take away is completely dependent upon our responses and associations with the material. The company manipulates our experience by providing stimuli to draw the eye or the ear and thereby capture the brain's spotlight of attention. The compelling stimuli become significant as an afterthought, when the conscious brain begins to piece together a subjective narrative based on an interpretation of the events recovered through memories of the sensations.

In contrast to the distant, often passive, stimulation of attendant sensation produced by DogTroep is the active and often violent attack on attendant sensation in the work of Survival Research Laboratories (SRL). SRL is more shocking than a simple cognitive mismatch that attracts our attention. Rather, it provides extreme traumatic stimulation that overloads our sensory system triggering the "flight or fight" systems that kept us alive through the millennia. Mark Pauline, its founder, explains that "The vision for SRL was always about creepy, scary, violent, and extreme performances that really captured the feeling of machines as living things."[49] He animates machines to trigger a response from his attendant to get them to treat and respond to these machines as real threats. A disgruntled attendant wrote a letter to the company describing the danger inherent in attending a SRL event. She went through a litany of injuries her friends suffered at a performance; one was lacerated by falling debris, and another was sprayed with BB pellets and suffered a cracked tooth. She complained to staff, but was rebuked with the response that injuries were to be expected. She could not understand why SRL created fear, destruction, and problems without solution. Why create actual danger? It did not match her expectation for what art is.[50] Having signed a liability waiver, she should have realized that there would be more to the event than a conventional artistic invitation; however, the jarring nature of having our expectations violated when we are immersed in an unfamiliar situation frustrates the conscious mind's desire to make sense of the experience. The event forces us to rely on instinct and experience to navigate its duration. To make sense of what the event may be expressing needs another analytical approach.

On their surface, the SRL events are violent, bone-chilling experiences. Gary Morris describes that in *Art Space*, Pauline:

> talks about the desire to "manipulate audiences . . . trap them." In one of their most combative pieces, audiences stand perilously on a moving catwalk while the aforementioned giant finger comes at them, backgrounded by what Pauline calls "a sickening vibration" that causes headaches and nosebleeds in onlookers. Encouraged to interact, some brave watchers hit the robots with a stick that's then partially devoured; others scramble away.[51]

Regardless of whether we are attentive to what the sound vibrations, ground tremors, or air temperature is, these stimuli are working on our physiology triggering emotional or instinctive responses. The stimuli will shape our experience and create neuron firing and teach our plastic brain something about the world. At first it may be unfamiliar and unpleasant, but with repeated or related exposure, the previously unforeseen patterns may become pleasurable and increasingly meaningful.

What effect does the barrage of sensation have on us when we consider the feelings and emotions generated as a result of the stimulation? Greta Dayal describes *Ghostly Scenes of Infernal Desecration* (2006):

A giant golden statue of a man resembling Atlas dropped golden balls and was subsumed by surrounding flames. A remote-controlled vehicle drove around, spitting fire. Balls of fire and gray clouds of smoke illuminated the sky above. . . . If anything ever resembled the end of the world, this was it. Huge, freakish machines, which appeared to do their bidding sans human involvement, ran roughshod over an empty lot behind a Silicon Valley building. Robots breathed fire and battled each other to untimely deaths. Flames streaked the night sky; orange sparks fell like rain; 10-foot-tall bolts of lightning flew from a giant Tesla coil. Explosions punctuated the silence as machines lumbered through the lot.[52]

One could speculate about how this is a commentary on the consequences of mechanization in our society. We are biological creatures attuned to the natural world that has created a dangerous and unpredictable world filled with machines. We are beyond the human and our bodies have not adapted or evolved. Perhaps Pauline is forcing us to glimpse the world where we will have to adapt or die—who is best adapted and receptive to the adaptation necessary to live with robots?

SRL comes close to doing this—literally forcing us to adapt to the huge robots destroying each other. Their Flame Hurricane uses five 150-lb-thrust Pulse Jet engines to produce a rapidly rotating column of hot, high-velocity, hurricane-like fire. Our eardrums could be shattered with the Shockwave cannon, a giant stationary device that forms vortex rings of air and projects the rings at high speeds. David Garver uses the experience of the attendants as a means to suggest how SRL can be understood:

[The Robots] do not speak from a particular subject position but, rather, quiver and shake like a demented body in the throes of fever or death. This is not a spectacle with which an audience could ever become comfortable. It threatens violence to the audience, presents a world independent of human logic and agency, and suggests that this inhuman world is, in fact, one that we make for ourselves. Presenting a spectacle with these three inimical perspectives both entices the audience to view it and prevents the audience from finding a safe vantage point for their spectatorship.[53]

SRL places the responsibility of understanding the experience in the lap of the attendants. Sensory data must be restructured by cognitive thought to contribute to conventional means of visual or cultural analysis. Garver's analysis shows us how these events take on meaning in a culturally or aesthetically significant way. He continues:

SRL turns this technology into nightmarish visions that match in their fiendishness the effect our technological obsessions have on our society. Yet, unlike more conventional indictments of social injustice, SRL's spectacles do not allow their audience to rest comfortably with a self-righteous message. For SRL, violence takes precedence over social critique. The implicit social critique in the shows is there mainly to prevent the violence from becoming a morally neutral spectacle, a commodity in what Debord calls "the society of the spectacle." SRL events speak against the enslaving passivity of spectatorship by offering a spectacle too conceptually dissident to be integrated into the sparkling surfaces of social spectacle.[54]

The effect of the performances provides a means to understand the ways in which both unconscious and conscious stimuli become culturally significant. In turn, the events change the way our brains operate.

Not only does the brain shape culture, culture shapes the brain.[55] As our adaptable brain becomes stimulated it begins to modify itself, because repeated exposure breeds change. Doidge explains, "Neuroplastic research has shown us that every sustained activity ever mapped—including physical activities, sensory activities, learning, thinking, and imagining—changes the brain as well as the mind."[56] He cites research describing the way in which men addicted to internet pornography slowly rewire their pleasure centers to respond to erotic imagery on the net, each time creating a rut that demands more and more stimulation to fire off enough neurons to excite the brain. To wean these men from the internet stimulation, they had to rewire the brain back to human-to-human contact in the bedroom to restore the connection to their partners. We change our embodied responses with each new habit that we develop.

The difference in how this occurs comes as a result of the ways in which media stimulate our organism. The hypnotizing qualities of television come from its constantly changing flashes of light. Our eyes are attracted and cannot make sense of the stimulation. Ultimately, we respond like deer in the headlights, staring, frozen. Movies are different as well, because they are a series of still images that are not pieced together. Again we respond in rather predictable and unstimulating ways. What is important is that notion of movement and continuity used to trigger visceral responses from viewers. All these forms of media are capable of triggering mirror and empathy responses from attendants, but those activities that stimulate the regions of the brain tied to action stimulate us in a much more holistic way. It provides us with an in-between state of response; we are experiencing this as if it is real, even though we are fully aware that it is fiction. We are learning through this experience and are strengthening neural networks making neural pathways habitual. As we gain exposure, we strengthen the plastic brain's pathways and what is familiar is most pleasurable. Art can literally pave the way for experience making strong the neural pathways that our brains use to experience, interpret, and conceive of the world around us.

At the heart of artistic production and experience is the human body. As humans we seek out traces of the human form wherever we are. The world around us triggers emotion, feeling, and consciousness within, and from those responses we generate our conscious attitudes and beliefs about the world. Our perceptions emerge out of the stimuli we encounter:

> We begin with an organism made up of body proper and brain, equipped with certain forms of brain response to certain stimuli and with the ability to represent the internal states caused by reacting to stimuli and engaging repertoires of preset response. As the representations of the body grow in complexity and coordination, they come to constitute an integrated representation of the organism, a proto-self. Once that happens, it becomes possible to engender representations of the proto-self as it is affected by interactions with a given environment. It is only then that consciousness begins, and only thereafter that an organism that is responding beautifully to its environment begins to discover that it is responding beautifully to its environment. But all of these processes—emotion, feeling, and consciousness—depend for their execution on representations of the organism. Their shared essence is the body.[57]

This is why we must look to the ways in which artists have been using tactics to stimulate the body and the brain by using materials that actively stimulate the nose, ears, eyes, tongue, and skin. Our internal responses color our perceptions of the world and, to some extent, though our cultural and social training will color how we respond to certain stimuli, the origin of that stimuli is consistent across cultures and therefore is consistent enough to consider as a means to plan how one might trigger responses from another human. It is through this stimulation that artists actively manipulate and change their audiences.

Recent scientific discoveries about brain function open up the possibility that we can think about the nature and value of theatrical practice by way of lived experience. Theatrical and other live artistic creations capture the attention of the neural networks of the body and make real experiences that might not be accessible in our everyday interactions. Through art we are able to offer experience and knowledge that change the attendant at his or her core. We can live vicariously in art and gain experience that has the potential to affect our everyday lives. After a theatrical event we can never be the same. Doidge uses the simile of brain activity as Play-Doh, where we can endlessly mold new shapes out of the material and return it to something resembling the initial shape. The material may look superficially the same, but it has been reconfigured: "Outcomes that are similar are not identical. The molecules in the new square are arranged differently than in the old one. In other words, similar behaviors, performed at different times, use different circuits."[58] The participants of Burning Man are right. Their experiences over the course of the festival have changed them and, as a result, they will never perceive and interpret the world in the same way again. As they return each year, the values and the stimulation will become more pleasurable and more inculcated in their understanding of the world. Artistic compositions that utilize active sensorial stimulation do have the power to affect human minds, and as such, can also be seen as dangerous. This brings up ethical and moral questions about what we ask actors to do and about what experiences we subject audiences to. Also, the consequences of manipulating sensory experience could have unintended uses, such as mind control by corporations to get you to buy their goods, or stores piping smells or sounds to get you to spend more money or buy certain goods and not others. In any event, the lived quality of theatrical entertainment has the potential to shift attendants experience and perception of the world around them.

2 Scintillating Visions and Visual Perception

How Light, Movement, and Stage Space Capture Our Attention and Stimulate Our Brains

Vision is one of the most investigated aspects of the role of the senses in theatrical performance, though its mechanisms are seldom investigated. Here I want to consider the role light and movement have upon our physiological perception and the ways in which theatre practitioners have manipulated physiological traits to keep us stimulated and interested in what is happening on stage. Visual stimulation entices our brains to pay attention to what is going on during the theatrical event. In fact, it is the moving image in front of us that distinguishes the theatrical event from other visual media. Movies are made up of still images that our brain blurs together and reconstructs into moving images; therefore, it is processed differently than live action. By stimulating sight through performance, we invigorate the rest of the information that we receive from all of our sensations. What are the implications of the recent discoveries and ways of thinking about sight on the theatrical event? Can these revised means of understanding how we process visual stimuli help the theatre reclaim its importance in the role of live mimetic representation?

THE PHYSIOLOGY OF SIGHT

As a child, I thought that the most horrible calamity for me would be to go blind, and I am not alone, for sight is often thought of as the sense that most people value more than all the rest. Eyes enable us to see and interpret the shapes, colors, and dimensions of the world's features and the objects that fill it by processing the light they reflect or emit. What we think of as seeing is the result of a series of events that occur between the eye, the brain, and the outside world.[1] To see something, the eye must first focus on an image, then the correct amount of light must be admitted to the eye so that light rays can be focused on the retina (the inner layer of the eye containing light-sensitive cells that connect with the brain through the optic nerve). Light reflected from an object passes through the cornea of the eye, moves through the lens that focuses it, and then reaches the retina at the very back, where it is absorbed into the photosensitive pigments in the rods and cones. Before the neurons of the brain and spinal chord can react to light exposure, the stimulus must be transformed by receptors into nerve impulses that must be transmitted to the visual areas of the cerebral cortex. When a photon of light from a candle burning on stage meets one of the photoreceptor cells of the retina it will be absorbed into a receptor protein, where transduction simplifies and integrates visual information for its travel from the eye to the brain by way of the optic nerve.[2] The retina is made up of the fovea, macula, and peripheral regions, where each performs a distinctive function. These different functions operate simultaneously and blend into each other, so we do not consciously differentiate them. The fovea is packed with color-sensitive receptor cells called cones, each with its own nerve fiber. Surrounding the fovea is the macula, an oval body mostly composed of cones. Macular vision is quite clear, but not as clear and sharp as foveal vision, because the cones are not as closely packed in the macula as they are in the fovea. We use the macula for reading or watching television, among other things. As we travel further away from the central portion of the retina, the character and quality of vision changes, and the capacity to see color diminishes as the color-sensitive cones become more scattered. The eyes see from slightly different positions, and the light criss-crosses while going through the cornea, so the retina receives the image upside down. The brain must mix the two images it receives to get a complete picture, with the brain then perceiving the image right-side up. Whatever the means—taste, touch, or color—when a physical stimulus acts on a sensory receptor cell, the energy of the stimulus is transformed into a reception potential that can offer news from the outside world in an electrical signal the brain can understand. In other words, whatever light that enters our eyes goes through the process of transduction, which results in the firing of neurons in our brains. The more complex the input, the more stimulated our brain becomes.

Most objects reflect light, and because light travels at high speed, it is possible to nearly instantly assess their shape, size, position, speed, and direction of movement. The light rays reflected by an object are gathered and focused onto an array of photoreceptors. For example, an object reflects light that will enter the eye passing through the retina. Our rod and cone cells will send out signals that travel to the brain, then the optic nerve until they reach the lateral geniculate nucleus. Electrical impulses describing elements of the object will be sent out the areas of the primary visual cortex. Then, signals will fan out to describe more global aspects of the object in higher areas of the cortex. Here, shape, color, and motion are determined. Activities generated in the different photoreceptors by the light interact to produce a two-dimensional representation of the object, which is transmitted to the brain. The brain then reconstructs a three-dimensional representation. The end-products of the activity of the visual system are sensations that represent the object and its surroundings and can be used to guide our immediate behavior, or they can be stored for future reference.

We can see in a great range of light intensities from dim moonlight to bright sunlight. Light is a form of electromagnetic radiation in the visible spectrum that our eyes are able to detect a small portion of. Our visual system is sensitive to the spectrum of visible light from violet through red, but we cannot see infrared or ultraviolet. The eye is able to detect bright light or dim light, but it cannot sense an object when light is absent. Because all light that enters the eye must be admitted through the pupil, the primary way of controlling the amount of light entering the eye is by means of the iris, which has the ability to adjust the size of the pupil. In bright light, a sphincter-like muscle in the iris contracts to constrict the pupil to a small opening that keeps out as much light as possible, whereas in dim light, contractile cells dilate the pupil to let in all the light possible. In those darkest moments onstage our eyes adjust and work to see the movement that occurs there. We seek out light and the information that it conveys to us. Seeking out light is one of our most basic preoccupations as a human organism. Rod cells are extremely sensitive to light and respond well to dim light, thus enabling us to see at night. However, they cannot detect color, and the images they produce are of poor quality. Cone cells, which need bright light to work, produce fine detail and color. Rods are found mostly in the peripheral regions of the retina. Night vision relies almost entirely on the rod cell receptors of the peripheral region of the retina, which because of their neural connections and physical makeup, are very sensitive to light. Rods need about a half-hour of dark or dim red light to activate fully, and then, it is claimed, they have the capacity to detect the flame of a candle that is ten miles away.

We have three types of cones, each sensitive to a different color of light: red, blue, and green. In combination, these three cone types enable us to perceive color. Each type absorbs wavelengths over about one-third of the visible light spectrum, causing red cones, for example, to absorb light from the red, orange, and yellow wavelengths. The chemical reactions in cones also generate electrical impulses. Impulses from the rods and cones are transmitted to ganglion neurons, which converge at the optic disc to become the optic nerve, passing through the back wall of the eyeball. In the cortex, the responses from these three types of cone cells are compared to interpret colors. Within the layers of the retina, light impulses are changed into electrical signals. Then they are sent through the optic nerve, along the visual pathway, to the occipital cortex at the back of the brain. Here, the electrical signals are interpreted or "seen" by the brain as a visual image. Actually, then, we do not see with our eyes but, rather, with our brains. Our eyes merely are the beginning of the visual process.

Basic visual information is processed before being sent to the brain. The retina has three layers of cells. From back to front they are the photoreceptor layer (rods and cones), the bipolar layer, and the ganglionic layer. Once the rods and cones are stimulated by light, they pass a signal on to the bipolar cells, which then stimulate the ganglionic cells, whose axons make up the optic nerve and carry the processed information to the brain. Retinal process-ing involves a lot of summarization of information because there are over one hundred photoreceptor cells for each ganglionic cell. All the light that hits all these cells is distilled into the output of the one ganglionic cell. Other pro-cesses enable them to detect contrast within an image, indicating an edge or shadow and recognition of horizontal, vertical, and diagonal lines. All of this output fed to the brain by the optic nerves is then unpacked and interpreted.[3]

Vision requires distilling foreground from background, recognizing objects presented in a wide range of orientations, and accurately interpreting spatial cues. For example, as children, when that orange Tether ball came whipping around towards us, we could see its color, shape, and motion all at once, even if our bodies were not coordinated to react and smack the ball back to our older brothers. The eye and brain break up the visual world into various aspects, such as color, form, motion, and depth and deal with each of them separately. These pieces of the picture are interpreted in a complex network of processing centers. To form a coherent picture of the world, the eye–brain takes signals from the retinas, relays them through the lateral geniculate bod-ies, and then passes them on to the primary and secondary visual cortex.[4]

The optic nerve primarily routes information by way of the thalamus to the cerebral cortex, where visual perception occurs, but the nerve also carries information required for the mechanics of vision to two sites in the brainstem. This is the oldest part of the brain that is referred to as the reptilian brain, and it regulates the drives necessary for survival. The first of these sites is a group of cells called the pretectum, which controls pupillary size in response to light intensity. Information concerning moving targets and information governing scanning of the eyes travels to a second site in the brainstem, a nucleus called the superior colliculus. It is responsible for moving the eyes in short jumps, called saccades. Saccades allow the brain to perceive a smooth scan by stitch-ing together a series of relatively still images; in other words, it solves the problem of blurring that would result if the eyes could pan smoothly across a panorama. These are the reflexes that enable us to piece together the lights, costumes, sets, and bodies on stage and understand it as live.

Cells in the primary visual cortex are arranged in several ways that allow the visual system to calculate where objects are in space. Almost all higher order features of vision are influenced by expectations based on past experi-ence. This characteristic extends to color and form perception, to face and object recognition, and to motion and spatial awareness. Although such influences occasionally allow the brain to be fooled into misperception, as is the case with optical illusions, they also give us the ability to see and respond to the visual world very quickly. Alva Noë describes this as the brain's action potential, which scans the environment for optional responses.[5]

The senses do not operate independently of each other, as they are dif-ferent strands that our bodies weave together into a web of sensory data that enables us to perceive and respond to the world. Psychologically, light has three aspects we need to consider. It has hue, a quality correlated with wavelength and analogous with pitch in hearing. It has saturation, a quality related to homogeneity or purity of wavelength and comparable to timbre or freedom from noise in audition. The color of a light is a function both of its hue and saturation. Finally, it has brightness, a quantitative measure of the intensity of the light and somewhat analogous to loudness in hearing. The intensity of light is dependent upon the amplitude of its waves or, alternatively, the number of particles of light.

It is the cone receptors that contain the visual pigments that are sensitive to the color of light. The generally accepted color theory today proposes that there are three fundamental color sensations in human vision—red, green, and violet (or blue)—and that each has their own type of color receptor. A single cone captures light and communicates intensity, not color. Color identification comes from comparing a variety of inputs. As light signals pass through the different layers of the retina, aspects are picked out and compared with information from the next layer and so on.[6] Excitation of a given kind of receptor leads to the sensation of the appropriate color, and all other color sensations result from simultaneous excitation of more than one of these receptors. Thus, equal excitation of all three receptor types leads to the sensation of white light, whereas the appropriate amounts of excitation of red and green receptors yields the sensation of yellow, and so on. Therefore, we determine color from wavelength comparison of the object and its surroundings. For example, Robert Wilson can change the color costumes in front of our eyes by changing intensity and wavelength. In a rosy illumination, a yellow collar will reflect more long-wave light and may then appear orange, but its surrounding black cloth will also reflect more long-wave light. Our brains compare the two and cancels out the increase. For the human eye, any color experienced can be produced by a simple additive mixture of the correct proportions of red, green, and blue light. By analyzing the visual image in terms of color, form (edges), luminance, depth, and movement, the retina has achieved a degree of pre-processing of the image before it leaves for the visual cortex via the optic nerve. These criteria also describe the use of light in theatre, and thereby can be used to demonstrate the effects of light upon the attendant. How the body processes light and color triggers brain activity, which in turn produces emotion, thereby instigating the brain to find meaning in the processed stimuli. As attendants, we process all of the stimuli, and the body produces emotions and feelings, which in turn allow the conscious mind to make interpretations. Lighting is used in the composition of a theatrical event to trigger a physiological reaction within the attendant's body.

LIGHT DESIGN AND PHYSIOLOGICAL EXPERIENCE

The physiology of the eye and the nature of light are exploited by lighting designers. Max Keller, in his seminal *Light Fantastic*, describes the nature of light and conceives of it in the abstract aesthetic language of art:

Physicists and physiologists define the phenomenon of light as a small sector of the scale of electro-magnetic oscillations that convey a sensation of brightness via the human eye. It affects our perceptions by triggering a large number of different stimuli. Light unscrambles chaos, takes the grey out of darkness.[7]

For theatre attendants, light is our means of seeing the action and absorbing the details that allow us to make sense of the unspoken mood of the events.

Lighting helps describe the ways in which the sentient body responds to change and mood in indirect and unconscious ways, because it is in almost constant use during performance. Manfred Wagner describes its effect in performance:

> Ultimately, light defines spaces, makes them larger and smaller, lowers and raises them, creates illusions but also real conditions in a virtual world. Light is the advocate of elements of water, sky, fire and earth, but also of those psychological moods that have an elemental effect on events. The spiritual transformation of psychological states into matter, regardless of whether it is oriented towards individuals or masses, must be effective in terms of communication, and use all the special qualities of what is specific and unique on the stage as a bridge to everything that is specific and unique in the audience.[8]

As we pay attention, our mind concentrates and becomes conscious of a range of stimuli; some sort of change needs to take place to attract our attention and begin our conscious collection of the memories of that stimuli. The changing quality of light over the course of a production is guiding us to where we need to pay attention. Yet we also need the other material objects of design to see the light and the colors of the light that are used to build and create our experience of the theatrical event.

Another designer, Achim Fryer, describes this function of scenography as: "[t]o create an open and transparent vessel which makes wealth and character of the work experiencible and discoverable."[9] The theatrical event's job is to create a hermetically sealed world for an attendant to process, as the brain does not discern between reality and mimesis, but rather processes all stimuli received as a live experience. We attach meaning because we give the experience our attention and we consciously ascribe significance to the stimuli that the arts have crafted for us. A designer aids this process. We can consider Dieter Dorn's description of the designer's use of light as a means to stimulate our attention:

> In everyday contexts, light serves to make existing things visible. On stage, however, it creates a new reality. "Created" light helps us to thrust forward into spaces that establish and nurture their own reality,

helps us to thrust forward into dimensions that are different from the ones we experience everyday.[10]

We pay attention to the event because light stimulates our systems of visual perception.

Contingency is also an integral part of the theatrical event, for we can never be sure of how a particular effect will affect an attendant or how it will be understood; it is that imprecision that is a part of the precision of crafting the structure of an event that makes art so subjective. For Keller, this is intrinsic to the value of art:

> The success of the visual effect also depends on the individual's emotional state. Fortunately there is no generally valid reaction to lighting effects. Light, like music, is a particularly subjective sphere. Sensuous perception of light is seldom a conscious practice. Perhaps it is precisely because its emotional effect is unconscious that it affects our sensibilities so incisively.[11]

In effect, it does not matter whether we are conscious of perception:

> Theatre-goers experience light as a resource or a demonstration of cognition, regardless of whether it does so as a physical indicator or as a metaphysical transformation. And the audience almost always makes the leap with it, transferring light into the realms of optics, or into . . . aesthetics.[12]

There is nothing new about the ways in which artists make use of media to create experience; it is the fact that neuroscience is beginning to find scientific principles that explain how and why we perceive different experiences the way that we do. As Jonah Leher argues, we express what we see inside our heads through art, not science. The seemingly strange blotches of color on the canvas that shocked Parisians in the nineteenth century were representations of the ways that our brains picture the world. Leher explains:

> The shocking fact is that sight is like art. What we see is not real. It has been bent to fit our canvas, which is the brain. When we open our eyes, we enter into an illusory world, a scene broken apart by the retina and re-created by the cortex. Just as the painter interprets a picture, we interpret our sensations. But no matter how precise our neuronal maps become, they will never solve the question of what we actually see, for sight is a private phenomenon. The visual experience transcends the pixels of the retina and fragmentary lines of the visual cortex.[13]

Stimuli must be shaped and interpreted by the brain to become meaningful, and biology leads us through the world aided by experience, thus teaching us how to interpret. Our internal processing systems are so complex that they must guess to keep us seeing the world in a useful way, and sometimes those guesses are incorrect, but we learn to see and guess more and more proficiently over time. Leher continues:

> that code of light, as Cezanne knew, is just the start of seeing. If sight were simply the retina's photoreceptors, then Cezanne's canvases would be nothing but masses of indistinct color. His Provencal landscapes would consist of meaningless alternations of olive and ocher, and his still lifes would be all paint and not fruit. Our world would be formless. Instead, in our evolved system, the eyeball's map of light is transformed again and again until, millisecond's later, the canvas's description enters our consciousness. Amid the swirl of color, we see the apple.[14]

Our innate biological survival systems have adapted for us to understand and appreciate the stimuli that art produces; it is almost as if it is a way of keeping our brains alert and adaptable. In the same way that dogs circle and protect us as we walk down the street or jump into the pool to protect us from drowning, our sight practices using our senses as they were evolved to do. One of theatre's intrinsic values is to keep our minds supple and to allow us to gain experience even when we are not directly experiencing a threat.

Richard Hudson's definition of scenography as "Choosing what the audience will see" shows us that the eyes and visual processing of lighting are an essential quality of theatre performance.[15] Though our awareness of the world is individualized and we interpret it according to our personal experience, we share our biology. As such, the way that we gather and sense the world is consistent. For example, Keller explains:

> The eye is able to register: differences in brightness, color differences, shapes, movements, and distances. Lighting is intended to make it easier for the eye to fulfill these functions, or even to make it possible in the first place. A certain minimum illumination is needed for seeing, perceiving and recognizing. Perception is an individual process, invoking a sensation, triggered by the psychological and physical effect of the five points mentioned above.[16]

Though we have been developing these principles intuitively since the advent of modern lighting technology, science has only now demonstrated the neurobiology that makes these theatrical effects successful. To pay attention to the stimuli that we are reacting to strengthens our conscious interpretation of a given theatrical event.

The effects of a work's composition stimulating the perceiver's body have been described in various ways. Wassily Kandinsky instinctively understood that color triggers neurons within our brain and can produce an emotional response: "Colour is a power which directly influences the soul. Colour is the keyboard, the eyes are the hammers, the soul is the piano with many strings, the artist is the hand which plays, touching one key or another, to cause vibrations in the soul."[17] Take, for example, the ways that Wilson uses color as an expressive element within his compositions. It is the last detail he overlays on his artistic composition. Not only does it manipulate the different emotional atmospheres of the space, but also it fills the space. Wilson predominantly uses white, gray, and blue and occasionally uses red, yellow, and green to create a flood of color against the cyclorama that functions in ways similar to those used by Mark Rothko for dividing the composition in his late minimalist paintings. The geometric shapes composed of simple color washes are meant to evoke a transcendent spiritual reaction within the attendant. As Kandinsky describes, "Shades of colour, like those of sound, are of a much finer texture and awake in the soul emotions too fine to be expressed in words."[18] However, as with Rothko's work, some people relate to Wilson's work and others find it formal and empty.

Wilson projects color or images upon a seamless cyclorama, thus creating gargantuan pictures, where forty- by-twenty-foot swatches of color create a potent physical reaction in the body. In *Maladie de la mort* (1991), as we watch these scenes, the color triggers involuntary physiological reactions, such as crying for no apparent reason. The work is entrancing because of the sheer scale of the scrim bathed in color. As the play progresses, the lines change, and the color is blended before our eyes. There is always something to watch. Sometimes Wilson uses a pure color like blue or red and gradually blends them with other colors to control the change in mood or scene. We suddenly become aware that the background is a shockingly different color. Gray can blend to form white or to form black, depending on the sentiments of the characters, and our emotional responses darken accordingly. A blue can brighten in its value or change hues completely. A pin-spot may pick out a hand or prop with light, and color may be projected upon a costume, thereby emphasizing a moment in a character's emotional journey. It is as if we are watching the act of painting as it happens. Keller reminds us of the effect color can produce:

> The use of colors, whether painted, as material or in the form of light, makes a definite statement. As we know, colour is created by light. Thus everything we see stems from the interplay of chromatic colours. The achromatic colours white and black do not occur in the spectrum and thus exist only as surface colours, and they produce the strongest and most radical contrast. Interplay results in a large number of intermediate colours. All these intermediate tints, including the six primary colors, affect us psychologically: coldness, warmth, joy, sorrow, beauty, ugliness, hardness and tenderness.[19]

The colors that Wilson achieves are more brilliant and noticeable than is normally seen in theatre. His control is so masterful that the changes become fluid. The plays are unified, seamless experiences whose scene changes are not a distraction because they work within the cohesive whole.

Wilson's most spectacular use of the visual comes with the ways in which he uses color in a three-dimensional space. In *Hamlet: A Monologue* (1995), Hamlet stands holding a dagger in the air against a great wash of crimson red filling in the space behind him. The color is an expression of the abstract emotions of the character, and in turn, influences our feelings and emotions. Despair may overcome our emotions as the oppressive grays become more intense. Its beauty and intangibility stuns the attendants and distances them from the verbal logic of the play, so they just experience what is unfolding in front of them. It does not only serve to highlight mood or be incidental detail, but also can take an active part in the unfolding of the event in time and space. The concrete changes in visual stimulation are guideposts that lead the attendants through the event. The color can make and organize time like a measure in a musical composition. Intensity and duration act as visual crescendo and tempo. Again, Kandinsky describes the effect of color: "Blue is the typical heavenly color. The ultimate feeling it creates is one of rest, when it sinks almost to black, it echoes a grief that is hardly human. When it rises towards white, a movement little suited to it, its appeal to men grows weaker and more distant."[20] The color is expression that is conveyed over time. In *Maladie*, the colored background transforms in a symphony of tonal gradation. Color can be used to mark out sections in play, act as an organizing principle, or serve an abstracted non-illustrative function. As with a painting, theatre spectacle can be organized with fragmented structures; a cubist painting can offer up as pleasurable experience as a pop art painting. Their aims and techniques of presentation are merely different.

Sometimes, the figural or sculptural image can remain the same, but with a simple blending of color, or color change, the entire world of the stage can shift to a whole new plane. Manfred Wagner suggests that:

> The chromatic type, achromatic type, color degree and brightness of a color hue lead to a certain perception of colour. Unlike the ear, the eye is integrative. For example, if the ear is trained, it can distinguish the upper harmonics of a sound. But the eye is not able to recognize the individual components of a beam of light. Given the same brightness and the same chromatic type, the eye is able to distinguish about 120 tints.[21]

In the same way that we become conversant at deciphering pitch, tone, and melody as significant, we learn to understand changes in gradations of light as it creates mood, although we can never see how the mixing of red and yellow photons produce orange. But to be aware of the process allows us to monitor how the light is affecting our perception of that it illuminates. These instantaneous changes done before the eyes of the attendant are surreal. Color changes mood, setting, and shifts the impact of the images. These changes can lead us down a path or bring us on a journey to somewhere new. Color can provide an abstract narrative. Color and light can shape the space by making it shallow or deep, tall or short. Light and its absence can transform an enormous orchestra hall into an intimate bedchamber. The color and the darkness guide us through the experience. The light can be made to dance or its movement can mesmerize, as does the spaceship in *Einstein on the Beach* (1976), and it can adjust the perceptual experience by capturing our attention. Its movement provides rhythm and shape to the temporal unfolding of the play.

In some ways, Wilson's work is reminiscent of the Light and Space artists of California, such as Robert Irwin, James Turell, and Bruce Naumen.[22] These artists created compositions that made use of changing light qualities as a means of affecting and calling attention to perception and our physiological responses to light. An artist such as Robert Irwin controls spaces and creates an aesthetic experience based on light and dark and subtle changes in the environment. Most are imperceptible to human senses because the changes are so gradual. On a typical day we barely acknowledge the changes are a result of variations in lighting as the sun crosses the sky. It is only when we come in from the bright day to a dark room or vice versa that the change is startling or noticeable. The changing conditions of light on stage offer the potential of an aesthetic experience. Wilson harnesses this effect and uses it as an element in tandem with dialogue and the movement of three-dimensional forms in creating a theatrical event. The principal concept of light and dark is used in the theatrical experience in tandem with dialogue and the movement of three-dimensional forms in space.

Jan Butterfield explains what effect this has:

> The participant in a work of Light and Space slowly lets go of rational, structured reality and slips into an altogether different perceptual state. In this "double depth of the dreamer and the world", the *presence* of light, the *sense* of color, and the *feel* of space merge, becoming far more real than any representation of them could be.[23]

A dreaming perception of a created reality suggests that the attendant's response is irrational and based solely on sense reception. When the form of the artwork is also its content, the reception of the experience becomes an intuitive process that resists definitive interpretation. Wilson uses light as if it is paint, to layer color across the stage, and transform objects from one thing to another as if by magic. Using light and shadow, he creates rhythm and tempo. It is a technique to create intimate or social spaces based on how much of the void is illuminated. Light guides the attendants to focus on the details that propel the event forward. Once we become aware of the sensory stimulation, we are able to monitor the changing nature of the stimulation and make use of our innate ability to process that data into meaningful interpretations.

MOVEMENT AND ILLUSION

One of the amazing things about the way that we see the world is that we are deceived by our own brains. Our control over what we think that we see is immense; we see what we think we ought to see. Gustav Kuhn and Michael Land have been studying magic tricks as a means to understand how the mind perceives illusion. They argue that magicians have an ability to distort our perceptions to get us to perceive things that never happened.[24] They chart a slight-of-hand trick called the "vanishing ball," where a ball apparently disappears in midair. While we scan the environment, we have an impression that what we see is the real world. However, what Kuhn and Land demonstrate is that the way we see the world is more strongly dominated by how we perceive it to be rather than what it actually is: "Our results show that an observer's percept was driven by the magician's cueing."[25] Even though the ball never left the hand of the magician, observers believed they saw it leave the hand. This is a result of our expectation that the ball would leave the hand. Our beliefs about what should happen override actual visual input. Even though attendants did not see a ball they perceived one because the cues from where they were watching suggested that a ball would be tossed in the air. Their belief system was tricked. Kuhn and Land found that observers spend a lot of time looking at the magician's face even though they claim that they are looking at his hand. Social cues influence how we perceive—whereas our eye movements were not fooled by where the ball was, our perception was. Not only does the eye detect the raw stimulus of the object's movement, it interprets the data according to social experience.

How does this fooling of the brain happen? According to Mark Changizi, "Illusions occur when our brains attempt to perceive the future, and those perceptions don't match reality."[26] Our brains only work on a few second time-lapse. Think of the way a progressive DVD works, going a bit ahead of where it is being projected to adjust if there is a skip. If a drunken lout lunges out at us as we walk down the street, our bodies will respond before our brains will register it. Our brains need to piece together the different bits of neural information for our consciousness to perceive it. Bryner explains:

> Humans can see into the future, says a cognitive scientist . . . we do get a glimpse of events one-tenth of a second before they occur. . . . it starts with a neural lag that most everyone experiences while awake. When a light hits your retina, about one-tenth of a second goes by before the brain translates the signal into a visual perception of the world. . . .

foresight keeps our view of the world in the present. It gives you enough heads up to catch a ball (instead of getting socked in the face) and maneuver smoothly through a crowd.[27]

This time-lag enables us to move fluidly through the world. Amusement park rides and three-dimensional movies make use of this neurological system to give us a thrill. As the illusion of the Borg assimilator in the *Star Trek Experience* dives towards our head, and its chair mechanism prods us, we automatically shift our head to try and avoid the collision even though we know we are in a fictional setting.[28] Changizi explains the brain function that enables this response:

> The converging lines toward a vanishing point (the spokes) are cues that trick our brains into thinking we are moving forward—as we would in the real world, where the door frame (a pair of vertical lines) seems to bow out as we move through it—and we try to perceive what the world will look like in the next instant.[29]

In this way, we can predict and respond accordingly to the world as we travel down a hallway.

Imagine running through the forest: It is important to be able to tell how much we ought to adjust our path to avoid a tree or dodge a branch. In the motion-simulator rides at Disney, the event designers exploit our experience navigating the world to play with our senses. Changizi elaborates on this process:

> In real life when you are moving forward, it's not just the shape of objects that changes. . . . Other variables, such as the angular size (how much of your visual field the object takes up), speed and contrast between the object and background, will also change. . . . For instance, if two objects are about the same distance in front of you, and you move toward one of the objects, that object will speed up more in the next moment, appear larger, have lower contrast (because something that is moving faster gets more blurred), and literally get nearer to you compared with the other object.[30]

In our run through the forest we need to segregate figures from background, predict which objects are stationary and which are mobile, and to be able to respond and adapt to those changing circumstances.

Our reptilian brains are activated when they are sensitized to movement. We begin to process divergent bits of information and put together a sense of motion. Motion sensation is possible because magnocellular neurons (MT cells) are triggered when part of an image of an object moves across their receptive field. The cells' resulting impulses are transmitted to the lateral geniculate nucleus (LGN) and onward to the primary visual cortex.

Impulses from an array of MT cells become sensitive to the direction that the object moves.[31] As a baton flies into the stage picture, our brain begins to process the new inclusion in a different manner than before. Our brains become active in the processing of the new data. This excitation is integral to the simulative processes that are inherent within the theatrical event. However, the data that it has processed might be misperceived. In our everyday lives, this may cause perceptual anomalies that misrepresent movements or colors, but in theatre, that may have been deliberately triggered so that an illusion may be perpetrated. These misperceptions—or theatrical misdirection—are a result of the way that the brain amalgamates fragmentary information. In the perception of color or of motion our brains may base their view of the circumstances on imperfect data that can be read in a variety of ways. If we catch sight of a falling branch out of the corner of our eyes, direction-selective cells in the motion pathway will pick up a bit of the event. In this case, the cells would register the diagonal orientation of the branch, but not register the movement of the object as a whole.[32] Our brains can be said to autocorrect to some extent to make sense of various bits of data it notices. There is yet another layer to motion perception, where our chemical possessing centers filter out unnecessary information to better make use of the relevant information it collects. Our brains are able to integrate motion information taken in from a large panorama. Whereas an MT cell might respond to a motion in one spot in the visual field, it will still processes what is going on in the area around that spot. It is sort of like when we look across to a train on the other track at a station. As it starts to move, we feel like we are moving because we note a change and it takes a moment to register the other contextual clues to allow us to understand that we are stationary.

Researchers have been measuring MT firing rates in relation to background texture. They have found that MT firing rates intensify if a background moves in an opposite direction to a moving object. This is why we notice a soldier as he moves across a stand of trees. MT cells detect motion contrast. However, if the background moves in the same direction we do not respond. We filter out static forms and colors. We will detect a moving object much more easily if its form or color strongly contrasts with its background.[33] If we recall the little girl in the red coat in Steven Spielberg's *Schindler's List* (1993), standing out in contrast to the black-and-white surroundings of the camp, we can understand the effect of the brain's filtering of unnecessary detail. The contrast of the red coat against the grey background gave her focus and began to manipulate our perception of the little girl using the symbolic and emotional resonances of the color red. We are able to make sense of a crowded scene because of our biological make-up and our ability to select details to focus on.

Though there were hundreds of surrounding people moving in different directions, we did not have a problem detecting the little girl in a red coat walking along. Our visual system uses the coat's color to filter out all the irrelevant noise around it and homes in on the moving object of interest. What designers and directors have known for years is that static forms and colors do not attract the focus of the attendants, but rather a moving object grabs focus, especially if its form or color strongly contrasts with its background.

As theatre is time-based art where movement plays a major role, setting, sculpture, lighting, and architectural space are in constant flux. In Wilson's theatre, the transitions between scenes have a profound significance on the content of the images. Whether the changes are discernible, contrast with what came before, or unfold at a constant rate are factors that contribute to the attendant's experience of the event. The work of mimes is especially good at this style of communication; they can create a space simply by reacting within it. The ways in which their body reacts within those bounds demonstrates the ways in which the space is conceived. The changing of that space becomes the expression of the event transpiring. Fluctuations in spatial relationships dictate a context in which a performer reacts, thereby creating an abstract visual experience with a beginning, middle, and end. One of the most startling techniques that Wilson uses is the slowing of stage time. The closest aural comparison is with his sometime collaborator Philip Glass. In a similar way to the repetitions and gradual changes in pitch or pattern of the music, Wilson's images can remain virtually static over long periods. Tempo and movement of the objects, such as the runner in *The Life and Times of Joseph Stalin* (1973) who did laps around the stage, can dictate the weight of the space between things. The technique asks us to linger visually more than we might normally in a single moment. In this way, when change does occur, it takes on significance. Also, as a figure or object moves slowly across the stage, the attendant is drawn to the motion and is allowed to scrutinize the lines and shapes of the object. By doing so, we are able to consider the nature and qualities of the image as it is, rather than by where it may end up. Transformation and its causes are revealing of the spatial dynamics, which compose the expression of the performance.

The rhythm of its movement is as important as the duration of the unfolding of the play. The music of *Einstein* has a deliberate tempo; changes or shifts in tempo and rhythm are noticeable. The pace of a particular event is determined by the time that Wilson believes it necessary to absorb the visual elements of the scene. The opening curtain in *Maladie* was a black and gray color scheme, and then as the play progressed, it used a bright blue palette. The progression of the color scheme slowly changed as the emotional involvement between the characters built. Environmental change occurred parallel to the dialogue and action and amplified the effect on the attendants. More extreme was the tempo of the movement in *Deafman Glance* (1971) of the figure of a Victorian lady in the process of moving across the stage over the course of a half-hour. Attendant response varied, in that some people claimed to see things that were not there, whereas others fell asleep. We do not experience that type of opportunity on a daily basis and thus a regulated rhythm over a long period in the theatre can be an unsettling experience.

Adaptation is an important function of the senses; our bodies need to respond when encountering changes in the world. Thus when change occurs, the brain pays attention. Everyone has experienced the ways our eyes adapt when we go inside from a bright day into a dimly lit room, such as when moving from the sunny street into a darkened theater. At first not much can be seen, but, after a short time, our ability to see clearly returns. This increase in sensitivity of the retina is called "dark adaptation." The reverse condition, termed "light adaptation," is when an increased sensitivity, followed by a decrease in sensitivity on emerging from the dark theatre back onto a sunny street, also occurs. Dark adaptation is a photochemical process.

In effect, in the arts we are creating circumstances that exercise our pupils, our muscles, and our senses, and that is why even fiction can transport us into an emotional state. We are making use of the tools of the body to create a sensory-rich mimetic representation. We are primed for any type of stimulation; sport is one, and theater another. Both are performative because they make use of creating a particular physical and mental state excited by the event that we are experiencing. We exercise our bodily responses and keep them stimulated. If we were in the wild, these would be stimulated by scurrying lizards or hissing snakes; instead we need to approximate experience to gain experience so we are rehearsing physiological and emotional experiences to keep us exercised and to build our experience. We learn through mimicking and exercising our physiological response. In this way, we remain flexible and we can keep on developing brain cells and neural pathways. Inherent in each discussion of the visual mechanisms in Wilson's dramaturgy has been the notion that each element is seen in relation to the whole. Any spatial change has an effect on the objects within that space. Actors move, setting changes, light and color change in intensity and value. The pace and rhythm of these changes moderates the attendant's response to the whole theatrical experience, thereby providing it an overall shape.

Keller instructs us that:

> Light is existential for all of us. As well as its biological effect, it shows us reality in constantly changing ways, thus opening a number of visual impressions that affect our perception emotionally. Light is with us night and day and makes life possible. The colour of light is also very important for people as organisms. Colours motivate, enliven and worry us. They signal danger or sound the all-clear and control our subconscious.[34]

As a teenager, my friends and I would go to a place called Horse-barn Hill late at night. We used to like it there because it was a wide open space

where we could watch the stars, yet we often used to make ourselves fright-
ened because of what the landscape evoked for us. Keller tells us that "Any
visual experience is dependent on light, which does not merely enable us to
see but also conveys atmosphere and drama."[35] Theatre uses light to create
mood, to fill in the details of the world that is being represented. For the
imaginative teenager, the silhouette of a hill with a lone tree atop its peak
and a full moon evoked a tale of werewolves triggered by the sounds of
howling wolves nearby. Sven Nykvist rhapsodizes, "Light can be gentle,
dangerous, dreamlike, bare, living, dead, misty, clear, hot, dark, violet,
springlike, falling, straight, sensual, limited, poisonous, calm and soft."[36]
The way that light suggests for us how to feel is essential to our world. It
gives us a way to use our experience to understand what to expect from the
world. Do we know how to see the world? The villages along the coast of
Indonesia that survived the tsunami saw that there were differences in the
tide and in the way that the world felt and knew to go to higher ground.
They survived. In another context, we are able to enjoy a sensual moment
because we have been prepared by the candlelight and close proximity to
our lover. We know what it is supposed to look like, or how culture has
suggested that it ought to look like.

As the technology of lighting has improved, so too has the range of media
that is available within theatrical events. What we could do on stage inside a
building was in part limited to what we could effectively see. As more of the
stage became illuminated, then we began to use the stage space in a different
way. As we began to use more space, Appia and Craig considered how to
make that space as evocative as music or verse. Light became metaphor, and
it began to suggest that what happens on stage could be understood or experienced as real. Once Wagner turned off the house lights, we were forced to
focus on the illusion presented in front of us without distraction. Our attention was directed towards the stage, and light attracted our interest.

THE ELEMENTS OF VISION

Vision is so rich in theatre and so well studied that I limit my examples to
Wilson's compositions because they are widely known and demonstrate
the ways in which theatrical form stimulates our attention through visual
means and offers excellent examples of the use of light as a primary tool
for guiding the attendant's focus over the duration of a performance. David
Bradby and David Williams encapsulate the basic components that are
essential to both Wilson's work and the visible in theatre:

> Wilson's anti-intellectual aesthetic is built around furnishing the spec-
> tator with an implacably beautiful flow of images, in the widest sense of
> the word: temporal and spatial configurations of sound, movement and
> their relationship to space—above all, an architectonic arrangement

of simultaneously superimposed elements, like overlaid slides, the contents of which are above all their form.[37]

His productions are a flow of images whose expression is the relations of objects arranged in architectonic theatrical environments. He consciously manipulates aesthetic concepts gleaned from the fine arts to create three-dimensional theatrical compositions. These can be categorized as "scopic building blocks"—that is to say, visible mechanisms used in the compositional structure of his theatre work. He uses a stock of these visual techniques to create the content of each work. In Wilson's work, spatial relationships are often the content. That means that the images filled with objects, shape, and color, are the visual spine that triggers the attendants' responses. By using spatial dynamics, the visual elements serve as a ballet of spatial components that propel the compositions forward and captivate us regardless of the textual narrative.

In contrast to a fixed medium such as a painter's canvas, the theatre allows light, color, mass, and movement to interrelate in three dimensions. Wilson describes, "This chair, or this line, or this cat . . . this cigarette, you, my words, the light, it's all . . . part of one thing. And in the theatre you can be all of it. I think that it is important to express that."[38] A greater whole can be made up of an array of objects whose individual qualities do not detract from the perception of that whole. We watch it transmogrify as it moves through time and space. The theatre medium enables many different elements to exist side by side and to communicate in very different ways, because time allows for change and transformation. A light can be a light, but it can also be a part of a different contextual situation. The moment before influences what comes after. Similarly to a retinal image, the first stage image stays in the attendant's consciousness and cannot be omitted. Each new image carries with it a residue of its own past.

Tadeusz Kantor describes the component parts of abstract visual expression: "The square, the triangle, the circle, the cube, the cone, the sphere, the straight line, the point, the concepts of space, tension, and movement—are elements of drama."[39] Physical forms or emblematic poses are broken down into their component lines or relationships to each other. Sorrow may be triggered by a curved line, and joy may be triggered by an upward fork. Abstracted theatre creates three-dimensional images using line, weight, color, movement, and sound to create metatheatrical experimentation with form. Wilson's plays are constructed of scopic elements that make up their composition. Images may be framed behind the proscenium arch, built by painting with light, adding human figures, props, and blending them with sound. The constant interrelationship over time of all these mechanisms provides the attendants with activity to keep their senses stimulated. These images do not necessarily convey any one possible interpretation, but are presented to affect the attendant on a sensorial level.

Whether images change or remain the same, they become an "invisible event." When they change, they represent a series of minute and mundane occurrences, which, when taken together, create a monumental image. As Robert Stearns claims, Wilson: "Uses the stage (among many arenas) to focus *our* attention on the world around us, on the things in it, and ultimately on the beauty and mystery of human endeavor."[40] Even the interrelationship of geometric forms demonstrates change. Again, Kantor describes how abstract elements create a dramatic occurrence:

> One person draws a CIRCLE. Another one draws this something that is in opposition to a CIRCLE, that is, a LINE. Dramatic tension appears and increases when the line gets closer to the circle. When the line passes the circle and moves beyond it, the tension decreases. Repetition makes one think about infinity, about our life and its relationship to infinity.[41]

The visual experience triggers thoughts, which trigger other thoughts. Through seeing visual elements, we follow a path laid out by the artist. Ad Reinheart made black square paintings. To comprehend these pictures, we must examine them for a long time, so that our eyes adapt to the sensory stimulation. Scrutiny opens our eyes to the nuances of shading and texture within the black square. Wilson's images can be understood in that context. For example, think about his affection for juxtaposing two unlike material objects. Only by noticing the differences between them, can we notice the "objectness" of each. In other words, the qualities of two unlike objects or components can be seen better when placed next to each other—that is to say, when it is seen as a Brechtian *Verfremdungseffekt*.

The image's texture and structure work together to provide experiences for the attendant:

> Wilson began to create a kind of dramatic "space/time" through contrasting the front stage with the action on the main stage. This technique has the same effect as juxtapositioning two unrelated images, another postmodernist strategy used by the artist. Once, during an interview, Wilson placed a beer can next to a piece of pre-Columbian pottery and commented, "The two things are more interesting than just one because they are so different. They're out of context, but they help you see. My works are like that."[42]

Each object can be seen for its own unique qualities because the incongruity of its context highlights what this object is. Each object's formal qualities stand out discretely against the alien context. In a sense, a third aesthetic relationship is created that has a greater effect than each of the objects displayed on its own. The techniques of juxtaposition, collage and overlay are also exploited using the theatre's ability to synthesize many threads. His medium becomes extremely flexible and he is able to use it to be self-reflexive. The structure ensures that the disparate stimuli work together to attract our attention to the details of the form.

Even when Wilson deals with canonical texts such as *Alcestis* (1986), the abstracted images constitute the content of the story. Words are not the primary communicative material. Wilson explains:

> Theatre doesn't live in words . . . It lives in space. A director works with space. Light lets you see the architecture of the space. Other directors pore over the text. I draw space. I always start with light. Without light there is no space. With light you create many different kinds of spaces. A different space is a different reality.[43]

Therefore, the visible components are parts of occurrences that make up the event. Physical imagery can convey meaning as effectively as a text-driven narrative, but in a different manner. Choosing to use one component over another component offers a different type of perceptual invitation to the attendants. By conscious use of both forms of expression, the artist has a wider palette of expression.

Form, light, and space are all aesthetically captivating separately, but often they are not noticed until someone points them out as worthy of contemplation. Image consciousness gleans a different level of understanding of the theatrical medium. Symbolic evocations of abstracted feelings and concepts are embedded within the communicative medium. In *Maladie*, projected drawings of a room comment upon the action, and the colors are physical manifestations of the characters' emotions. We notice the subtitles of color projected on the cyclorama and the ways in which it progresses from light to dark, blue to red, or yellow to green. These changes can trigger emotions such as jealousy, depression, lust, or any other emotion. It is the stimuli and processing of these pictorial constructs that strengthens our ability to generate personal interpretation of the event.

Wilson coordinates scopic elements with aural elements to create theatre that is a blend of dance, sculpture, painting, and performance art. Heiner Müller enjoyed working with Wilson because the text and images need not work together towards the same goal. They have different aims and, when juxtaposed, each retains its own character. With Wilson's theatrical performance, each element operates autonomously, neither functioning in an illustrative capacity in relation to the other. The textual and the visual exist side by side, each creating its own part in the whole of the performance: "You've got all these textures and structures, and each one on its own can be very different, but together they offer something else. And it's how they counterpoint one another; how they can be put together structurally so that we can taste and smell and experience them. Each element, whether it's light or a gesture or an object, is thought about as something that has its own validity."[44] The performance becomes a barrage of stimuli, where elements drift in and out of perception as they relate to the other elements. The experience of watching occupies the sentient being. Its ephemeral nature keeps the viewer involved with the experience. Philip Glass described how the three predominant visual themes or images of *Einstein on the Beach* were conceived:

> Bob often mentioned that he envisioned them in three distinct ways: (1) a landscape seen at a distance (the field/Spaceship scenes); (2) still lifes seen at a middle distance (the Trial scenes); and portraits seen as in a closeup (the Knee Plays). As these three perspectives rotated through the four acts of the work, they created a sequence of images in an ordered scale.[45]

The different genre paintings serve as techniques to achieve different desired effects. Throughout his entire theatrical output, Wilson has used an array of common scopic mechanisms as elements in his dramaturgical composition. These elements help show, in general, the ways in which theatre can exploit three-dimensional imagery to attract the attention of our visual systems.

SPATIAL ORGANIZATION AS A MEANS OF CONTEXTUALIZING EXPERIENCE

Robert Storr's description of the work of the sculptor Tony Smith is also useful as a description of spatial organization in the theatre:

> Space is not just the context in which art takes place—the void that is filled by objects and images—but is, instead, among art's basic raw materials—something to be taken hold of, studied, and shaped. Thus the architect frames emptiness to consolidate volumes, while the draftsman or painter divides space within the confines of the white page or the blank canvas, and the sculptor anchors the environment around him with physical mass or embraces the atmosphere with armatures.[46]

The theatre artist divides space within the confines of the stage, frames it with setting, and anchors the environment with props and actors. Our experience of the stage space is as integral a component of the theatrical experience as the text that actors speak.

When discussing the shaping of space, the parameters of the visible stage space become variables. Each choice has many consequences for the effect of that space upon the attendant. A deeper stage makes more space available in which actors can interact or in which to place large sculptural objects. Wilson's *Forest* (1988) uses deep staging, which allows the stage space to be divided into separate playing areas that act independently of the rest. The human figure can exist at one depth, birds in another, and a log in a third.

The easiest way to visualize the placement of the objects in space is to use the Cartesian coordinate system. The horizontal is designated as the ordinate (x), the vertical as the abscissa (y), and the depth as (z). The biological object exists in an environment in relation to other masses. The appearances of its placement in space carries with it emotional connotations for us. For example, in *Orlando* (1989), the stage space is horizontally divided into two different zones. If the darker color moves down the x-axis, the space becomes endowed with a sense of weight and pressure upon the characters. As the objects change values for x, y, and z, the movement through space offers a visual narrative of changing spatial relationships. If the black scrim descends on the x-axis, our impression of the way in which Orlando occupies the space changes, thereby triggering feelings that influence a different understanding of Orlando in the context of what came before.

The grid pattern used in *A Letter for Queen Victoria* (1974) shows how deep in space the figure moves. The relationship between the figure and the space creates different effects depending on its placement in the architectural environment. The linear perspective of deep space is dependent on the place in the house in which we sit and thus introduces different complexity to the design of stage setting. Attendants sitting on one side of the theatre see the action at a different angle than those sitting on the other side. Thus, the spatial relationships of the objects on stage are seen differently by the two groups. Wilson must choose whether he wants the variability to be a component in our response to the scene. In contrast, Wilson created a shallow light show for *Lohengrin* (1991). A shallow stage pushes all the action to the front of the stage, allowing us the same planer view of the stage space as we have of a flat painting. The relationships within the composition minimize the distortion of linear perspective of three dimensions. Wilson frequently uses a shallow staging. He therefore must utilize the principles of plane geometry; in other words, he works primarily with the horizontal and vertical x- and y-axes. In either example, Wilson must decide whether to limit or broaden our range of responses to the given moment.

Barnett Newman's compositions demonstrate the ways in which planer geometric shapes are organized, and in turn trigger an attendant response. In *Canto VI*, a single vertical strip cuts across the right side of the black rectangle confined by the edge of the page. The space is divided into three distinct zones. Each has its own size and dimension, but is also seen in relation to the whole. Likewise, in *Hamlet*, Wilson divided the stage into distinct zones on the vertical. Both have similar divisions of the confining space. One-quarter of the right side is lit, whereas three-quarters is blocked by black scrim. For example, in the performance, Hamlet jumps out from behind and disappears periodically behind the scrim as the verbal thread repeats. One possible interpretation of the staging is that the image is a physical manifestation of the verbal idea that was beginning to form. When Hamlet jumps out of sight, the image repeats in the same way the text repeats, thus giving us a physical experience of an abstract concept. Later,

Wilson opens three-quarters of the stage, contrasting it to the three-quarters of darkness that is set on the closed vista of the one-quarter stage. The variant space creates a tempo that structures the visual content. The pacing of the play is carried by spatial dynamics rather than verbal rhythms, and the visual stimuli guide the attendants' focus. The painted light divides the planer surfaces of the stage space. There, the spatial composition is determined by where the line cuts through the horizontal and vertical axis.

Wilson's use of stage space is analogous to the concepts applied by Rothko to his compositions in which he utilizes horizontal geometric shapes to organize spatial arrangements. In *Number 61(Brown Blue, Brown on Blue)*, the weight of the brown zone pushes down the bright blue strip that rests atop a darker blue rectangle. Each component part has an effect on the reception of the composition. Colored shapes are the content and the form of the painting. Rothko believed his paintings possessed the ability to provoke spiritual transcendence, which he intended viewers to achieve by looking at the paintings. Wilson plays with the manner in which viewers understand space as a communicating medium to convey something about the character of the idea contained therein. *Orlando* shows Orlando recumbent on stage in a narrow horizontal band of blue light. The height of the frame is only several feet. The weight of the blackness pushes down on the narrow band of space, making what looks like a coffin. The weight of the blackness suggests the ways in which the life force, the blue color, is constrained by the grip of death, the black color. The image looks two-dimensional despite the presence of a sculptural entity. Again, in both artistic compositions, the space is arranged in a similar manner, thereby, the colored planes are the forms that convey the expression of the images.

Another, more radical, use of space is divided staging. The attendants for *Death, Destruction & Detroit* (1979) had to swivel between one of three stages to watch the action. There were the three playing areas surrounded the attendants; simultaneous staging gave multiple images from which to choose. Divided staging exists when the stage space is partitioned into distinct playing areas. A stepped wall created several levels on which to present action. In an interview with Stefan Brecht, Wilson describes the way in which he devised the spatial organisation of *The Life and Times of Sigmund Freud* (1969):

> The stage is divided into zones—stratified zones behind the other . . . in each of these zones there's a different "reality"—a different activity defining the space so that from the audience's point of view one sees through these different layers, and as each occurs it appears as if there's been no realisation that anything other than itself is happening outside that designated area.[47]

Each stage division contains its own content so that when seen in relation to the rest, the space has a life of its own that contains the actions within.

Another example is the setting for *H.G.* (1995), where the experience had a phenomenological rationale, by which our perceptions were heightened, and perceptual manipulation played a major role—the space and image were designed to be experienced in the same manner as walking through a building. After we pass through the Victorian dining room at the entrance, we discover the rest of the underground space at our own pace in whatever order we come upon its constructed images. It is of little consequence whether we found the Mummy in the misty tomb, or the rows of hospital beds and vats of bloody water. The act of negotiating the terrain of the dank, dark vaults is as much a part of the event as are the brightly lit still lives of different epochs and places.

The space in which the visible elements of theatre are displayed contributes to the ways in which these elements are perceived. Wilson frames the stage space variably using height, width, and depth to limit the space into a contained environment for attendants to view. He also divides the stage space to present simultaneous multiple frameworks to shape the content of each theatrical presentation. The different techniques are effects he applies to shape the space into a desired overarching effect. He also uses light and dark to contain the images within the stage space. The space is organized so those sculptural objects can relate within their setting. The relation of these objects within the space becomes the event. Accordingly, these techniques demonstrate Wilson's overt use of the vertical and horizontal and his overt "foregrounding" of depth and flatness to organize space. This structure provides him and, hopefully us, a meaningful context for interpretation of the event.

THE SETTING AND THREE-DIMENSIONAL PERCEPTION

A theatrical setting serves a variety of functions. It may denote time, place, and mood; act as punctuation where design strategies advance narrative propositions; act as embellishment where decor displays an elevated style; act as artifice where design is patently unreal; act as narrative where a single setting is self-reflexive; or act as an acting machine. However, when looking at it in relation to the senses, setting is most like a landscape. It depicts a place made of forms in a contained space. A landscape setting can encompass the more traditional definition of setting, as well as serve as an artwork in its own right. Its form and content communicates to the viewer. Wilson's installation work can show the ways in which setting can be evocative on its own. The *H.G.* installation is also a theatrical event that only uses a visible setting. The ephemeral presence of H.G. and the inhabitants of the world that he presented became the protagonists of the event. Moreover, the movement between scenes and the duration of the event depended upon the attendants, who were the actors following the random path of H.G. bouncing through history. The sculptural properties that compose the still lives or landscapes of the installation have a history that we as attendants unearthed in an analogous way to archaeologists who reconstruct ancient civilizations based on relics they find. Often, very little else is given by way of action or dialogue to inform the attendant. Thus, the setting becomes the primary conveyor of sensory stimulation.

The presence of an object changes the narrative. In *H.G.*, there are nineteenth century objects scattered through the settings. Within the mummy's tomb, towards the back was a flask engraved with the initials "H.G." We took notice because our eyes were attracted by the light highlighting its presence. This discarded human article suggests that H.G. had been there before us. Finding the flask in the proximity of the mummy changes the story of the space. It suggested that others have walked here before us and others will follow. As other environments have other objects, a relationship between H.G. and these sites becomes apparent. We have walked this earth for thousands of years, and different refuse remains as evidence of past life. Coke cans and bottles populate the scene, as well as eighteenth century portraits. Our objects tell the story of our movement through history during our own transient time and our ultimate death. Other sites suggest that humans can die by extermination (pairs of tagged shoes like in German death camps), die of disease (influenza records strewn about the medical ward), or die in war (arrows across the sky in the Classical ruins).

The decor may ground the scene into what is recognizable. A bedroom suggests one thing, a drawing room suggests another, and a room filled with objects that are too large for it yet another. The setting tells the attendant what kind of distortion, or what type of illusion, is expected. The form and content of the setting carries thematic implications. The visible whole world of the play is communication that conveys story or place. The information attendants glean from the component elements of the picture is one form of expression. Images carry the show and bind it together into a visual unity. The function of the words is not unimportant, only they are not the primary mechanism that unifies the theatrical experience in Wilson's works. Words are elements that clarify, direct, or suggest contexts in much the same way that sets in conventional works may punctuate, denote, embellish, or narrate.

A more traditional and recognizable landscape is of the homestead. An American colonial home appears in *Edison* (1979) and *Time Rocker* (1996). The colonial home is emblematic of the American consciousness of history and of a sense of nationality. Bachelard professes: "For our house is our corner of the world. As has often been said, it is our first universe, a real cosmos in every sense of the word. If we look at it intimately, the humblest dwelling has beauty."[48] In *Edison*, Wilson goes a step further and projects a landscape upon the colonial house. These landscapes are emblematic of themselves as much as they are of illustrative locations in time and space for the characters. They serve as more than mere setting because they shape the space and add to the total fabric of the visible theatrical composition.

The shapes that are formed on a painted canvas capture particular moods or feelings. The advent of photography in the nineteenth century freed the art of the twentieth century to explore the unreal or the abstract; in other words, to explore what cannot be captured or defined by mere reflective representation. Theatre has always had this ability, and Wilson exploits it to depict the fantastic on stage. In *Time Rocker*, a fish skeleton can be a time machine transporting the characters into unknown dimensions. Through the arrangement of forms in space, he is able to convey dream elements with the illusion that they are real. The transformations of those forms match the fluid quality and fractured logic of the mind flitting from one idea to the next. Nick and Priscilla have travelled from one environment to the next witnessing different events. Though there were songs and text, these different worlds were described only by the components that made up the landscape and the different characters dressed in costumes that further defined the world that they inhabited. These places were clearly fantasy locales, even if one seemed primitive or another seemed Egyptian. Human figures were depicted in abstracted human situations. The impression that attendants were left with does not so much concern where the characters were, but rather what type of qualities these places possessed.

Like a painting, a play can have visual texture that is an apparent rather than tactile quality of a surface. Whether a visual surface is smooth and silky or rough and jagged affects the ways in which the attendants respond to the image. Within Wilson's images, the different components have their own qualities. The woman in *Maladie* wears a silky gown, whereas the dancers in *Time Rocker* wear angular, stiff clothing that resembles crumpled newspapers. One effect of the silky curves and the satiny texture of the colors of the setting are that they promote a sensual quality to the intimacy of the piece. In contrast, the rough crimped lines of the *Time Rocker* dancers' costumes and hair distance the attendants from the experience. Setting also has shape and texture. In *Maladie* the chairs are slender curves resembling the beauty of a woman's shape, and in the dance scene of *Time Rocker*, the hair and the small city props that fill the space are all angular. Not only do these objects shape space, but they also give the stage image a feeling of texture. The materials of the clothing, the shapes of the props, and setting all work together to create the texture of the images. Curves and silk help contribute to the sensuality of the images in *Maladie*, whereas angles and rough material contribute to the mechanistic feel of *Time Rocker*. Therefore, visual texture is both a visual and haptic form of touch that we actively assess synchronously to identify its qualities.

Wilson also shapes the architectonics of the space by creating artificial locales and interiors as setting. In *Maladie*, he projected charcoal-looking line drawings on the back wall to create a hotel room in various perspectives. Only general indications of the room's walls and window were needed because the bodies and the interaction between them made the space seem real. Other architectonic mechanisms anchored the narrative to the immediate visions of the body. The slender art deco lines of its furniture played against the curve of the actress' body. The charcoal drawings were abstracted and unreal, and the sensual beings were real and sleek. These are a physical realization of the sexual fantasy playing itself out in the abstracted space of the mind. An architectural landscape became the landscape of the imagination. With *Maladie*, Wilson takes on a design and directorial role, but the technique he used gave life to the Duras text as a component of his own theatrical expression. The attendants are allowed a glance into the "interior screens" of the figures onstage; that is to say that Wilson talks about the imagination or conscious self as interior screens.[49] Staging imaginary landscapes makes the theatrical medium stretch in a different direction than the more conventional mirror to nature. These plays are visions in three dimensions. The landscape and the figures are portraits of feelings, moods, and unreal fantasy. The stage and the transformations of color and perspective can shift as the thoughts and dreams of the narrator shift. The play becomes the staging of impossible landscapes.

The genre of landscape painting has provided Wilson with a device in which to place his actors. Like a painting, the component parts of the landscape's composition contain a visual narrative. In *The Forest*, the rocks and creature that move across the stage are indications of the events that are transpiring. Each object is on stage for a reason. It is those forms that convey a part of the theatrical experience. Its textures of jagged rock or its sculptural forms of biological entities guide the attendants to an understanding of the space. Wilson's most commonly used settings are composed briefly with line in the form of recognizable locales. Above all, as with orthodox theatre practice, the setting provides a context for the events of the play. The environment and the ways in which the environment changes are how the play progresses through time.

SCULPTURE

Wilson uses figures and objects to shape and sculpt space in different configurations as a play changes from scene to scene. He can create different sculptural shapes by placing different objects together. Human forms can be manipulated using costumes or masks to change the line of mass of the figure. The interrelationship of these elements also changes the nature of each element, as well as that of the space. The shape, texture, and movement of the human figure can be adjusted to broaden the possible creations that can be constructed. Movement of the figures can be seen from different perspectives. The architectonic setting also bears on the nature of the construction because its mass shares the space with the sculptural objects. Together they give a sense of whether it is confining, crowded, vast, or small. Wilson's installations can be considered sculpture. By setting up a classical colonnade or a row of beds, he is organizing and dividing the installation into three-dimensional landscapes. This mutability molds the contexts that the attendants view and experience.

Sculptural objects—whether biological or inanimate—shape the emptiness around them. For example, in *Lohengrin*, Wilson begins with an empty stage, for, he claims, "There's nothing more beautiful than an empty space."[50] From there, he adds human figures and objects to his theatrical stage. This highlights the ways in which forms within that space change its qualities. Two objects in the space are what they are and together they are the sum of what they are. Like Wittgenstein's reversible duck/rabbit picture, the spatial area we choose to focus on changes our perception of the image. In one case, the lines form a duckbill; in the other, rabbit ears. We can focus on the objects onstage or the space between them. By vacillating between the two images, the mind processes information from two different visual sources. In the theatre, the character can be shown one way while reacting to the other characters in a different way. We can focus on the individual and on the relationship between individuals, thus creating two perspectives simultaneously. Sculpture's relation to other sculpture and architecture offers several avenues of communication that can elicit many things for the viewer. All these manners of suggestion are pasted together into a collage of impressions, as is the case in *Time Rocker*, where Priscilla and Nick relate to each other as well as to the different worlds they visit. With sculpture, the curve of a line or the colors of its context can trigger emotional reactions. The ways in which the visual artist arranges and manipulates the objects creates an atmosphere, or world, that the attendants of the experience can respond to in a variety of ways. Intuition, convention, and cultural codes guide them to what feels like a harmonious arrangement of form and context. These arrangements are the stimuli for the attendants to experience and augment the other communicative mechanisms in operation in the work. Wilson's aesthetic operates within a given set of cultural and social conventions.

The sculpturing of human figures is an essential part of Wilson's dramaturgical composition because figures shape space and augment "liveness." His forms become bio-objects, the "biological symbiosis between actor and object."[51] Theatre highlights "objectness" because it uses self-propelled human figures as part of the visible components of the stage. Critics often describe actors in Wilson's plays as furniture. In fact, Wilson choreographs their movement and records it on videotape so they can learn the appropriate gestures, body shapes, and movement. They are meant to be tableaux vivant, expressive of the shape and spatial relations that Wilson intends. At the other extreme, props can become animated. The flying bird from the Knee plays in *The CIVIL warS* (1984) takes on life at the hands of the puppeteers; here, "furniture" becomes a biological entity. In *Hamlet*, a shovel stuck in the ground moved around the stage of its own accord. The inanimate objects begin to have their own personality and also tend to lend an air of humor to the piece. The shapes and movement of objects can change the composition and the nuance of the space.

The space between things is also important in dramatic expression. According to Susan Cole:

> Wilson is characteristically concerned with "the space around the movement": "the space under the arm." It is part of his concern with ways of seeing: "In the theatre you always have to fill the auditorium with presence . . . the weight of the gesture has to get to the exit signs. And the space around it helps us to see it . . . as I've said many times . . . a small dot in a large room . . . will fill the room simply because of the space around it."[52]

Form shapes space and space shapes form. As studies in kinaesthetic theory show, basic human physical behavior and interaction is a readable language.[53] Different cultures have prescribed ways of interacting that is inculcated in the individual during social development. The proximity of two people defines the formality or intimacy of the relationship at that moment.[54] In its most conventional forms, it can tell us whether two people are feeling affectionate, are friends, lovers, business partners, or of higher or lower status. In the staging of *The Meek Girl* (1994), three actors move through the architectural space and adopt poses or gestures reminiscent of nineteenth-century tableaux frieze. Their poses are mirrored in the other's gestures. They inhabit different places on the stage, yet retain a balanced pictorial composition. It is the space between them and the manner in which they interrelate that is evocative of the content of the piece. A usurer tries to understand why his wife committed suicide and relives their sadomasochistic hell filled with silence, passion, and contempt. Sculptural movement or posing sets up the relationship between the movable objects and the static objects, and thereby, stimulates the attendant's awareness of the figural interrelationships.

Costume can shape or stand in for the bio-object. In *Hamlet*, Wilson used the costumes of all the dead characters, in the final moments, as a sort of summary of all the deaths in the play. The clothing became a litany of senseless death. In *H.G.*, the props were strewn around the tunnels as a reminder or evidence of past human exploration. They become evocative of larger issues, such as the holocaust, cycles of mortality, and contemporary humanity's place in history. The objects can be thought of as a type of ready-made sculpture acting as a surrogate to human corporeality.

A recurring object can suggest a recurring theme. A train, suggesting the industrial age, is a recurring image in *Einstein*, and the repeated identical movement of bars of light in *Lohengrin* is a reminder of earlier material. One sculptural object in a particular time and place will resonate with another in a different time and place, thus adding structural integrity to the composition. Our own personal associations with the images have a bearing on the way we experience the event. The presence of a particular object can plant seeds of ideas within our subconscious. How much is suggested from the introduction of that element depends on visual, cultural, and educational literacy. The ambiguity inherent in the structure, form, and content provides enough flexibility to transcend cultural or literal specificity, yet retain a controlled range of meaning. As on the outside of a church, where the relief sculptures on either side of the door will balance each other, a visual stage composition can be arranged to highlight a particular element or to visually rhyme with other elements. The composition may be balanced asymmetrically, as, for example, when Wilson places nonidentical forms to either side of a balancing point in such a way that the two sides seem to be of the same weight.

Sculptural objects serve as compositional elements whose arrangement and rearrangement create a fluid image of spatial relationships. The "objectness" of each figure, prop, or set piece helps to convey an emotional or formal relationship. Watching the ways in which these forms occupy space, and the ways in which their character is used in the overall framework of the play, creates an experience that is, in part, the content of the play. Their characteristics trigger mental associations in the manner described by Rudolf Arnheim's theory of visual thinking. A visual language triggers a range of perceptions within the attendant. These sculptural forms inform the attendant in non-verbal ways, and their lighting provides the illumination to focus attention on them.

LIGHT AND DARK

Without light, only a void exists, but with it, shape, depth, mass, and lines reveal themselves. Light is one of the most essential mechanisms that Wilson uses in the construction of his images; after all, as Hubel and Livingstone have shown, our brains are interested by shadows and curves.[55] With light, Wilson is able to illuminate and delineate forms and shapes. Orlando stands at the division of the cyclorama into a black zone stage left and a forest green zone stage right. She holds a hat in the illuminated area and another object in the stage left area. If seen from head on, her body straddles the barrier of the two worlds. The contrast created between the figure and the ground highlights parts of the bio-object. The lighting organizes the space by breaking it into units, thus suggesting possibilities for interpreting the image as a character that hovers between two worlds. With lighting, a stage can become a bright ground whose figures stand out from the bright wash of color behind them: Orlando atop what looks like a staircase; its mass stands in relief to the planer colored surface of the cyclorama. The world around the solid mass is a blank canvas, whose color shows change, creates a visual tempo, and characterizes action. In addition, light can stand in relief to darkness and reveal the tiniest lips of an actor; A light picking out Hamlet's face, his jacket, and a glove puppet of the king who is murdered. Black, as a ground, is neutral background against which the minute shades of the other colors stand clearly forward.

From light and dark, there is also shadow and silhouette. Either they are used as an effect, or they shape the objects illuminated on the stage, giving them mass and depth. The silhouette is used as an effect to contrast the corporeal objects. At one point, Orlando stands posed upstage center closer to the back scrim. On the wall behind her is a shadow of her dress that lacks her head and her arms. The shadow is different from the bio-object on stage. Of course, this is a theatrical trick, but it acts as an image that suggests Orlando's sexual transformations. The setting becomes a place to contemplate the ways in which her other self is beginning to reveal itself. One interpretation shows, that shadows can have a variety of interesting effects. Holmberg interprets, "In *Quartet* Wilson used shadows to create a climate of menace and for psychological bobbling. When Merteuil saw her shadow, she screamed, exposing self-loathing."[56] Whatever associations are elicited by the uses of shadow, the device certainly calls attention to itself. These are instances where the effect plays with traditional notions of shadow and shading to create theatrical imagery that carries us through a theatrical presentation.

Projected line drawings on the back of the stage are also a type of shadow and shading. The line creates an effect of shadow that printmaking and classical painting use to create effects of depth or weight to a two-dimensional object. Wilson most often uses this technique when he is using shallow staging that renders the stage practically two-dimensional. The three-dimensional bio-objects stand out from the artificially projected backgrounds. In *Death, Destruction & Detroit*, a parachutist comes down across the charcoal-shaded sky. Rather than create shadows using beams of light against objects, the shadows are drawn by way of projections. This enables Wilson to light the figures independently of the visible landscape. The reverse is also true. Rather than changing foreground, in *Maladie*, the background changes from time to time, thus changing the emotional climate of the environment. Just as dialogue between the characters can reveal a shift in their mood, a changing background can make tangible the unseen emotional swing. At times there would be the black-to-gray shadowing, while at others the perspective lines for a room were drawn in. In this way, the space of the environment becomes highly artificial and contrasts with the bio-objects.

In *The Golden Windows* (1981), Wilson uses a picture of a house on a mountain, viewed at different times of the day, thus making light and shadow the structure of the play. Changes in shadow and the angle at which the house is viewed create a temporal light show. The light show is the content of the experience whose text serves as a counterpoint to the images. Lighting guides our perceptions of the environment. In turn, it becomes a mechanism to question the ways that changing appearance illuminates or obfuscates the event and the figures in the environment.

Even in a darkened space, we need light to see the forms in front of us. This was taken to the extreme in the *H.G.* installation. We were led into a dark, dank underground system of tunnels, where the only light was from his installations. We moved forward tentatively, testing the ground in front of us and feeling for walls. Form was revealed and shaped by light cutting through the darkness at different intensities. The objects took on a brilliant aspect when we emerged from the darkness into a brightly-lit hospital ward, or when we peeked through a hole in the wall and saw a cascade of arrows flying across an ancient colonnade. Some environments were purposely left dark allowing the attendant to question what lurked near the pole. We were H.G., stumbling through time and space discovering new worlds.

In *Hamlet*, the shades of darkness created one atmosphere, which then was contrasted to the bright light of another. The changes in intensity shaped the audience's perception of the characters and objects on stage. For example, in scene 3, the sculptural elements of Hamlet and a precipice he lain upon changed position as he spoke about "murder most foul," and the lighting in the background foregrounded the sculptural objects. The shifts in stance gave shape to the shifts in verbal expression and the silhouette of the setting took on a resemblance to a pistol. Wilson uses light and dark and its intermediary shadow as a painter would to give depth, shape, mass, or to create effects that become emblematic of concepts or ideas. Light and darkness lead the viewer to take notice of the significant moments that Wilson has made apparent in his structuring of the piece. The lighting reveals the journey of the images, and it is meant to trigger emotion or impressions of the space in a manner that is used for sculptural images. A shaft of light cuts the cube of the space, whereas floodlighting opens the entire vista of the confined space. Adding the color spectrum further highlights the progression of the play through lighting.

THE POTENTIALS OF SCINTILLATING VISUAL EFFECTS

I grew up in the countryside, so when the lights went out, it was pitch black, unless there was a full moon. I would pull up the covers under my legs and over my head to protect myself from the imagined creatures scurrying under my bed. Any form of light was reassuring. On the other hand, when there is a moon it is actually very light out. The sky is lit up by stars, galaxies, and planets. It is beautiful—we can pick out the distant starlight in an instant and the planes and satellites moving through the sky can keep a child dreaming for hours about flying saucers or Santa's sleigh. We are drawn to those pinpricks of twinkling lights. The stimulation that those lights provide keeps us feeling secure. Light regulates our daily existence. Spelunkers who spend extended periods of time under the ground find that, without light, their bodies convert to a twenty-four hour clock with a changing rhythm of the addition of one hour each cycle. What does this mean for theatre practitioners?

Theatre attendants share the same space as the stimuli of performance, watching what the artist shapes for us. As Manfred Wagner explains, the contrast between fiction and reality is at the heart of the experience: "Theatre lighting shows colours, spaces, shadows, objects, people and images, in short, the compressed world of the theatre in contrast with the real world, even in the attendants' area, which is physically the same size."[57] He continues:

> Theatre light is as virtual as the theatre itself. It never achieves natural quality, indeed is not trying to do that, and thus it creates the necessary distance between itself and nature. Theatre lighting insists that thinking and seeing are connected. It does not allow anyone to get away unless they shut their eyes, which are otherwise entirely at the mercy of what is happening. In other words, there is very little possibility of switching off and thinking about something else. Theatre lighting shows the virtual stage and the people acting on it from a different point of view.[58]

He suggests that although we are aware of the fiction of theatre, it is also physiologically real to the attendant; fiction and reality are merely different degrees of neuronal activity. Our embodiment makes real any stimulation and interprets it according to context, but it is also wired to respond empathetically. Theatre makes real mimesis through live shared experience. By making use of light, the artist is able to evoke for the attendant a fictive journey: "All these pictures show how differently light can define a situation and how the right light can, in fact, bring action into a picture."[59] Lighting thus focuses our attentiveness.

One of the most potent experiences that affected my state of being through vision was a visit to a Robert Irwin installation back in 1998.[60] He transformed two floors of Dia Art Foundation into a gauze-filled warren of rooms. Rather than using drywall to create the walls, translucent gauze was used. Natural light came in through the windows on the solid perimeter walls of the building. We could see others moving through the different rooms. Our minds began to wander, imagining what it would be like to stage a show there where the attendants would chase after actors moving through the space—a sort of murder mystery filled with ghosts. Over the duration of the visit, our eyes accommodated to the light levels. We scrutinized what we were seeing so intensely our vision took on an atypical crispness. After we left and walked down the street the facades of buildings were defined. The city took on a whole new level of interest as we took notice of light and shadow in a way that we had not done so previously. We entered into a store and had no interest in its wares. Instead our eyes were drawn to the storefront window that framed the traffic moving outside. This transition was exciting. It took a while for the detail to fade and our colored, meditative gaze to subside. The installation had primed our eyes to take control. Although we still beheld the street, our vision crated a new perspective in which to analyze the streets around us.

Another Light and Space experience calls attention to the adjusting visual perception systems. There are two installations at Houston's Menil collection. At Richmond Hall, Dan Flavin has neon lights set-up in an old deserted grocery store. He has positioned long green florescent lights along the perimeter of the outside walls of the space. Inside, angled foyer walls have matching sets of white, eight-foot light fixtures, mounted diagonally. The rectangular interior of the central space is flanked on opposing walls by four-foot, vertically mounted fixtures alternating pink, yellow, green, and blue lamps that are cut in half by a horizontal line of filtered ultraviolet. Here, color and light levels create a mood. As our eyes adjust from the bright Texas sun to the more subtle neon colors, another meditative state is produced. The second installation is in the Rothko Chapel. Although it is a religious site and particularly quiet and restful, the large grey Rothko compositions create a meditative mood. The pale grey colors give us something to stare at as we contemplate the nature of this faith, or contemplate the nature of aesthetic balance and symmetry. Both environments filter out the noisy outside world and allow quiet focus. Those states are evoked as a response to the way that color creates a mood within the space. The color stimulation of our eyes evokes mood, as Damasio has proven is tied together. We can sense even if not consciously and, as a result, a mood or emotion will overtake us.

Josef Svoboda describes theatrical design as "[t]he interplay of space, time, movement and light on stage."[61] This can also describe what we pay attention to over the duration of a performance. These compositional elements stimulate our vision and trigger our emotions and feelings, enabling us to make sense of the experience that unfolds in front of us. We pay attention because light, shadow, lines, and movements grab the attention of the perceiving body. This experience has the potential to make known worlds unknown to us. Another example of what potential paying attention to the ways that vision is stimulated in attendants can be seen with descriptions of Mark Morris' *l'allegro, il penseroso*. Joan Acocelle describes the opening of the performance:

> After the overture the front curtain rises, but we see nothing, just darkness. And what the tenor now sings is frightening. . . . The singer is wishing away these terrors, but that's not what we hear. We hear the long vowels, the liquid consonants—"loathed", "forlorn"–sucking into the void we see before us. We are in the stygian cave, in hell. But wait. A stripe of light falls across the stage, and suddenly people are running. Still there is no prose to rescue. The people look frantic; the stage remains mostly dark. We feel we are waking up from a nightmare, pulling cobwebs off our face. At last the stage lights go on, all blare.[62]

The blackness followed by light, in concert with the aural stimulation, evoked Hell and the terror of a nightmare. By watching and listening, our bodies begin to react. Our heartbeats increase and we begin to concentrate on the stimulation before us as if our lives depended upon it. When we trigger the reptilian response system, our emergency response sensations are making sure that we can respond to the danger around us. We focus on the stimuli. Thus the opening sounds are critical in capturing our attention and setting the context for what is about to occur. The stimulation is evoking a range of responses and associations to understand the subtleness of the expression of the piece. James Ingalls designed the lighting to work with the dancers as a means of conveying mood and expression. He tells us:

> I decided to use sidelight extensively and emphasize the various planes of the space, layers really, which open up and closed down for the different sections. But the design isn't only about how each dance section looks. The sequence of light cues has to make sense with the movement of the dance, the music and the changing space. The lighting and the set, in essence, are dancers, too.[63]

The physical properties of the material that artists present to attendants on stage are deliberately manipulative and designed to be of interest to our visual systems. Once our eyes are engaged, the brain will take over and begin to evoke the feelings and emotions that the stimuli is using to form an expression.

Hubel and Livingstone determined what shapes and shadows our brains like to pay attention to. They found that the cells within our eye were attracted to angles of lines and not by dots of light or light intensity. When they cast a sharp shadow onto the retina of a cat they were studying, the cat's brain activity went into action in a way that they had not seen when projecting pure light.[64] We prefer contrast over brightness, edges over curves. This discovery goes a long way in explaining why we are fascinated with the light shows at rock concerts and the colorful motions of the acrobat high above our heads. Our biology finds movement and shadow and angles exciting. Both Appia and Craig understood that as they outlined their principles for the use of light and shadow as a means of creating atmosphere and mood as evocative components of theatrical expression. It is the dance of light against a multi-dimensional plane that satisfies our innate need for capturing the attention of our brains. We were wired for this as a survival mechanism to catch food darting across the forest floor, but artists use this knowledge to create a stimulating and evocative theatrical event. Design practice has taught us that:

> Six principal angles are available if an object or space is to be lit. Choosing one angle is seldom enough to create the required effect. The fundamental question is: what is the composition supposed to look like?

> Beautiful, exciting, uncanny, lacking in contrast, boring? Each angle emphasizes a particular impression and suggests a mood or feeling to the observer.[65]

The live quality of this is important. Film, while stimulating, is a series of twenty-four still images per second. This is not a natural perceptive situation for the brain. We perceive the illusion of movement because our motion-processing system automatically fuses the images of legs that shift position slightly from frame to frame into the appearance of a walking character. If we are unable to perform this fusion we would see the world around us like a series of snapshots. Our motion system must match up image elements from frame to frame, over space and time. We have to detect which direction a hand is moving, for instance, and not confuse that hand with a cantaloupe when it reaches for a piece of fruit. Without the brain's ability to be attracted to movement and perceive the movement-to-moment connections to the world, the body is unable to respond. These stimulations are part and parcel to life, and we seek out that stimulation.

Of the elements in theatre and performance, utterance and image, the utterance is privileged, particularly in the mainstream theatre. Wilson's theatre depends on the eloquence of the set and the form within it; in other words, on what is seen. In most theatre, the visible elements carry a low level of narrative weight. They set time, place, and mood and subscribe to the generally accepted depiction of the real. Time, place, and mood are often conveyed by the visible elements through conventional generic strategies and conventional depiction of cultural contexts. Décor participates in the narratives that claim minimal description; that is, narratives determined to depict the familiar through verisimilitude. In Wilson's theatre, décor acts as a form of expression, thereby serving as a structure to the performance's composition. Scopic constructions metamorphose through time to form an aesthetic journey for the attendant of a performance. At its heart, Wilson's work is a series of drawings realized onstage through the layering of the visible components. When the performance is over, what are left are our embodied memories.

The scopic techniques discussed are visual themes that organize the experience, providing a way to make tangible what was seen and provide a vocabulary with which to describe it. These compositional elements do not work by themselves, rather they function as a web, connecting and building a structure for the whole experience. A better understanding of a play such as *Time Rocker* is developed by recognizing the ways in which music, dialogue, song, light, sculpture, movement, change, texture, repetition, and color are intertwined to create a painter's view of theatrical expression. These cues are the plot devices that can trace the journey of the play through the visual ideas expressing humanity's progress and development, which are central preoccupations of the work.

The work of Cirque du Soleil, whose acrobatics and technical effects astound popular audiences worldwide, demands a different way of watching. There is a flood of sensory information, much like the copious information flowing at us in contemporary culture. Their designer, Luc Lafortune, explains, "The eye, by nature is lazy. It's a bit like water down a river—it will follow the easiest path. By providing more intensity at one particular area on stage, they will want to go there naturally. In a stage such as this one, the possibilities are endless."[66] Wilson, on the contrary, has developed a specific language, which is far slower than most ordinary experience. It is about watching the minute details to understand what is going on. Like the experience of looking at a painting, it is in the infinitesimal components that convey the most information. The elements in Wilson are presented in such a way that the attendants must focus on visual change because it affects the way in which they will perceive the onstage environment. A change in spatial relation or in lighting modifies the experience. He orchestrates three-dimensional visible environments by choosing the visual and aural media that we will witness. He arranges them so that we can experience certain sensations and relate to different spatial relationships revolving around a theme. Our awareness of our sensations helps us understand visual theatrical events with great subtlety.

In rather disparaging terms, Pope Benedict XVI lambastes the nature of the experience of rock music, yet the same statement aptly describes the positive power of performance's evocation of visceral experience:

> "Rock" [music] . . . is the expression of elemental passions, and at rock festivals it assumes a cultic character, a form of worship, in fact, in opposition to Christian worship. People are, so to speak, released from themselves by the experience of being part of a crowd and by the emotional shock of rhythm, noise, and special lighting effects. However, in the ecstasy of having all their defenses torn down, the participants sink, as it were, beneath the elemental force of the universe.[67]

What Pope Benedict describes as the raw vulnerability of having our defenses down and being swept up by the experience of the moment is at the heart of the value of the theatrical event. The web of sensations that has been crafted for our benefit is a means of engaging us dynamically with the world. We are able to experience the elemental forces of the universe because all stimulation is geared to engage embodiment.

To excite our senses is to monitor the material world around us. Vision and touch are related by means of haptics; smell and taste are degrees of the same process. It is impossible to experience just one sensation. It is merely a matter of highlighting our attention towards one sensation. In traditional theatre experience sight and sound have been primary; however, the rest of the senses have never been ignored. The nature of the theatrical event is social and visceral by its nature. By calling attention to the means by which we experience the world, we can further understand the importance of sensation to the theatre's unique event-ness and we can understand the means by which artists have already and could potentially manipulate attendants into a meaningful expression of human experience. To understand the plight of Racine's *Phaedra* is not just intellectual, it is also about the effect of longing on our heartbeat and the feel of our lover's sweat. It is about the physical effects of frustrated love and passion and the knowing desperation of being spurned. What physical torment Phaedra experiences, it is not just a moral dilemma. The theater makes this so because of our close proximity to the actress playing Phaedra, as well as through our basic physiological neuron firings. Our perceptual systems allow Phaedra's plight to be real to us, even if we consciously know it is fiction.

3 Attendant to Touch
Cutaneous Stimulation and Its Expressive Capabilities

"Touch is our most social sense. Unlike seeing, hearing and smelling, and tasting, which can generally be done alone, touching typically implies an interaction with another person."[1] Various modes of theatrical interface suggest that our senses are intrinsic to our understanding of what we are experiencing and what the artists are trying to stimulate within us. Touch is central to the theatrical event—as it is intrinsically a social event where we come in contact with others while watching a group of performers. Though touch is an essential item in our conception of the social, it is also the most elusive and difficult concept to think about when it comes to theatre because, in our recent memories, it is more metaphorical and abstract as a component of the interaction between attendants and performer.[2] However, between performers or between performers and the props and set, touch is a meaningful signifier. More prevalent today than ever before are art experiences where touch is more actively sought as a means for the attendants to experience the work in a more direct fashion, cutting out the middle-ground of haptics or synesthethia.

Whether we acknowledge it or not, touch plays a vital role in communication and social bonding in any theatrical event. Rogue, a teenage character from *X-Men*, cannot be touched by others, lest she sap their life force from them.[3] Her tactile contact with others must be mediated through a prophylactic, thus shielding the touch of her skin from the skin of others. As a mutant, she is denied the one real human social tool; we know life through touch. Without touch, we can only know the world through distant proximate senses. As a result, her character is frustrated because she cannot know a kiss or the intimacy of love. In the end, she sacrifices her special abilities to be able to touch others without hurting them. Touch can send messages; it can comfort, arouse, repel, or seek out. Ancient conceptions of the senses extended touch to vision, seeing, and sound, suggesting that we knew the world by reaching out beams projected from the eyes or nose, caressing the world beyond us with our different senses. We have since proven that we are giant receivers processing all chemical and physical stimuli that our bodies encounter. Some go as far as to say, for example, that touch is our strongest contact:

Touch is ten times stronger than verbal or emotional contact, and it affects damned near everything we do. No other sense can arouse you like touch. We always knew that, but we never realized it had a biological basis. If touch did not feel good, there would be no species, parenthood, or survival. The mother would not touch her baby in the right way unless the mother felt pleasure in doing it. If we did not like the feel of touching and patting one another, we would not have had sex. Those animals that did more touching instinctively produced offspring which survived and had more energy, and so passed around their tendency to touch which became even stronger. We forget that touch is not only basic to our species, but the key to it.[4]

We are increasingly preoccupied with the role of touch in everyday life. The news is filled with examples of the healing properties of allowing residents in old age homes or hospitals to pet animals; in the computer business, there are studies dedicated to developing touch controls to make technology more accessible. A recent example is the success of the Nintendo Wii, which takes advantage of body movement in guiding video game movement. In the game *Frisbee Dog* you can flick the Frisbee to your dog and control the angles of the throw. These games make use of body movement to bowl or ski. As well, there are laboratory projects that are striving to give robots a sense of touch.

There are many examples of theatre actors making use of touch by exploring the environment or touching each other on stage. These are passive actions from the attendant's perspective. If the ingénue slaps her suitor during the play, we know the feeling of her hand against our cheeks and the sting of the slap upon the suitor's face. We receive the information by way of our gaze; however, mirror neuron response ensures that neurons will fire and stimulate the same part of brain that would respond if we were the character being slapped. But these are mimetic representations of touch rather than actual touch used to create an active mimetic experience. To fully consider the implications of an attendant's visceral reaction to the stage action, I am concerned with the ways that the attendant becomes blurred with the spect"actor," to borrow Boal's term, where stimuli reception is the piece.

Let us consider a rather straightforward example of how a theatrical event can be designed to use attendants' experience of touch to enhance the reaction to the event. In Ulay and Marina Abramović's *Light/Dark* (1977), two performers kneel face to face, their faces lit by two lamps positioned above them, with microphones hanging just above each head, and alternatively, they slap each other's face for about twenty minutes until one of them stops. We focus on their faces and the sound of the slap that is amplified each time. Working in much in the same way as whipping has been used in film to show the brutality of enslavement, the sound of slap after slap grates on the attendant's nerves and potentially becomes evocative of the brutality of interpersonal relationships. How long can we stand to watch this man and woman slap each other? Documentation photos show a young woman sitting in back of Abramović with sad eyes, mournfully watching.[5] Her empathetic response is visible. Whereas we have always acknowledged that watching painful behavior can create an emotional response within attendants, experiments with monkeys have proved that simply watching the action will cause a physiological response similar to the experience of Ulay and Abramović. We have experienced the event in as real a way as the artists, and walk away having been affected on a biological level. A neural pathway related to slapping has been activated as a result of what we have experienced.

To appreciate this opportunity to craft the personal experience of touch in the creation of a performance, one must have at least a rudimentary understanding of the basic physiological composition of the sensory system and the ways that the brain processes the data the body generates. Roger Cholewiak and Amy Collins define the modality of touch:

> Touch has been defined as the variety of sensations evoked by stimulation of the skin by mechanical, thermal, chemical or electrical events . . . Because there is such a variety of sensations aroused by stimuli interacting with the skin, it might be more appropriate to describe this modality as the "sense of touch." And, as befits such a symphony of sensations, there are a multitude of instruments contributing their voices, each in its own fashion. The mechanical and physiological characteristics of the skin and these receptor structures, as with those in the other senses, define and limit the sensitivity of the skin to stimuli.[6]

In other words, stimuli that come in contact with the skin offer the nervous system data that it communicates to the brain for processing. How much attention the brain pays to the data is dependent upon the way in which that message is generated. Touch is experienced as a deviation from homeostasis. What we are able to feel is constrained by our organism. That is to say, although we share the same biological language for processing the world by means of triggering the brain, we are limited in our experience of the world by our bodies. How we make sense of that data—such as whether the stimulus is pleasurable or painful—is affected by accumulated experience and cultural conditioning.

Our organism is able to process complex perceptual tasks as a result of our sense of touch. Typically we use touch to determine the material properties of objects and surfaces to identify what they are. Janet Weisenberger asserts that:

> The information available from tactile and thermal stimulation allows judgment of weight, stiffness, elasticity, material (e.g. metal, plastic, etc.), and roughness. This information is often rendered imperfectly

by other sensory systems, such as vision, and thus touch supplements visual information about size, shape, color, etc. in object identification. Equally important is the role of tactile feedback in the manipulation of objects, where touch and thermal information permit fine-tuning of the motor response in precision grip and movement.[7]

Imagine walking down a Chicago sidewalk on a windy night in February. As we approach the corner, we can feel the wind rushing around the corner of the cross street, we look to the pavement, and it appears to be clear of ice. We take a step forward and we next find ourselves flat on our backs, staring at the skyline. The slick, thin coat of black ice created by the whipping wind that coated the surface of the pavement was invisible to our eyes. We could have only know the texture of the sidewalk by testing it with our feet first; however, our eyes told us to ignore the pavement, our boots insulated our contact with the pavement, and we could not feel the ice's slickness until we were already on our way to the ground. Whereas vision and touch can provide some degree of redundant information about objects (size, shape, roughness, location), the tactile sense provides the most immediate and accurate information.

Without the sense of touch, we would not be able to navigate the world. To better understand the implications of the loss of touch, Robles De La Torre asked the question, "What would be worse, losing your sight or your sense of touch?" He found that major somesthetic loss cannot be adequately compensated for by sight. By describing what happened to a subject who lost his ability to feel, he proved that impairments of hand dexterity, haptic capabilities, walking, and so on were catastrophically impaired.[8] We usually think it is our hands that give us the most tactile information because we use them to manipulate objects, but everything we do, including sitting, walking, kissing, and feeling pain, depends on touch. Ainsley Iggo explains that introspection allows an object's qualities to be distinguished from vibrations, steady pressure, and light touch.[9] Touch a smooth surface like glass and our fingertips feel an even distribution of pressure; touch a rough surface, like whisker-stubble on our faces, and we feel a lot of little pressure points. On a practical scale, this becomes clear when we try and negotiate a slippery street, an icy ski slope, or rocky terrain. Learning whether something is rough or smooth, cold or hot is critical in order to avoid splinters and burns. And, without the sensation of touch, the pleasure of contact with our lovers, feeling silk, or floating in a pool on a hot summer day would be gone.[10]

We experience and move through the world as a result of data collected by sensory receptors lodged in the skin. The skin is the largest and most sensitive sense organ in the body: "After the differentiation of the brain and spinal chord, the rest of the embryo's surface covering, the ectoderm, becomes the skin, hair, nails, and teeth, and gives rise to the sense organs of hearing, smell, taste, vision, and touch."[11] Our skin and deeper tissues contain millions of sensory receptors. They register what is happening on our bodies' surfaces and then send signals to our spinal cords and brains. The nerves in skin receive the stimuli that are then interpreted by the brain as touch, heat, and cold. Contained within its layers are the structures responsible for our ability to "feel."

Our skin is layered. Its surface is made up of dead cell bodies that have worked their way out as the skin regenerates; below this is the epidermis; and below that is the dermis, a layer of nutritive and connective tissues. Our cutaneous end organs, the structures that are responsible for transducing mechanical, thermal, chemical, or electrical energy, are imbedded here. The Meissner's corpuscles, for example, are enclosed in a capsule of connective tissue. They react to light touch and are located in the skin of the palms, soles, lips, eyelids, external genitals, and nipples. It is because of the Meissner's corpuscles that these areas of our bodies are particularly sensitive. Most of the body's touch receptors sit close to the skin's surface; however, receptors such as the Paccinian corpuscles sense pressure and vibration changes deep in our skin. Skin receptors do not only respond to touch—they also register pain, as well as warmth and cold. Pain receptors are the most numerous—every square centimeter of our skin contains around two hundred pain receptors, whereas, in contrast, there are only fifteen receptors for pressure, six for cold, and one for warmth.

Touch, for the most part, is a proximal sense. That is, we feel those things that either are close to us or actually contact us. There are exceptions, such as radiant heat from a jet engine firing up on the tarmac, or the vibrations of fireworks exploding far overhead. These events produce changes in the skin that convert energy from one form into another to evoke sensations of warmth or movement, respectively.[12] When we feel the cushion of the seat below us and the warmth of our companion's arm brushing up against ours as we watch a play, "The sensations produced by these events are a function of the underlying morphology (form and structure) and physiology (biological functioning) of the neural end organs that lie within and under the skin."[13]

For our purposes, our skin is a giant pressure plate waiting to be stimulated. What information we pay attention to at any given moment is dependent on our consciousness—"Psychophysical measures of the skin's sensitivity can be affected by factors other than its physiology or stimulus conditions. Cognitive factors such as attention, motivation, learning, or task demands also have to be taken into account."[14] When a new stimulus is felt, then our attention refocuses upon it. That is not to say that the body is not processing millions of other stimuli simultaneously. Our brain is aware of the feel of our clothing upon our skin; however, it does not attribute undue attention to it. Weisenberger explains:

> The receptors for these diverse sensory abilities respond to several different forms of energy. Mechanoreceptors respond to thermal stimulation

of the skin; and nociceptors mediate pain sensations arising from potentially damaging application of mechanical, thermal, chemical, or electrical stimulation of the skin.[15]

Pain is our most significant alarm mechanism.

How touch messages reach our brains and the ways that it responds to those messages are the result of information gleaned from changes in the environment and our homeostatic state. Consider how our bodies responded to the environmental stimulation of heat, air, and vibration provided by SRL during the course of *A Complete Mastery of Sinister Forces Employed with Callous Disregard to Produce Catastrophic Changes in the Natural Order of Events* (2007).[16] Here, fire-breathing robots were brought into our immediate vicinity. As these robots raced around battling each other, shooting fire, jack-hammering the other robots, or banging into objects in their path, we felt the heat from the flames, the vibrations in the ground from their movement, and heavy-duty engines, and were startled by the crash of metal against metal. Bursts of air from the machines cause a physiological response, our heart beats increase, and our palms get sweaty. As the temperature changes, our bodies automatically respond to the stimulation; it is only later, as we reflect on our sensations, that we can make conscious sense of why we are responding in this way. Vibrations underfoot from the heavy machinery have got us on our toes; we can sense the machines moving closer. When the arm of the machine suddenly lurches towards us, we instinctively leap backward. These are not small machines; they are industrial-sized robots akin to the largest of bulldozers or backhoes. The scale of noise that accompanies them is comparable to their size.

As we feel the temperature changes related to the blasts of flame nearby, our skin registers the several-degree flash of heat and sends the information up the spinal cord. If the heat is burning our skin, then chemical messages will travel on short fibers. If a machine lunges towards us and we respond by jumping back, then the mechanical information generated by our movement moves up the spinal cord by way of large fibers. The speed and path are determined by the type of information. It crosses through the sensory cortex and is processed on the opposite side of the brain. Cholewiak and Collins explain what happens to the ascending information when it arrives at the brain:

> What has happened to the information that was encoded within the receptive field of a single unit? First, it has been combined with that from other first-order units and has been distributed among many other second-order units in the spinal chord. This convergence and divergence continues in the higher centers to produce finally a representation of the body's surface at the cortex (but on the opposite hemisphere).[17]

As stimuli reach the brain, it organizes and processes the data, determining whether any action is needed to regulate prioproception, temperature, and so on. When we sense a need to move away from the flame blasts, or we see the lunging motion of the machine and we feel increased vibration from the machine as it moves nearer, our brain will combine the information about the different stimuli and issue a command for our bodies to jump back out of harms way. All of this is pre-consciousness. Our system is monitoring the situation to keep us from harm.

Neuroscience and cognitive science study the paths through the body by which the mind becomes activated and provides us with awareness and a response to our surroundings. Current cognitive theories view the mind and body as a single system. If the brain is intact, then a mind will emerge.[18] This is important to the experience of the arts. We mainly pay attention to ideas that have already been filtered through social and cultural systems. We view this material by being attendant to sensory stimulation and beginning to make meaning out of the event that we are observing. If we are trying to stimulate a new system of being attendant to theatre and making meaning out of the sensory world, then we have to pay attention to our body's experience of those first stimuli. Understanding how they enter into our consciousness can assist us in attending to significant data to help reach a richer interpretation free from our habitual expectations.

How can we better begin to understand the implication of the dangers that artificial intelligence may offer than through our experience of SRL's antagonistic robots? Our fear of a seemingly and sometimes really out of control robot give us more immediate responses to the larger social and intellectual themes that are offered as a result of the entire experience of the theatrical event. The visceral fear of the vibrations and the heat and danger of damage to our bodies provide a vivid visceral message. It gives us a real-world experience of an artistically mediated experience. This performance, albeit unusual and, perhaps, unwise because it puts the attendants in danger from the machines, opens up a potential metaphorical world whose interpretation is powerfully reinforced by the tactile contact between the performing robots and the attendants. This is not so different than what has been going on for over a century within experimental theatre. However, awareness of more recent neuroscientific and cognitive theories related to the sense of touch have generated a new range of potential communication systems to capture that which is beneath the surface of things. It makes this world so much less alien and distant, and gives the artist a host of new tools to play with attendants. It is a means to cut through the conscious baggage that we carry and jump directly to our neural processes before they become influenced by prior experience.

TOUCHA, TOUCHA, TOUCHA, TOUCH ME[19]

The following examples extrapolate the intricacies of the tactile and the ways in which we can feel temperature, vibration, and pressure as meaningful stimuli generated as a part of the theatrical event. Actors make use of touch both to explore the environment and to interact with each other on stage. As discussed earlier, these are passive acts from our point of view. When Ulay and Abramović slap each other in *Light/Dark*, our nervous system reacts empathetically.[20] We may get information by way of the gaze; however, mirror neuron response ensures that neurons will fire and stimulate the brain as if we were the character being slapped. These are mimetic representations of touch rather than actual touch used in the theatrical event.

Sexual contact onstage between performers is another potent example of the activation of touch as a means of generating strong mimetic mean-ing-rich interaction in attendants. Sexual contact between performers and attendants has also been explored as a means of generating a direct visceral response in attendants. Ashley Montagu quips:

> The French wit . . . who defined sexual intercourse as "the harmony of two souls and the contact of two epidermis," elegantly emphasized a basic truth—the massive involvement of the skin and sexual congress. The truth is that no other relationship is the skin so totally involved as in sexual intercourse. Sex, indeed, has been called the highest form of touch. In the profoundest sense, touch is the true language of sex. . . . The lips and the external genitalia are especially well-supplied with concave, disk-like branched sensory nerve endings.[21]

How has theatre made use of these most sensitive touch receptors to create mimesis? Obvious examples are the live sex shows and pantomimes staged during Nero's rule in ancient Rome. In the realm of more contemporary practice, recent performances use sexual contact by staging close contact between naked performers and attendants, or the performers fondling atten-dants. A startled elderly observer recounted an example of this after attend-ing a performance at the Institute of Contemporary Art, London (ICA) where a naked woman hopped onto his lap and thrust her breasts in his face; he asked me what he was supposed to do; was it reach out with his tongue to lick her nipples? Field explains the dilemma: "Touch can have strong effects on our bodies because, when the skin is touched, that stimula-tion is quickly transmitted to the brain, which in turn regulates our bodies. Depending upon the type of touch we receive, we can either be calmed down or aroused."[22] Whereas the observer did not know immediately what to do in the social context performance, his body reacted simultaneously. The tactic, commonly used by live artists performing at the ICA in the 1990s, remains the same: make bodily contact with the attendants of the event to require them to consider why they responded in the manner that they did and reflect on its appropriateness. In a sense, it also brings to light the notion of paying for the contact, and in the context of the performance, the ideas of sexual exploitation and prejudice might arise within the thoughtful attendant.

Ulay and Abramović's *Imponderabilia* (1977) explores the potential effect of full-body brushes with genitalia. They greeted gallery attendants with a situation where a decision had to be made—if the attendants wanted to get into the gallery they had to pass between the artists who were flanking the doorway. Abramović explains, "We are standing naked in the main entrance of the museum, facing each other. The public entering the Museum have to pass sideways through the small space between us. Each person passing has to choose which one of us to face."[23] Why brush against the body? What is this communicating? As attendants, we had to make a decision to come in close bodily contact with naked bodies; we would feel the hardness of Ulay's gaunt figure or the suppleness of Abramović's breasts through our clothes. We cannot avoid touching another's intimate places, because if we try and pull back we will brush against the other artist's body, and have our own body touched by another. We are being forced either into an uncomfortable social situation or being aroused by the touching. Through touch, they are immediately bringing up social exchange and gender issues. The objective was to activate our awareness prior to entering the event and break the traditional public passive attendant relationship of the gallery. They exploited the live quality of the event to make direct contact with us to break barriers and communicate in a direct manner.

Why is this tactic so immediate? Firstly, it is a blend between public and private behaviors; secondly, the artists are making use of the areas of the body that are particularly susceptible to precise touch. To make accessible the areas of the epidermis where cutaneous receptors are likely to be stimulated brings culturally accepted touching conventions relating to gender into the foreground. The socially acceptable areas that a male can touch a woman are, for example, on the shoulder from behind or on the arm. These zones are less innervated. Cholewiak and Collins outline the physiological reasons behind this:

> The distribution of cutaneous end organs appears random when small areas are examined, but a regular gradient of receptor density exists across the body's surface. Cutaneous receptors are found to be tightly packed in regions such as the fingertips, lips and genitals. As one moves toward the body, away from fingertips, these become more and more rare as the palm, forearm, upper arm, shoulder, and trunk are examined. Furthermore, as one might guess, sensitivity to tactile stimuli is, in many ways, related to the density of innervation.[24]

Thus social conventions are related to the level of innervation of particular regions. Sexual congress is stimulated because touch is heightened in those regions. To make use of performance tactics that stimulate these regions borders on pornography and indecency, but they are also prime targets because they are so laden with meaning and speak so directly and immediately to the receiver. Artists can directly stimulate a bodily response by touching the attendant. For this reason, these touch tactics have been popular since the 1960s, when creative artists sought to challenge the passive relationships between actors and audiences. As well, they were creating art in alternate venues to expand the basic assumptions of how the theatrical event should be framed.

An example of breaching the fourth wall tied to a more traditionally conceived theatrical event is the infamous performance of Richard Schechner's *Dionysus in '69* (1968). To transgress the fourth wall and make theatre an immediate event where the spectators no longer sat passively in the dark, Schechner used full-bodied contact to reach out and touch the audience. A *Time* review reports:

> Sweaty, tangled heaps of men and women kiss and fondle each other from head to toe, all the while uttering erotic moans and groans. . . . the audience . . . is urged to join the act, in the name of "participatory, environmental theater." Sibilant seductive whispers invite the spectators to dance. Some playgoers are gingerly about it; others are the life of the orgy. . . . two or three members of the cast sidle up to a girl in the audience and begin speaking words of love in her ear. The girl may be induced to lie on the floor, where the actors rub against her and caress her.[25]

An attendant lying with the actors in a bit of public fondling is the most blatant transgression of the fourth wall. Here, we move from public passive attendance to a public display of private behavior. In its most immediate form, the attendant is addressed in sexual congress—the actors make use of the language of sex by making contact with the most nerve-enriched points of the epidermis. To reach out and touch someone in this way, this quickly, is a leap from the traditional actor–audience boundary. Schechner directly makes use of innervated contact to advance notions of participatory theatre, free love, and social transgression. This work has been synonymous with the definition of avant-garde theatre practice of the late 1960s and early 1970s counter culture. Through the use of touch, Schechner was able to blur the line between theatrical mimesis and identity politics.

Amiri Baraka's *Slave Ship: A Historical Pageant* (1967) used the setting as a means of triggering discomfort as a reaction within the audience. He describes the play's setting with the term "atmos-feeling" to heighten the sensorial qualities necessary to establish its stage space. Eugene Lee's set placed attendants on benches within the bowels of the slave ship and the actors performed the action of the play in close proximity, thus making the attendants part of the play. Henry Lacey describes:

> The set itself, a split-level wooden platform mounted on huge springs was a brilliant conception and the play's chief metaphor, suggesting with its rhythmic rocking not simply the swell of the ocean as the slave

ship sails across it, but also the structural insecurity of a black man both as a slave on his way to America and as a citizen once he has arrived and settled. . . . The lower level of the set, the dark hold . . . forced the audience to hunch over in order to see what was happening during the first part of the play.[26]

This, combined with music, made manifest the atmos-feeling of the slave ship and created the physical reality of the ship for the attendants; thus, we became aware of our bodies or the state of our bodies in the uncertainty of confinement of the captive slaves. To call attention to a somatic awareness became a potent, evocative tool for the designer.

The consequences of breaching the fourth wall and bringing in the attendants as an intimate part of the performance are to allow us a means by which to make conscious the accumulation of sensations that will enrich our conscious interpretation of the themes and actions presented during performance. Attendants of *The Slave Ship* were confronted with a semblance of the crowding and discomfort that the slaves experienced in the hold of a slave ship, thereby making us more susceptible to the play's themes of militancy and revolution.[27] Iggo observes the physiological process that allows this:

When we are aware of ourselves and of the immediate environment and of our effects upon the environment, then we can be said to be conscious. Mental processes then take on an additional quality, and are described in terms of qualia, whereby we refer to our phenomenological experiences comparatively.[28]

Therefore, in our experience of *Slave Ship* we can describe our perceptions of the intensity of the odors of the sweating actors and the bright lights from above. These subjective statements reveal our personal awareness. On the other hand:

Mental processes, as distinct from objects in the world . . . are about things, and this can be said to mean that our mental states are differentiated on the basis that we have beliefs *about* things, or we can remember things, or that we perceive things or that we think about things. We do not simply believe, remember, perceive, or think in the abstract.[29]

In effect, the experience of the theatrical event becomes a part of our physical memory. We are affected physiologically by the experience, which changes our belief about the objects we encounter.

Whereas olfactory memory remains with us the longest, touch is the most immediate and tangible of the senses. Weisenberger argues that research indicates that touch:

can convey certain object aspects more accurately than other senses, in particular object properties such as surface texture, compliance, and thermal conductivity. In addition, the sense of touch is unique among the human senses in that it is the only system that simultaneously interacts with objects in passive perception and active manipulation.[30]

As we interact with the world through touch and our passive comprehension of touch qualities, we are able to put that data to use immediately. It is logical then that performances that make use of touch in a direct way will have meaning-rich expression. To activate touch in this context is to make accessible the material qualities of the art object presented. The artistic context made the senses accessible; we were asked to make use of Paccinian corpuscles to trigger our reception of the object.

TOUCH STRATEGY: ARTISTS AND THEIR INVITATIONS TO TOUCH

Exploiting the attendant's sense of touch is an invitation for our physiological response to a theatrical event. The following examples move from common experiences that most theatre attendants encounter to the types of touch experiences that are integral to understanding a piece in a nuanced and complex manner. The most accessible and evocative examples of events that make deliberate use of touch are the participatory performances of the *Rocky Horror Picture Show* (1978), where fans act out the movie in front of the screen. We became a part of the performance by talking back to the screen, answering the dialogue, or commenting on the dialogue. This is supplemented by the throwing of toast, toilet paper, water, and other objects on cue. The line between cinema actor, live actor, and attendant blurred.

Another example of blurring the line between actor and attendant was used to disturbing effect in a performance by Argentina's *El Periferico de Objetos*. Daniel Veronese, Emilio Garcia Wehbi, and Ana Alvarado created a political and confrontational production by giving attendants a numbered ticket, similar to the way we get at a raffle ticket. They staged *Máquina Hamlet* (1998), aka Heiner Müller's *Hamletmachine*, using a combination of puppets and life-size effigies with actors onstage. At Dublin's Project Art Centre, after milling about for an hour waiting for the house to open, little numbered tickets were passed out to us. Having no idea what we were lined up for, we entered the theatre and sat down to watch actors create a world that mirrored the military dictatorships of Argentina. This was brought home by way of the tickets. At one point the actors called out a number and we all looked to our ticket. Suddenly, a life-sized effigy planted in the audience was singled out, the ticket taken off its body, and the figure was forcibly dragged from the audience to the stage. He was arrested and tied up against the rear upstage right wall. Immediately after the "disappearing" of this "member" of the audience, we remember feeling relieved that our number was not called. Another audience member was pulled from the audience and handed a gun. He was commanded, taunted, and threatened with his life until he shot the effigy. The performers easily enticed many of us to participate in their deconstruction of Hamlet. At other points, a Hamlet puppet was dismembered. The violence and brutality of the actions were effective because the effigies and puppets were ripped from the communal body of the audience. Our mirror responses quickly made empathetic connections with the figure. In a way similar to a subject's response when Ramachandran smashed the table with a hammer, we felt Hamlet's dismembering. Through touch, we were drawn deeper into the mimesis of the performance. Touch was a bridge into our means of understanding the action.

The material qualities of the setting of a performative event can manipulate us into feeling and experiencing the world in a particular way. For example, one brisk October night in 1999, I wandered Chicago's Logan Square through Red Moon Puppet Theatre's Halloween bash. They had large bonfires in several locations along the center of the space. In one, large fire-puppets danced a macabre ballet; in another, fifteen-foot puppets interacted. We had to push between the crowds to see the action and music that drew us from mansion to mansion to see the individual acts. We could feel of the heat of bonfire in the air, the contrast between the cold air against our skin, and the waves of heat from the crackling logs made the event festive. Smoke clogged our lungs, drums vibrated one's bones, and the bustle of the crowds kept us aware of our surroundings. The temperature of the fire and the warmth of the crowds drew us in to each new experience. The setting, the stations, and the actions of the puppets created a theatrical event, but as much meaning came from the active effort it took to see the different acts and to find a view of the Halloween celebrations.

Another type of audience enticement to participate physically in an installation is the manner in which one has to negotiate the space. In a piece at Houston's DiverseWorks Art Space by an artist I have long since forgotten, we had to get on our knees to see a reliquary. The artist got curious attendants to crawl on the floor to enter through a low opening. Once inside, we could stand up and look at the religious art artifacts displayed against mirrored walls and illuminated with colored lights. Ingeniously, by getting us in that position, he set us up as unwitting supplicants to the objects within the sanctuary. From there, all the conceptual meaning followed when the conscious mind, thus influenced, gave us a clearer vision of the cultural and religious significance of crawling on one's hands and knees in relation to religious artifacts. These types of activities, coupled with performance, elicit meaning-rich sensations.

As a means of opening up a dialogue about the objectification and abusive exploitation of women, Karen Finley has used a number of viscous, metaphor-laden foods, such as chocolate and honey, as a medium to costume her body. In July of 1998, those of us that attended a performance of her *Return of the Chocolate Smeared Woman* at the Flea Theatre in Tribecca, New York, witnessed Finley auctioning off a chance to lick chocolate off her body. Instantly a man reached into his pocket and offered twenty dollars. She asked where he would like to lick her and offered up her forearm, calf, and elbow. He immediately amplified the sexual contact and instead chose to lick her across her belly. This request gave her pause. Trying to hold her ground she again offered up the "socially acceptable" places to be licked in public. As explained elsewhere, the concentration of nerves are least on the forearm and calf and greatest in areas such as the genitals and belly, making these areas especially taboo. Although being licked in public by a stranger when we are naked and covered in chocolate is hardly acceptable social behavior under any circumstances, she was intent on pursuing a political message highlighting the abusive exploitation of women. His touch was paid for, and seemingly had the authority of the consumer who paid for touch. By choosing to lick her across her belly for twenty dollars, she actually made her point about the objectification and prostitution of women quite effectively. He did not choose the least nerve enriched zones of her epidermis, rather he chose a highly enriched zone. We could see the explicit message that her body was a commodity to be used as this man wanted. The most intimate of sensory experiences was instigated by an offer to accept money from a stranger to lick chocolate off her body. This was also amplified by the memory of the television cameras in the audience moments before she auctioned the lick, where reporters questioned her about the Supreme Court decision that had come that day about the pending pornography charges levied by Congress in regards to the revocation of her National Endowment of the Arts (NEA) grants. On that same night, the Supreme Court decision in the "National Endowment for the Arts v. Karen Finley" case upheld a congressional "decency" test for federal funding in the arts, thereby revoking her NEA grant. Human touch in public, as mediated by an audience, can be considered gratuitous. As touch is real, it cuts to the chase. Was the line between art and pornography breached because the lick was real? Layer upon layer of meaning was instigated by merely touching and watching touch. The attendant had the ultimate sensory touch experience because his tongue came in contact with her flesh, whereas we watched and had a passive touch moment. Above all, all of us paid to watch this event. Was it art or a peep show?

In contrast to the politics of touching women is the implication of handing male bodies in two performances by Michael Mayhew, where attendants' touch sensations were integral.[31] In the first piece, reminiscent of Yoko Ono's *Cut Piece* (1965), Mayhew stood there wearing a white tee-shirt and attendants could pick up a razor blade and cut through the shirt to find small stickers with words printed on them. We had to rip through the cloth to get it to tear, and then we had to pull away a sticker entangled in his hairy body. This was an uncomfortable sensation for us, because we did not like touching him or his clothes or bringing a razor so close to his skin. We did not want to cut him, so we were tentative and halting. Handling a razorblade so close to flesh elicited a phobia, for me, of shaving while being naked. The idea of an open blade near sensitive skin is frightening to me—I remember the movie *In the Realm of the Senses* (1976) where Sada Abe strangles her lover in ecstasy and slices off his genitalia so that they may be one.[32] Perhaps for me, if it was a woman performing the piece, there might have been an erotic thrill—a type of foreplay to sex. I also see that there could have been a sadistic desire to hurt him. Being in proximity to the man in relation to the razor blade with the permission to cut set up the context for touching, as well as the context for responding to and thinking about my reactions and his reaction. I recall that women who cut his clothing at the same time as I did were more comfortable with cutting and taking the sticker off his sweaty body.

Mayhew's *The Doctor's Note* (2001) was a reenactment of a 1999 performance where he lost control, got drunk, and had to be taken to the hospital. His reenactment and verbal deconstruction of the piece was accompanied by vodka shots at various points mapped out on the floor. As he made his point, he gave all the attendants vodka too, and provoked us into pairing off and dancing with strangers. In a mock high-school dance, in a darkened classroom, we leaned against a sweaty stranger and felt the warm, damp body next to us sweat off the booze. Although we remember moments of story and reenactment, what we most remember is clumsily stumbling cheek-to-cheek, embracing a woman that we do not remember. Is this lack of memory like the lack of memory he has of the original event where he was drunk, threw himself to the ground, and injured himself in a drunken stupor? Was it the alcohol that made it possible to be enticed into dancing with a stranger in a darkened classroom during the day midweek? Why was that social contact more memorable than the art that inspired it? In this sense, I read experience from a different angle—further amplifying my experiential and cultural associations with touch—sexualized, homophobic, but always social, always evocative, and meaningful exploration. If image reception is culturally conditioned—or alternatively, sexually driven—our pleasurable or painful reaction would be different. The alternate readings are no less significant or less meaningful in context; it is just that the touch experience leads me to a different reading of the experience than one predetermined from the cognitive facts. The senses give us perceptions that we can understand through a cultural, aesthetic, or political perspective. It is how our consciousness attributes meaning to these experiences that makes the reactions mean something; even our bodies' experiences of these events is close to our bodily experience of the work.

We are all familiar with the joy of cold water splashing us on an amusement park log ride, or our experiences of revulsion when sweat or spit from a performer flies out and splatters our face while we are sitting in the audience. What are some of the consequences of becoming attendant to one's touch sensations, and how do they commingle with our cultural experience to begin our journey of questioning? How can we make sense of our cutaneous perception? We remember not knowing what Franko B was spraying in the air when we saw his *Mama I Can't Sing* (1996) and was afraid of coming in contact with the red mist floating in the air. After having seen the rest of the effluvia smeared on his skin, and the vials and flasks of blood and urine on the stage, we feared that he was spraying blood into the air. We did not want to come into contact with bodily waste or contaminated blood. That fear of blood was directly related to the tactile. This is in relationship to my knowledge of a history of performance, where effluvia and other contaminated paraphernalia were placed in close proximity to attendants. Was it not true of Ron Athey's ritual scarring pieces, where a critic claimed that Athey was pinning blood-soaked bandages and rags on a clothes line and pulling it over the heads of the audience and blood was dripping on their heads? Whereas the description was exaggerated by a critic who was not present at the performance, it is true that there was a clothesline with blood-soaked bandages in proximity to the audience where blood could not contaminate them, but it highlights this notion of coming in contact with the performer or his or her body or its effluvia. Then there are the moments in Annie Sprinkle's performances where she has us walk up, crouch between her legs, and shine a flashlight up her vagina to look at the make-up of female anatomy. There is also the event where she pees in front of us and wipes herself with a tissue. She then leaves the tissue on the stage before intermission with a tease that someone can take it. It disappears at intermission. Someone, either a stagehand or one of us, has picked up the tissue from the stage and taken it away. Touch is indeed integral to our participation and reception of the performance. Theme park attractions offer radical examples of the ways in which cutaneous stimulation can be exploited to guide attendants to have visceral reactions within designed contexts.

TOUCH AND THE STAR TREK EXPERIENCE

A motion simulator ride is a prime manifestation of the way in which touch can be harnessed to create a mimetic experience. Amusement park attractions such as this create a live-action adventure for attendants to feel what it is like to be a part of the world of their favorite television shows and movies. These adventure rides range from *Alien Encounter* (1995), where attendants experience an alien attack, to a Lilo and Stitch adventure, where kids get a chance to experience life as it exists in a cartoon. One can appreciate the potential for building a sensory-rich analysis of a mediated entertainment by considering the array of touch stimulation types possible on these rides. *Star Trek: The Experience* (1998–2008) was a combination of a theme park attraction and an interactive theatre experience revolving around Star Trek and its various incarnations. In *The Klingon Encounter*, actors take us on an adventure to rescue Capitan Jean-Luc Picard and repair a rift in the time–space continuum, whereas in *Borg Invasion 4-D*, we help defend against the evil Borgs. There is no pretense that this is a serious artwork; an element of self-parody is built into the structure. They could have made it a much more intensive experience by attempting to create a more immersive environment, but they chose to create a largely accessible and friendly experience. Throughout the spaceship, there is evidence of the theatrical workings in the form of spike tape, employee entrances, and masking. Furthermore, the theatre space itself is a museum displaying "historical" future technologies and clothing of the Star Trek universe. To immerse the attendants in this universe, we must first walk through the museum installation to get to the disembarkation area. Characters from the Star Trek opus walk around and interact with us through conversation, jokes and taunts. Though there are lines to get on the ride and other theme park accoutrements, this interactivity with the characters helps make the wait a part of the adventure. Once the rides begin, the characters guide us through the adventure and the context attempts to incorporate our presence into the fictive framework. We are both attendant and subject of the event.

Our experience starts as we walk through the "History of the Future" museum, which winds us down a chronology of all Star Trek episodes and movies. Video clips and montages of the Star Trek history are projected on TV screens positioned through the space. The exhibit also weaves in history, such as the moon landing, to give credence to the plausibility of the fictitious advancement of space flight, which led to the Insurrection that comprises the plots of the last episodes of *DS9* and *Voyager*. As well as biographical information for the most famous Starfleet officers, there is a collection of Star Trek props and costumes, such as Communicators, phasers, and other technology used by Starfleet Command and aliens. Following this are anthropological displays featuring the Klingon, Bajoran, and Borg.

As the focus of this event is our experience of the action, the plotting is simple and makes use of the most known elements of the franchise. After passing through a set of doors, we are abruptly transported to the Starship Enterprise and informed that we have been transported to the twenty-fourth century. We are told that someone in the room is the ancestor of Captain Jean-Luc Picard, and the Klingons, in an effort to terminate their archenemy, has created a rift in the space–time continuum. They have sent an army to come to the present to assassinate this relative to prevent Picard's birth. We become a part of the ensuing adventure to evade them. Fans are often taken by the detail, attending multiple times to figure out the transporter effect. They love the control panels and costumes, giving them a sense that the crew is actually working on the ship, loading and unloading cargo in the shuttle bay. The crew guides us through the plot, putting us in a position to experience directly the actions in the fictive world. We respond physiologically rather than intellectually or aesthetically, as is usually offered in a live theatrical event. We are participants in this imagined universe unimpeded by the screen separating the video world from the real world of our living room.

Initially, we are herded into a small room. As the doors slide shut, Starfleet personnel mundanely lecture us about Star Trek while a small device displays scenes from several movies. We are led into another room and the lights go out. Attendants most often blog about the flickering flashes of light, the sounds, and cold air blasts that that create simulate the "transporter effect." Once the lights are turned back on, the room has transformed into the transporter room from the USS Enterprise-D.[33] On the transporter pad, a Starfleet officer meets us and explains that we have been beamed aboard the Starship Enterprise and are in the future. We then follow him to the Bridge, where another crewmember explains that Captain Jean-Luc Picard disappeared the moment the group beamed aboard the Enterprise, and describes our predicament. As we stand between the science stations and the tactical station, crewmembers contact Commander Riker, who promptly appears on the monitor. Apparently, our only choice is to board a shuttlecraft to escape the ship and go through another temporal rift to return us home to the dawn of the twenty-first century.

In a travel review, Mitch Mandell recounts his amazement of the beaming effect. He cannot figure out how we move from a small, square, industrial enclosure to an open, round, multi-color room on a spaceship. Before he can figure it out, we are rushed to board a turbo-lift.[34] What follows is the most intense use of sensorial stimulation. The Klingons attack the Enterprise while we are in the turbo-lift to the shuttle bay. During the attack, there are several jolts from phaser hits that toss us around and there is a malfunction in the turbolift, which results in what feels like a free fall. Finally, we arrive at the shuttle bay deck, where we are rushed onto the shuttle (flight simulator) and strapped in. As we take off, we can see open space out the front of the simulator, and can sense the movement through space by avoiding three-dimensional obstacles and by the changing direction of the craft. The real excitement begins with a battle between the Enterprise and a few Klingon vessels. We cling to our seats as we are tossed back and forth, brought to abrupt stops, absorb hits from phaser attacks, and feel changes in direction and variable speed. At one point, the shuttle goes into warp for three seconds pushing us back in our seats and drops into the rings of a planet. As the shuttle completes a mission, we are forced to engage in several aerial battles. By this time, our palms are sweaty, our heart rates have increased, and our muscles have contracted.

We are thankful when the ride smoothes out and feels more like an airplane coming in for a landing. The shuttle returns through the temporal rift to present-day Las Vegas. A Klingon vessel also follows and locks a tractor beam on the group's shuttle—another twist. But luckily, the Enterprise comes to the rescue, allowing us to land at the Las Vegas Hilton. Before we disembark, Captain Picard speaks to us by video thanking us for "restoring his existence." He proclaims, "While only one of you is my ancestor, each of you holds that same opportunity for the future. Guard it well." The shuttle doors open, and we are led out to the Deep Space Nine Promenade and Quark's Bar and Restaurant.

The second ride is *Borg Invasion 4-D*, which uses many of the same devices, but adds mechanical sprays and three-dimensional glasses. Once again, we are ushered into a space facility that is attacked by aliens. This time it is the notorious Borgs—they are sort of half human/half robot killing machines that transform a human into one of them through a process known as "assimilation." We are again walked through an installation where live actors provide the action happening all around us when Borgs break through the frontlines and kill Starfleet personnel. Bloggers are enraptured by the design elements, describing what sounds like an earthquake complete with a shaking floor and flickering lights to give the effect of an attack.[35] All around us is chaos; sporadic gunfire punctuates our race to safety through the labyrinth of passageways. We never know whether a Borg will jump out at us or kill the crew around us. Out of the corner of our eyes, we see the Borg army annihilate everything in their path. However, the crew does its job and leads us to the escape pod. At this point, the action shifts to a theatre configuration. We pick up three-dimensional safety goggles and sit down in the shuttle. We see imagery that suggests we take off from the station. On our race to escape Borg horde, our pod bucks and jerks with each laser blast. However, our craft is pulled inside the Borg Cube. Special effects blow open the front of our ship, and small Borg probes enter and spray us with nanoprobes. We feel them in our skin because we are being prodded by our seats—it is rather like a massage chair. Though mild, the sensation can be startling; we can be surprised by water droplets, wind bursts, and aggressive jabbing—in the back and under the legs. All this happens as the three-dimensional image of the probe lunges a needle toward our eyes.

We are primed as living beings to react to sensory stimulation. These amusement park designers are making use of technology to control our experience of mimetic events by manipulating our senses into a particular experience of the world. Bursts of air, sprays of water, and variations in temperature, body location, motion, and speed are all combined with three dimensional projections to override our basal sense awareness, and create a new prioprioceptic illusion of the world. This virtual world allows us to perceive non-real experiences in those worlds as real.

In contrast to the pleasant stimulation of the aforementioned examples, these events have the potential to trigger extremes of emotion from the audience response. The narrative context framing the *Alien Encounter* (1995) ride at Disney World had a malevolent theme of an alien invasion, and the type of sensory stimulation used, such as binaural sound, triggered terrified attendants. It took place in the dark, forcing us to cope with its effects using our other four senses. Because aliens breathing on us in the dark were so terrifying, its narrative context was redesigned into *Stitch's Great Escape!* (2004). Many of the same effects and set pieces are used, but are transformed because of its new narrative into a benevolent experience. This technology can give us a real experience of the remote fantasy worlds offered in film and television while remaining a passive and safe experience because it is controlled by the construct of the amusement park structure. We are granted a glimpse of what it feels like to be a part of the fantasies that we watch on the big screen. It is the act of making real the remote experience. It suggests for us a new way of knowing about the world without being at risk—it has only the illusion of risk—though its effects have to be tempered. It shows us the lengths that we have to go to capture the playful abandon we once experienced as children experiencing the unfamiliar.

BECOMING ATTENDANT TO TOUCH

As we become accustomed to and crave the mediation of the screen, we become increasingly cut off from human contact, we are in increasing need of reclaiming mass public interaction to provide us with proximal human contact. We have bleached out personal smells, animal smells, and tastes from our world. It is a comparatively sensory bland environment that our animal brains crave stimulation to mimic the hunt, to savor the smells, tastes, and touches of the natural and social world. As a result, there is an ever-increasing need to create events that stimulate our bodies as well as our minds. Popular interactions, such as dance, drinking, and other amusements provide contact and release. Amusement parks and theatre share a common goal of providing sensory-rich experience for us to satisfy our need for touch, interaction, and sensory stimulation.

If theatre, the quintessential art form, is to survive, it will have to adapt to satisfying the physical social needs that we crave. The deeply unsettling feeling of the world reflected in contemporary practice is a shift in thinking. With this in mind, our models for interpreting our experience of theatre must be shifted. When we follow the physiological processes of receiving, perceiving, and interpreting our experience of the world, we can begin to build a procedure for understanding what we experience in the fictive reality of a theatrical event. Edward De Bono describes the physiological model, where:

> The first stage of thinking is the perception stage: how we look at the world, the concepts, and perceptions we form. The second stage of thinking is the processing stage: what do we do with the perceptions that have been set up in the first stage. Logic can only be used in the second stage since it requires concepts and perceptions to work upon.[36]

Thus, changes in the nature of our world have changed the way that we monitor and react to theatrical events. William Rushton explains:

> As we process sensory evidence into perceptions these understandings become available for use by higher-order processes that involve language, whereby our perceptual experiences may be described. They are also available to memory, where they may be retained for later use, and in thinking, where the information may be used creatively or to solve a problem.[37]

An understanding of this perspective can enrich our view of performance and theatre, as well as look at how these assumptions provide us with tools to create a viscerally exciting theatre fit for today.

What does being attendant to touch enable us to understand as attendants to theatrical events? As a part of an American Society for Theatre Research field research seminar in Las Vegas, our task was to try and make sense of Vegas through the lenses of the participants' research. I was working on the notion of the how the senses were stimulated by the theatricality of Las Vegas. Being particularly sensitive to noise and chaos, I despise Vegas. We had to reconnoiter the banks of clinking, buzzing, dinging, and flashing slot machines to discover the labyrinthine path to find the elevator to go to our rooms. When we went outside, the winds off the desert ripped into our skin and got into our eyes. Whenever we sat down, the chair was uncomfortable. What we did find was that the more money we spent, the more comfortable and quiet the setting. As active participants when we sit down at the poker table, then the edges are cushioned with smooth leather so that our elbows do not get bruised and we do not notice the time passing, and the lighting was directed onto the table so that the world around us disappears into the periphery. Our whole attention gets focused on the task at hand—to spend money. Likewise, only when we eat at an expensive restaurant, such at *Emeril's New Orleans Fish House*, will we be comfortable again. The only oasis against the discomfort, noise, and lights is in environments where large sums of money would be spent. Silence as an escape was only available through the power of the dollar. What we learned on our visit was that, through comfort and discomfort, we were able to make tangible the means by which the city was designed to prod us into spending money. Department stores, the city, and casinos are designed to guide us through multiple locations and try and distract us into spending more of our time and money in attractive places. Once we deviate from the city's set paths, we entered a no man's land of deserted alleyways and sprawling parking lots. To become aware of these processes is to become aware of the ways in which our senses are manipulated in society to try and entice us to behave in a particular manner.

At the most basic level, touch is activated from the moment we begin our journey to the theatre. We must negotiate the world to travel to the theatre.

We will feel the touch of the handle on the door that we open to enter into the theatre; we will brush against and bump into the other attendants of the theatrical event. In Miami, the contrast between the hot and humid tropical air outside and the chill of air-conditioning are noticeable environmental factors walking into any theatre. If we are in the Arsht Centre in Miami, we feel the crush of the carpet in the concert hall beneath our feet. If we were at the Performance Garage in New York, we feel the hard, decrepit texture of the crumbling concrete stairs. As well, how many others are crammed into the space has an effect. In the Project Arts Space in Dublin, the long benches can accommodate one person or fifty people in the row depending on how close people seat themselves. If we are all sitting cheek by jowl, our close proximity sitting up against people will change our reception of the art event.

At the Globe reconstruction in London, whether we are milling about in the pit, shifting from leg to leg through the duration of the piece, or feeling the boards of the benches in the galleries bite into our glutei maximi, we are attentive to our bodily state as we watch the play. Does getting involved in a production, so much so that whenever we stop paying attention to the details of comfort or discomfort, determine a good theatrical event? Likewise, outdoor factors, of course, have an effect on our awareness of our bodily state. When attending a performance of the Australian company Strange Fruit's *Swoon!* (2007) on a Miami patio at noon in May, with the sun blaring down in a temperature of over ninety degrees, sitting on a plastic lawn chair, mostly we remember the sweat dripping down our bodies, rather than the acrobats twirling in the sky or floating in space in a fusion of dance, theatre, and circus. It is when these factors are controlled deliberately by the artists that the information becomes significant and meaningful.

Do we realize the consequences of our touch upon others? The power of cutaneous perception has the ability to incite us to question in an immediate way both our nature and that of the world in general. *Epizoo* (1994) is an interactive media event that highlighted the sense of touch via proxemic or haptic stimulation, where the touch of a computer mouse called into question the nature of mediated interaction and reality. Though we were in the same space as the artist, the presence of media distanced us enough to cause us not to realize immediately what we were doing or how we were touching the artist through the computer. The performance installation by Marcel Li. Antunez Roca is an interactive media event in which Roca submits himself to the whims of the attendants. In it, he hooks his mouth, nose, ears, glutei, and pectorals up to a pneumatically movable machine. This machine is connected to a computer with a touch pad. The attendants use the pad to click points on an image. This sets in motion animation movies, sound, and compression relays and triggers the machine to contort his body.

We enter a dark, open space. Loud techno music blares. There is a machine with a stainless steel cap; it has wires and a flame-thrower on it.

The machine is set up in the center of a bank of screens, on which is projected animated films and the screen of a computer desktop. A video camera records the attendants' entrance; we see ourselves on the projection screen milling about the space. There is a message telling us that we are part of an interactive performance and that we should go stand near the machine if we want to play. The computer hardware is on a raised platform, or control station, in the space directly in front of the machine. A few of us are really excited to play, and we do not have to wait long before Roca enters wearing a red loincloth. He puts on the parts of the machine—the helmet, a waistbelt, and tongs in his cheek.[38] Roca attaches the machine to his body so that his epidermis will receive stiumuli telling him that he is being poked, prodded, or licked. As Weisenberger explains the sense of touch:

> The Cutaneous senses are inherently multimodal in nature. The receptors under the skin surface are responsible for conveying sensations of light and deep pressure, vibration, temperature, and pain. Further, some of the same receptors also work in concert with motor of limb movement. The ability to sense the position of the body and limbs in space is referred to as proprioception, and the sensing of body and limb movement is called kinesthesia.[39]

Roca has attached this machine to mechanically regulate his bodily response by experiencing the stimuli received from the machine. We, as attendants, are in close proximity to his body and touch him indirectly through the mediation of the machine.

We are invited to send shocks of pleasure or pain to Roca. Using the computer, we can manipulate the machine, spinning him around or contorting his body: Touch the buttock image, and without mercy an electronic knife hacks into it. Press the pectorals, and a virtual dog's tongue caresses his flesh. But at the head, a touch will cause his mouth, ears, and nose to be pulled in various directions. When the attendant/controller steps away for the next person to manipulate his body, the lights go down on him and burning gasses spout out from his head. It is like watching a cartoon with a real person getting all of the abuse; Roca has a release button if he becomes over stimulated.

As we enjoy the sociality of the club, we jockey for our turn to get our hands on the controls to manipulate the morphing screen images . . . and, well, to torture Roca. Whereas the attendants may think they are not culpable for what is happening because of the distance, they are actively manipulating the performance—they are part of the performance as instigators pushing the action forward. What fun, mediated sadism, where the attendant's actions and indirect touches inflict pain on another body. Part of the allure of this experience is in its danger to the performer and to the attendants. What would happen if the machine went haywire? Do we have a responsibility to consider the safety of the person to whom we are inflicting pain and pleasure? What are the implications of watching this and participating in this activity? Are we, as attendants in proximity to this action, voyeurs or sadists? What are the ethical considerations of participating in an event like this? How does our relationship with technology inadvertently affect others? Are we really inflicting pain? Weisenberger tells us:

> Haptic perception refers to the combination of cues provided by tactile and kinesthetic receptors during active manipulation of objects in the environment. When stimuli are presented to a stationary observer, the cues arising from tactile receptors are referred to as passive touch.[40]

Is this haptic perception? It is only a click of a mouse, and we do not actually touch flesh upon flesh. How much we get out of the experience has to do with how much we think about our relationships to the event, and are aware of our reactions to the presented stimuli. Sensations trigger thought processes, which in turn begin the interpretive process.

Our bodies are wired to respond to certain types of stimuli—in Roca's case, literally. Arnheim explains why these sensations are critical to human thought: "To interpret the functioning of the senses properly, one needs to keep in mind that they did not come about as instruments of cognition for cognition's sake, but evolved as biological aids for survival."[41] When artists use these types of systems, they are tapping into our pre-linguistic models of experience. Roca literalizes these stimuli in his body by actively shocking his body through our passive touch. Thus, by becoming aware of our passive touch having an actual consequence via the computer mouse, the piece highlights our lack of sensorial awareness in our own bodies during the event. We are cut off from our experiences with those around us, and need to reach out and touch flesh against flesh in pursuit of social activity. On the other hand, we may feel that we are making contact and affecting the performance and the experience of the artist through our touch and our proximity. It is the ultimate sensorial social relationship. It is a twisted sexual congress. He gets us to pay for his masochistic pleasure, while we get no actual touch benefit from the experience; Roca gets off from our caresses and whipping. Perhaps, it is we who are not getting our money's worth. In this way, we immediately are confronted with the implications of touch within a social and artistic situation.

4 Noses, Tongues, and Other Surprising Possibilities
Harnessing Olfaction and Gustation in Performance

Smell and taste are our chemical senses, and with them we sample our environment for information, continuously testing the quality of the air we breathe to alert us to potential dangers, such as smoke, as well as searching for other relevant information, such as the presence of food or another creature. Smell, similar to sound but unlike taste, can signal over long distances. The emotions of others—for example, fear, contentment and lust—may also be experienced and communicated by smell. Smell is said to be the most direct route to memory, and the longest lasting. It can influence mood, memory, emotions, mate choice, and the immune system. With taste, one or a combination of sweet, sour, bitter, salty, and umami alert us to vital information about anything we put in our mouths. Both smell and taste, though little talked about in theatre practice, have their place in performance. What are the ways in which artists have used smell and taste to communicate? How do these senses evoke memories or convey messages? In what way can harnessing these alert sensations intrinsically define theatre as a live event that connects the attendant to the artistically mediated environment?

In contrast to vision, which many say is their most important sense, the consensus seems to be that smell is the least important sense. Constance Classen, David Howes, and Anthony Synott note that, when surveyed, most respondents said it did not matter whether they were able to smell.[1] However, when that sense of smell is absent, one's sense of well-being is unsettled. They evoke Oliver Sack's patient's realization of what anosmia—his loss of smell—had cost him:

> It was like being struck blind. Life lost a good deal of its savour—one does not realize how much "savour" is smell. You *smell* people, you *smell* books, you *smell* the city, you *smell* the spring—maybe not consciously, but a rich unconscious background to everything else. My whole world was suddenly radically poorer.[2]

Our sense of smell enriches our experience of the world and is a vital component in our connection to those around us. John Leffingwell confirms that smell is a primal sense:

Smell (or olfaction) allows vertebrates and other organisms with olfactory receptors to identify food, mates, predators, and provides both sensual pleasure (the odor of flowers and perfume) as well as warnings of danger (e.g., spoiled food, chemical dangers). *For both humans and animals, it is one of the important means by which our environment communicates with us.*[3]

We use it to make sure that we do not burn down the house with a piece of toast, to find where the rotting mouse is under the washer, and to detect a sore throat. Smell depends on chemoreceptors that respond to odors made up of chemical molecules floating in the air that enter the nose. With every breath we take, inhaled air swirls up into the nostrils, dissolving in the mucous of a tiny patch of tissue (the olfactory epithelium) located high in the nasal cavity, which contains millions of olfactory receptor neurons. The olfactory epithelium is made up of sensory neurons, each with a primary cilium, supporting cells between them, and basal cells that produce replacements for those that die. Next, the cilia of the sensory neurons are immersed in a layer of mucus. Molecules that we can smell (odorant) dissolve in the mucus and bind to receptors on the cilia, sending a message concerning whether the smell is noxious, pleasant, or bland through the olfactory nerves, then to the olfactory bulb. In essence, it is a biochemical reaction that creates a pathway for the generation of an action potential, also known as a nerve impulse. The impulse is conducted back along the olfactory nerve to the brain. Before the brain receives the information for interpretation and recognition, the bulb receives input from other brain centers that modify the neuronal activity and enable smell to interact with other information, such as memory, physiological and psychological states. The brain then evaluates this in tandem with other olfactory signals to identify odor quality and intensity and discriminate between odors. This information is the basis of the perception of smell.

Recent research has shown that emotion can be communicated by smell. Karl Grammer has demonstrated that women can discriminate between armpit swabs taken from people watching uplifting films and people watching depressing films.[4] The emotions of others—for example, fear, contentment or lust—may therefore be experienced and communicated by smell. Denise Chen demonstrated the ability of underarm odor to influence mood in others.[5] We respond to smell in an involuntary way. Part of this is due to the way in which the olfactory pathway is wired to our most primal region of the brain, called the limbic system. Tim Jacob and his co-authors explain:

The limbic system is a collection of brain structures situated beneath the cerebral cortex that deal with emotion, motivation, and association of emotions with memory. Only after this relay has occurred does the information arrive in the higher cortical brain regions for perception and interpretation. Smell is unique among the senses in its privileged access to the subconscious. The limbic system includes such brain areas as the amygdala, hippocampus, pyriform cortex and hypothalamus. This complex set of structures lies on both sides and underneath the thalamus, just under the cerebrum. The limbic system is increasingly recognised to be crucial in determining and regulating the entire emotional "tone." Excitation of this, by whatever means, produces heightened emotionalism and an intensification of the senses. It also has a lot to do with the formation of memories and this is the reason that smell and memory are so intimately linked.[6]

As smell is directly wired to this primitive subconscious region, we are often at a loss to describe its characteristics. Our conscious mind has already been influenced by smell, and our bodies have already responded to the stimuli, often before we are aware of its presence. It shapes our world in profound ways, even if we are not able to consciously articulate what those ways are. To be able to better identify smells and be aware of their affect, we can consider how scientists are trying to broaden our vocabulary.

Our conscious ability to identify, classify, and describe odors and flavors is limited severely. As a result, we are reluctant to speak about smell, and we are cautious in our use of smell as evidence in complex intellectual arguments. We do not teach smell in any systematic way. Most often, as anthropologists tell us, our acknowledgment of smell is tinged with shame. It is this imprecision in our conscious articulation that leads us to distrust smell. Whereas we can organize colors into a spectrum, or musical tones into scales, there is no way of organizing smells. This vagueness is not limited to our everyday interactions. Scientific research has not discovered a unifying theory of olfaction. As Classen et al. remind us, "Smell . . . is a highly elusive phenomenon. Odours, unlike colours, for instance, cannot be named."[7] Though scientists still do not fully understand the way that the brain is able to identify smell, there are four major competing theories of olfaction: molecular shape, diffusion pore, vibrational theory, and the spectroscopic nose. Molecular shape theory posits that there are seven primary classes of odors and seven kinds of olfactory receptor areas, places whereon odorant molecules could lodge when adsorbed in the olfactory sensitive area, and that the odorous molecules have shapes and sizes that were function like a lock and key.[8] In other words, they are complementary to the size and shape of the seven receptors.[9] Diffusion pore theory posits that olfactory molecules diffuse across the membrane of a receptor cell, forming an ion pore in its wake. The different odor would cause a different size pore and therefore a different receptor potential, giving rise to a particular firing quality of the odor.[10] Vibrational theory posits that infrared resonance, a measurement of a molecule's vibration, might be associated with odor. Compounds with distinctive odors vibrate at different infrared frequencies and are associated with different smells.[11] Finally, the nose as a spectroscope is a controversial theory suggesting that the olfactory organs might detect molecular vibrations. Receptors are therefore "tuned" to the vibration frequency of odorants.[12] Though researchers may not agree on how olfaction occurs, its importance to human survival is clear. Furthermore, due to its preconscious nature, by mimicking the triggers of smell response we can get attendants to respond involuntarily to odorant stimuli.

We recognize seven primary odors that help to determine objects: camphoric (mothballs), musky (aftershave), roses (floral), pepperminty (polo mint), ethereal (dry cleaning fluid), pungent (vinegar), and putrid (rotten eggs).[13] According to accepted theories, every aroma we inhale is made up of some combination of these odors. We have a huge palette of aromas at our fingertips. No two substances smell exactly alike, each odorant activates a unique set of olfactory receptors, and the current understanding of smell discrimination means that there are an infinite number of odors to which we would be sensitive.[14] Our sense of smell is based on a combinatorial approach to recognizing and processing odors. Scientists have adapted the different approaches to describe the ways that the nose can interpret such a variety of odors.[15] Leffingwell explains:

> Instead of dedicating an individual odor receptor to a specific odor, the olfactory system uses an "alphabet" of receptors to create a specific smell response within the neurons of the brain. As in language (or music), the olfactory system appears to use combinations of receptors (analogous to words or musical notes, or to the way that computers process code) to greatly reduce the number of actual receptor types actually required to convey a broad range of odors.[16]

This alphabet does not need to be the same each time for the same odor, but can change its characteristics depending upon the previous stimulus, thus explaining how we can be sensitive to odors we have never previously experienced.

Smell signals a variety of physiological states for us and has the power to influence our bodily functions. Men rate women as more attractive during ovulation and less attractive during menstruation. We smell different when we are ill; illnesses (such as diabetes) can be diagnosed by their associated smell (acetone). Sexual attractiveness, bodily functioning, and emotion are known to have a direct affect on our olfactory system. The well-known notion of menstrual synchrony was tested by taking armpit swabs from women during their menstrual cycle and wiping samples beneath the noses of recipient women. Researchers found the scent sped up or slowed down menstruation in the recipients.[17] Though we do not know how, we possess the ability to chemically relay information to others, such as communicating sexual virility through the release of pheromones. Scientists are experimenting with chemical compounds to determine if they can be used to alter mood. The applications of these studies are of intense interest to the perfume and retail industry.[18] Likewise, the potentials for theatrical representation are fascinating. We already know that smell and memory are closely linked. In Socìetas Raffaello Sanzio's (SRS) *Il Buchettino*, the odor of cedar chips evokes memories of lying in bed next to the closet at night as mother read a bedtime story.[19] These memories enrich the theatrical experience and add layers of intimacy to the performance.

One direct response by an artist to the scientific experimentation of women being able to detect what fear smells like was an exhibit created by Norwegian artist Sissel Tolaas for *The Fear of Smell—the Smell of Fear* (2006). Since 1995, Tolaas has been working with researchers to examine the effects of scent on human behavior. For this exhibit, she collected swabs of sweat from men suffering from extreme phobias of other people. She broke down the scent into its odorant components and then chemically reproduced the aroma of each man. Next, she mixed the product into a special formula of wall paint that was applied to nine panels in the exhibit. Attendants walked up to the gallery wall, gently scratched the paint, and cautiously moved closer to capture the smell that might reveal a potent odor similar to that of the stench of an unwashed male armpit. The curators framed the exhibit by posting explanations for the attendants so that they could make conscious sense of the experiences. Tolaas conceptualizes how smell is involved in making judgments about people:

> Body odor is a universal phenomenon, but people have failed to find words that describe specific, individual smells uniformly across language and cultural barriers. That, together with difficulties in capturing and archiving smells, makes odor-based artwork rather rare—with the exception of flattering scents from the perfume industry. "We are judged by the eye most of the time, we perceive reality through the eye more than any other sense."[20]

Visitors were hit by the strong odors wafting from the exhibit when they walked into the reception area of the gallery. How they responded to the exhibit was determined by how active they wanted to be and how curious they were about the fragrant stimuli. Sarah Cowan reports:

> The walls release what is distinctly the stench of body odor, and while rubbing a wall in a gallery seems unusual and tempting, the revulsion of the smell sends most people away from the walls instantly, with grimaces and, well, a little of the smell on their fingers. . . . Tolaas keeps her subjects anonymous except for labeling one through nine "Animalic sweat, Asian sweat, Buttery sweat, Coriander sweat, New York 1, 2, and 3 sweat, SM sweat," and finally, "Whiskey tobacco sweat". . . . Four perfume bottles labeled with the numbers wait on a wall, offering anyone daring enough to spray the condensed sweat on.[21]

According to Cowan, the exhibit instigated a dramatic response from those who have attended. Mark Linga, a museum official, reported that:

> It's really interesting. Some people actually enjoyed the piece to the extent where they have gone to every single panel to kind of see the differences in the various scents coming off the wall. . . . Other folks have had a very visceral response where they don't want to relate to the piece. They kind of hurry through the piece.[22]

He believes that the scents present sensorial images: "It is almost like portraits, but there is no visual correlation except for the shifting tone in paint . . . [it] is not about who they are or what they are. It is about the body as a tool of communication, what happens when the body speaks, through odor, to your nose."[23] The unspoken signifiers wafting through the room are able to characterize the people that they originated from. Is the person we detect healthy, fearful, happy, or sexually virile? Our senses are able to perceive more than we acknowledge without the aid of the eyes and the ears. The potential of identifying people through smell is so strong that U.S. government anti-terrorism experts see applications of this work in tracing terrorists using their body odor. The government has invested significant money into scent tracking technology and other sensory-intelligent means to detect terrorism through uncontrollable aspects of physiology, such as the body's release of chemical markers. Tolaas' works were designed to be interactive, involving not just the observer as in a traditional museum, but also the hearer, the feeler, and the smeller. Her exhibit made use of experiential works to stimulate the attendant's use of their senses, not just their intellect, to understand the exhibit. The provocative exhibition challenged sight, the dominant sense, to make room for taste, touch, smell, and sound. What does this all mean to us? Tolaas further comments that, "It is about learning about smell and then figuring out how to communicate smell in language. We only have the connotation of smells in terms of bad and good, so I am teaching myself to be tolerant. We have to go back to the body, back to nothing."[24] By calling attention to smell rather than image, she uses olfaction to make us attentive to the world around us in a novel manner. As we monitor our responses and try consciously to figure out what the stimulus means, we train ourselves to acknowledge the role of smell in everyday life.

Another important aspect to consider is that odor memory falls off less rapidly than other sensory memory and it lasts a long time.[25] This process has become known as the "Proust Effect," where odor is associated with experience and a smell can recall the memory. For Proust, his famous madeleine cookie evokes his childhood obsessions. Time and time again we see this device used in television and movies, where a scent is used to try and trigger an amnesia victim to remember. It is true that smell is better at this memory cue effect than the other senses.[26] This is a result of the olfaction system's connection to the hippocampus. Once electrical signals about smell pass through the olfactory bulbs, they work their way through the brain into our most primitive portions, such as the hypothalamus, which controls appetite, anger, fear, and pleasure, whereas others continue into the hippocampus, which regulates memories, or travel into the brain stem, where such basic functions as remembering to breathe are regulated. This is why aroma can generate powerful emotion and trigger memory. Each time that I smell freshly cut wood inside a building, the backstage space of Jorgenson Auditorium in Storrs, Connecticut, is evoked. As a young apprentice I used to have to sweep up piles of freshly cut 2 x 4 when we built scene flats. When this aroma is perceived, I immediately recall that summer and the crush I had on a cute redhead. Through this simple example, we can begin to see the potential for using odors to evoke deeply personal memories quickly.

Our brain continually learns and adapts to the world around us. Smell research supports the idea of brain plasticity by showing that smell memory is context-dependent and can be modified by new experience.[27] Our olfactory sense is continuously adapting the world we live in as we experience new things. If we encounter scent in a new situation, such as a performance, there is the potential that our perception of that smell can be influenced, and that sensation can be taught to associate itself with a particular memory. Whenever I smell cedar chips I think both of a closet and of the SRS's theatre space for *Il Buchettino*. It evokes a sense of the comfort of one's bedroom, and in turn, SRS used this scent to evoke that very thing as a mood in their production. Now, the odor immediately accesses my memory and brings to consciousness what I have experienced during performance and from my childhood. These new associations show how theatrical representation is a powerful media endowed with the potential to change how our brains and our memories operate.

Odor offers the theatre a powerful tool to have an effect on our feelings and emotions during performance. Jacob argues why smell has an influence:

> The effects of smell on emotion and mood are most likely to be the result of conditioned association. Strong emotional responses to olfactory stimuli are rare or idiosyncratic, much more common are minor mood effects and mild affective states. The mood effects are likely to parallel the hedonicity of the odour (pleasant odours give rise to pleasant mood states while unpleasant odours give rise to unpleasant moods).[28]

If we smell the fragrance of Channel No. 5 and we associate it with rich French women, our memories and associations of that scent will affect a physical response as we inhale the scent when an actress walks onto the stage wearing it. For example, if we smell Annette's scent in Yasmina Reza's *God of Carnage* (2008) as she walks onto the stage, we inevitably make subconscious assumptions and feel a certain way about her character. The scent of her perfume will affect our future judgments about her. Her wealth, sense of fashion, and her perception of her femininity could become evident with one sniff of her fragrance.

There are many additional recent examples of the ways in which theatre practitioners are responding to the awareness of new understanding of the senses in concrete and physical ways. For example, IOU Theatre Company worked with artists, hospital patients, and staff throughout the United Kingdom to create a production that makes tangible the emotions and symptoms of illness. Joan Beadle describes her journey through the installations of *Cure* (2000):

> The unmistakable odour of disinfectant mingles with the chill night air as we descend into the subterranean vaults of the theatre. Smell is the first of our senses to be awakened and stirred during *Cure*. . . . After meeting a gigantic inflatable leech—part blood sucker, part bouncy castle—we are plunged into the world of the patient, each of us becoming temporary outpatients as we wander through the wards of this improbable infirmary. . . . All this is linked by a haunting soundscape of music and song delivered by disheveled musicians clad in dressing gowns. We empathise with and are entertained by the experiences of the hapless patients of this hospital as we hold the talking colostomy bags close to our ears.[29]

The immediate context for the performers was set up by the activation of our olfactory awareness. As a result, attendants began to make associations with what they saw with memories, feelings, and emotions evoked by the smells. Does the disinfectant remind us of sitting for hours in a National Health Service emergency room in South London, or does it remind us of the pain we suffered as children when we were admitted to a hospital for an appendectomy? Such evocations place us in the right mental context to make sense of the critique that the production offers us of the health care system. We relate to the event because we remember the sensations of being present in a hospital. Controlling what the attendant smells and for how long is a major obstacle in the success of the deployment of scent in performance. Exploring how creative artists have made use of aroma strategies will help demonstrate the power of scent in performance.

THIS MOVIE REALLY STINKS: TECHNOLOGICAL EXPERIMENTATION AND OLFACTORY ACTIVATION

There are a variety of Scratch-and-Sniff and Smell-O-Vision projects that demonstrate the efficacy of aroma as an expressive device in theatrical representation. The film *Scent of a Mystery* (1960) was an early pioneer in scent deployment making use of aroma technology. Smell-O-Vision was a gimmick to thrill audiences by getting them to smell objects they see on film. When the projector hit a specified point in the action, air blew over a rotating drum and pumped into the cinema.[30] The movie has a murder–mystery plot that is set in Spain. Smells highlighted key moments in the plot, such as the release of the aroma of a smoking pipe that became associated with an assassin.[31] Due to technical difficulties, the movie was a disaster, but it was an attempt to harness olfaction to make rich the attendant's experience of the film. The novelty of experience of Smell-O-Vision made it memorable, and as it was produced for a mass audience, its techniques are widely known. Randall Fitzgerald recollected that when mid-twentieth century filmmakers used fans to disperse odors to audiences, they were unable to clear the scents. As a result, rather than having a precise synchronized smell journey, the theatre became an odor garbage dump.[32] This difficulty of controlling the duration of the effect is only now being controlled with any measure of success using computer-controlled aromatic oils.

The most famous of these types of experiments is John Water's *Polyester* (1981). Set in a middle-class Baltimore suburb, it tells the story of Francine Fishpaw, whose husband Elmer, a polyester-festooned oaf, runs a XXX theater. She is ashamed, as neighbors picket her house in protest, her son is a nefarious foot fetishist, her dirty-dancing daughter is pregnant, and her husband is unfaithful. Smells that punctuate the action included the scent of flowers, pizza, glue, gas, grass, and feces. Waters' earliest films were low budget and sought to affect spectators by depicting trangressive and gross behavior. One blogger recalled getting his "Odorama" card when he bought his ticket. He knew he was supposed to Scratch-and-Sniff the scents when one of the ten numbers flashed on the screen because he saw *Pink Flamingos* years before. However, his friends were shocked when they scratched and got a rotten egg smell for when a character farted, and when they got a whiff of natural gas when a character stuck his head in an oven.[33] The use of smell is one element that contributes to the tone of the movie, which is overtly a camp send-up of bourgeois middle-class America. Not only are conventional characterizations subverted by the use of transvestitism, its everyday aromas, which attendants are instructed to sniff, include scatological samples. This is hardly a pleasant experience, but it points to Waters' use of the form of his artwork as a means of subverting conventional expectations about what a movie-going experience should be. He mischievously violates the contract between viewer and filmmaker by training us to sniff on cue, thereby tricking us into sniffing something we normally would not and turning our stomachs with fetid smells in the process.

There were other attempts in the 1990s where Scratch and-Sniff cards were distributed as promotional gimmicks for such movies as *Revenge of the Nerds IV: Nerds in Love* (1994), and television shows such as *Living Single* (1993–1998) and *Married . . . with Children* (1987–1997). In 2007, this gimmick was brought back in to mainstream popular culture with an episode of *My Name is Earl*.[34] Less offensive than Waters' choices, the smells included on the Scratch-and-Sniff card were a dryer sheet, Oreo cookies, cinnamon buns, popcorn, new car smell air freshener, and cologne. Smell called attention to the small details in the program that would get its viewers involved actively. While we watched for the cues to use the card, our anticipation kept us alert. As a result, we noticed small off-hand gestures, such as when the central character Earl sniffed his overalls. Was this the time to sniff? It was a quick gesture, but it became important because watching how his face registered the smell allowed our brains to fire off sympathetic smell responses. Likewise, when he introduced Oreo cookies, not only was the aroma of the cookie evoked, but also the taste of the filling that he was licking off. Some of us began involuntarily to salivate. We could squirm when Earl handed a moist, half-masticated cookie to his brother to ingest, remembering when our brother used to do the same thing to us. This in turn stimulated an active search for other smells that might trigger our memories. At one point, Earl walked into an appliance showroom that had air conditioners blowing on him, with streamers waving in the air, thus suggesting that we could feel the damp and cool air. He talked about the smells up front, calling attention to cooking cinnamon buns.

As we watched the episode, the activity of sniffing the scents helped focus our attention on the characters' actions. Becoming attendant to the cologne that the salesman wore connected the character's physical actions of spraying it into the air and stepping into it to the ritual of applying cologne. The cologne also made use of a "smell refrain" when the salesman snaked Earl's client away from him. When the salesman brought this female customer in close, we knew she could smell his cologne. We too could smell this smarmy guy, and the scent helped us feel appalled by his behavior; smell reinforced the effect of the action. Another smell refrain joke came from violating our expectation of how an air freshener was going to be used. Perhaps thinking that it was going to be in an employee locker, we were shocked when it was used by a character to give character to a sex doll. Characters in the TV episode talked about baking the doll in the oven or microwaving it so that it felt real. Another character, Darnell, snuggled up to the mass next to him in bed thinking that a sex doll was his wife. Then he smelled air freshener, which was associated earlier with the doll, and which in turn triggered him to throw off the covers, revealing the doll. Though flippant, the episode shows the potential power of paying attention to the senses as they are highlighted in performance, and how our awareness of these unusual stimuli gets us thinking about and noticing both the world of the play and the world around us in a different way for a short time. It is about noticing the world and showing how artists are directing our attention so that we are aware of the sounds and smells around us. In the same way, our exposure to the world is harnessed by the artists to give us more joy at our attentiveness to the sights, sounds, and smells of the world.

Another fanciful exploration of the joys of a sentient life was imagined in the classic film *Harold and Maude* (1971). Liesl Schillinger describes the use of an imaginary machine that plays recorded scent compositions:

> The scents she has hoarded are not Joy or Chanel No.5, they are everyday smells from a long fully enjoyed life—roast beef, old books, mown

grass. "Odorifics," Maude calls them. "Here's one you'll like," she exclaims, plunging a canister into the contraption: "Snowfall on 42nd Street!" Harold inhales. "What do you smell?" she demands. "Subway?" he asks. She nods. "Perfume. Cigarettes." He coughs . . . then there's a pause. With quiet wonder, he says, "snow."[35]

Schillinger captures an essential element in the evocation of aroma as a memory device. By harnessing the powerful propensity that aroma has to trigger memories and evoke our emotional associations, the film directs us to make use of our memories to identify and appreciate our exposure to the fragrances that accompany our day-to-day existence. Merely identifying and savoring the aroma of snow was depicted as a pleasurable experience preserved by memory and passed on by an older member of society. Whereas the use of aroma is metaphorical in the film, the ability to actually stimulate our sense of smell is possible today, although we have not made significant attempts to harness its use. A range of commercial applications exist to manipulate the buying experience or create a mood within the home. Demeter Fragrance Library sells "Crayon," "Dirt," and "Laundromat"-scented colognes, and AromaComposer promises a "smell synthesizer" where "a completely new aroma can be directed to the user in a matter of seconds, providing for quick changes of mood, dramatic effects, or healing scents."[36] These aromas are used to create an ambience or a hint of elegance at a party. Imagine preserving the scent of a loved one after they have died. The film industry occasionally attempts to make use of these new technologies. For example, Terrence Malick's *The New World* (2005) used computer-controlled smells to release smells in the theater to match scenes relating to a love story set seventeenth-century North America. In these "aroma scenes," seven types of aromatic oil were emitted from devices placed near seats. Using computer controls to release the smells at the right time, a forest scent came at the start of a journey through the woods, floral scents were matched to love scene, and peppermint and rosemary were released during emotional scenes.[37] Movie audiences are a bit skeptical of the applications of these technologies because they are still in such a primitive state. Our audiences want more immersive experience like those offered at theme park attractions. When my wife and I were at *Shrek 4-D*, she insisted that she smelled onion while the lead characters raced away in a chariot made of onions. Because we had been splashed, had air blown on us, and been prodded she expected to smell as well. Attendants can get too excited by the technology. Bloggers comment that rides like *Alien Encounter*, which had effects in complete darkness, like blowing hot air on your neck to make an alien breathe on you and drool, and dripping blood on you to make real scenes where personnel were killed were the most effective.[38] Total immersion seems to be the desired goal of these attendants. They would like to have each of their senses stimulated in such a way that they lose their sense of disbelief. As our brains can only focus on one interpretation of a stimulus at a time, if our senses are being directly triggered, we do not have time to doubt the skill or veracity of the aroma, the drip, or the jolt. Our brains will experience the event as if we have lived through it. In that way, it becomes a part of our lived experience, and what we take away has changed us or shaped us in some small way. As a result, our descriptions will become more evocative of sensation.

If we are more attendant to the ways that olfaction has been stimulated, then it stands to reason that our descriptions in turn will become evocative of the feelings, moods, and atmospheres that were perceived by our brains. Matthew Reason describes a performance review of *Balti Kings* (2000) by the Tamasha Theatre Company as evoking the smells of foods prepared on stage as evidence of how the use of olfaction creates authenticity in performance. He quotes a review by Susannah Clapp, where she describes the smell of coriander and its relationship to the curry cooking onstage. He explains:

> The logic of smell as an authenticating device is clear; the stage setting is so real that it smells real. Indeed the ability to match smell to its source (whether cigarette smoke, cooking, or incense) clearly marks the event as real and returns us to the linguistic importance of being able to identify visually the "odor designator."[39]

Reason is interested in defining how the evocation of a scent serves a descriptive function. If we can designate an odor, we can articulate a mood or atmosphere in a concrete way. He goes on to quote another reviewer describing a performance of *Ghost Ward* (2001) at the Almeida Theatre, where he thinks that the reviewer uses evocations of smell to evoke a sensual response. What these reviews show is that these shows activated these reviewers' senses and they began to chart their olfactory experiences of the performances. Their interpretation of the particular performance is tied to their involuntary responses to the smells and the feelings and emotions that were evoked. They begin to describe the performances as if they were describing any other lived experience. For example, Lynn Gardner recounts her attendant responses: "The experience is fleeting, fragmentary and mysterious. You walk down a corridor that smells of cabbage, peer into rooms where a nurse sits next to a bed in which a striplight flickers faintly on and off, and pass another where a pair of children's shoes lie abandoned."[40] She is aware of the lighting, the aromas, and her body is actively engaged in exploring the space. Her feelings and emotions that are evoked as a result of what she sees are affected by her neurological responses to the smells in the environment. Like the Proust effect, her own subjective journey through the space is elicited. As Synott expresses, "olfactory likes and dislikes [are] based on emotional associations. Such associations can be powerful enough to make odours that would generally be labeled unpleasant agreeable, and those that would generally be considered fragrant disagreeable for particular individuals."[41] Associations with smells are a powerfully evocative result of sensory stimulation.

By manipulating the context of smells we can change their associations. In the same way, by tying an image to a smell we can create a new association. If Gardner was fond of cabbage she might have found the image of a sick child in bed unsettling and associated the smell with a hospital; if she found the aroma abhorrent she may have associated the nurse next to the bed as the harbinger of death and disease. This manipulation of the context and images has great potential to shape our current experience, and perhaps even future experience, of some part of the elements that made up the moment as experienced during the duration of the performance. To further explore how practitioners have tried to make use of scent as a means of affecting interpretations, I will describe how several productions failed on the technical level because scents did not dissipate.

HISTORICAL FORAYS INTO OLFACTORY STIMULATION

The use of smell communicates to us in an intimate way. We try and regulate our proximity to noxious or pleasant smells, and limit what others can smell of us. Classen et al. assert:

> Smell is not simply a biological and psychological phenomenon, though. Smell is cultural, hence a social and historical phenomenon. Odours are invested with cultural values and employed by societies as a means of and model for defining and interacting with the world. The intimate, emotionally charged nature of the olfactory experience ensures that such value-coded odours are interiorized by the members of society in a deeply personal way.[42]

When we harness smell in performance, we are invading or impinging upon personal space. We cannot escape the smells of the theatre. In the early twentieth century, Modernist practitioners experimented with olfaction. Mary Fleischer catalogs Symbolist use of scent as a practical means of achieving their aesthetic aims. She describes:

> Smell might well have been the Symbolist sense par excellence. While the Naturalists and Realists used detailed descriptions of smell as literary device to imbue the environment with a moral atmosphere or to enrich the verisimilitude of their works, the Symbolists used smell in suggestive, mysterious, and expansive ways to dissolve barriers between subject and object, individual and environment. The idea that art should be an evocation of a hidden reality through symbolic means was a central belief of the Symbolists.[43]

By activating a sensation that cannot be easily put into words, they were further able to create a mysterious atmosphere in the same way that they were using lighting and other scenic effects. There were several productions that made use of perfume or smoke to evoke mood. What these effects may have meant to attendants is not know; however, several scholars have investigated the effectiveness of scent strategies.

In describing the effect of smell in Andrei Bely's *The Jaws of Night* (1907), Fleischer interprets what this may have achieved:

> Here, actual scent could be used onstage, but more importantly, the qualities of its smoke are abstracted and intermingle with the play of light and movement; the sound of the censer echoes, perhaps suggesting church bells, an alarm, or the vastness of the empty space. Although incense and perfumes have been used in several Symbolist productions, it is not always evident whether the scent was simply dispersed for a general atmospheric effect or whether the scent was somehow orchestrated into a synaesthetic kind of experience.[44]

However, as the symbolist theatre strove to emphasize the subjective nature of interpretation, they made traditional theatrical techniques seem strange, such that audiences were at a loss to cope with the new production practices. The earliest experiments with the use of smell suffered from the invasive nature of aromatic stimulation. A failure to clear scent after it was deployed doomed its use. In 1891, the were two performances of a *Cantique des Cantiques* adapted by Paul-Napoleon Roinard at the Theatre d'Art that exploited smell as a means to communicate the unseen elements of life that cannot be expressed by words alone. *Cantique des Cantiques*, or *Song of Songs* or *Song of Solomon*, is based on the Hebrew bible story of the sexual relationship of a woman and her lover, and attempted to convey the underlying emotion of the verses through scent. Kristin Shepherd-Barr argues that the play was staged: "expressly to present a new idea of theatre as total art by engaging the visual, aural, and olfactory senses of the audience . . . 'music, words, colour, even perfume, were to be harmonized; all the senses were to be involved, simultaneously, in the one overwhelming experience."[45] Paul Fort's direction made use of an arsenal of scents that were meant to be symbolic in a way similar to and icons. However, as this was a new production method, it was decided to support the experience with a plethora of explanatory material. The program contained essays highlighting the meaning of the scents. Shepherd-Barr continues:

> According to the outline Roinard provided in the programme, nine scents were used: frankincense, white violets, hyacinth, lilies, acacia, lily of the valley, syringe, orange blossom, and jasmine. Each of these odours had corresponding orchestrations of speech (specific vowel sounds), tones (original music composed by Mme Flamen de Labrely), and colours.[46]

Claude Schumacher recounted the attendants' response: "a bewildered audience was doused with perfume and left choking in fumes of incense which the ventilation system of the theatre was unable to cope with."[47] Shepherd-Barr points out the shortcomings of utilizing scent in performance and how it is a subjective experience. However, the subjective nature of interpretation according to an intuitive lived experience is part and parcel of the Symbolist movement, and their instigations have made it possible for lived experience to be both real as the realists or naturalists would have wanted, but also spiritual in that it communicates to the intuitive parts of the brain that do not consciously ascribe meaning and logic to its lived experience. In fact, technology has improved in the century since the play was performed and we have a greater control over the deployment of the scent. We also understand that the subjective emotional associations of the mechanism are essential to the device. The intimate connection between smells and the feelings that they evoke is powerful; "The perception of smell, thus, consists not only of the sensation of the odours themselves, but of the experiences and emotions associated with them." [48] Fragrance was used to create aromatic imagery:

> Roinard adapted the eight "songs" of Solomon so as to make the literary text a sensory narrative as well, and it is the latter context that frames and dominates the production. From his detailed descriptions it appears that Roinard sought to de-emphasize the over eroticism and physicality of the original and, as one would expect in a symbolist theatre, to guide his audience instead towards the mystical and spiritual meanings of the text and its allegorical figures. The focus is on the orchestration of sights, sounds and smells to bring out the imagery of the text, rather than on the text itself.[49]

The language of the nineteenth century evoking the soul and spirituality can make way for the concrete perceptions of the mind given validity by science. Though attendants were confused despite the linguistic cues given to help them understand, a greater awareness of the scents and what they were doing to the attendant was the real guide. It is not that jasmine means one thing or another; it is that our experience of the scents that were meaningfully laid out gives us a means to experience the sensations, which in turn can communicate in varying levels of meaning. Classen et al. explain: "Smell can evoke strong emotional responses. A scent associated with a good experience can bring a rush of joy. A foul odour or one associated with a bad memory may make us grimace with disgust." [50] The more we associate jasmine with the Bible we can make deeper connections to the metaphorical imagery. Those associations will in turn evoke memories of the theatrical event and the content of the *Cantique des Cantiques*.

However, the shock of the new, to borrow Robert Hughes' phrase, would have been off-putting for the attendants; "Each participant would have undergone a heightened degree of the emotional state evoked by the odour stimulus and an intense concomitant search for the meaning of the associative property within his or her memory."[51] They would have been so distracted by the novelty of the experience that they would have had difficulty putting together their physical sensations with their cognitive understanding. Without a system or awareness of how to perceive these sensations in a meaningful way, the attendants would have been unable to consciously understand the potential meanings that the aromas were meant to communicate. Shepherd-Barr concludes:

> The impact of each scent on Roinard's audience would have been most powerful on initial contact and rather than growing in intensity, the reaction to it would have been diminished during exposure. This makes it even more important that the scents be cleared away rapidly, yet once released into the audience the odour molecules could not be easily dispersed; thus the spectators would have experienced sensory fatigue, possibly negating of undermining the intended effect of the aromas.[52]

This was a meaningful artistic creation. Its lessons bring us back to *Harold and Maude*—it is possible with new technology to more precisely control the durational qualities of the aromas. *Harold and Maude* makes use of smell to heighten our awareness of the effect of action on the emotions of the characters. Their attention to sensation points to the times when we become aware of smell—their senses were alive when they were preoccupied with death.

Our sense of smell can sharpen when we encounter stressful situations. Wen Li tested volunteers who repeatedly smell odors distinctly different from those we encounter in everyday living. When Li gave mild electric shocks when volunteers smelled the odors, they were able to identify the odor more often than when not shocked. This experiment showed that there was a connection between shock and memory. Lauran Neergaard explains:

> There were changes in how the brain's main olfactory region stored the odor information, essentially better imprinting the shock-linked scent so it could be distinguished more quickly from a similar odor. That is certainly a survival trait evolved to help humans rapidly and subconsciously pick a dangerous odor from the sea of scents constantly surrounding us.[53]

We remember these scents and associate them with stress so that we are able to respond quickly if we should encounter them again. This type of experience enables us to learn and respond to the world throughout our life. When we depict events and stimulate the brain through mimetic representation, we can prepare our brains for a variety of unfamiliar experiences that we might later encounter.

Because of our brain's ability to reconfigure and strengthen neural connections, repeated exposure enables us to identify and respond to stimuli in practiced ways. However, we can also distort our perceptions through cultural conditioning and neglect to create erroneous connections in our brains to the information that aromatic stimuli communicate. In contrast to the cultural interference that humans cope with, other creatures simply respond biologically to the chemical world. Ants are social insects that leave scent traces as messages warning of danger, guiding others to food, and regulating behavior. However, we disregard or suppress smell, relying instead on sights and sounds.[54] Our cultural conditioning has dulled our ability to appreciate and become attentive to scent. Our brains can strengthen our conditioning in relation to scent if we begin to become aware of scent. Neuronal connections will be built and our brain will fire more rigorously when stimulated by sense with repeated exposure. Therefore, the potential to affect human experience, perceptions, and ways of thinking is potent if theatre should learn how to make use of scent in performance.

The commercial world spends large sums of money researching how to manipulate consumers using smell. Retailers make use of technological advances to shape the consumer's experience while buying. They use the scent of chocolate chip cookies while selling a home, or the smell of baby powder in the infant clothing section. These tactics create a setting that they claim is not manipulation, but rather an attempt to make the consumer comfortable. It is a strategy of making use of subtle stimulation to evoke mood and feeling.[55] It is easy to see the potential uses this might have for theatrical representation, as well as more nefarious subliminal thought control by the government and retail industries. It is up to the theatre world to find creative and exhilarating ways to harness this information in transformative ways rather than manipulative ways. However, are all aromas sniffed during the course of a performance relevant in meaning-making? What if a full garbage dumpster from a restaurant is sitting next to the back door of the theatre in late August and its fumes are seeping into the theatre? Although it might be convenient for a production of Oyamo's *I am a Man* (1992), about the African-American garbage strike in Memphis, to have the smell of rotting garbage permeating the auditorium one evening, it would be a different story if *Brighton Beach Memoirs* (1984) had the same smell wafting through the auditorium. The smell of garbage might unintentionally become meaningful even if it is just a coincidence.

THE PROBLEM OF UNINTENTIONAL STIMULATION

One evening while watching a production of David Mamet's *American Buffalo*, I smelled smoke. The aroma of tobacco filled the house long before we could determine from where and from whom it was emanating. Eventually, an actor tapped his cigar in an ashtray, and all was revealed. However, the question lingered of why the director used real cigar smoke when he did not use whiskey or other smells to fill in the aroma of the environment. Can smell ever be more than mere artifice used to make a bit of naturalistic mimesis authentic? Whether generated consciously, or created as a by-product of the actions of a piece, use of other modes of sensorial stimulation adds another dimension to information transmission. How do we talk about sensory perception in theatre, where many of the smells are mere accidents? How do these experiences break free from the production into a deliberate enrichment of the experience and shape of the event?

If smell guides us in everyday life by giving us key information (phero- mones for sexual attraction; disease with the smell of a festering wound; smells related to menstrual or lactation cycles), then why not shape it to craft experience? We craft scent in our day-to-day routine by wearing fra- grance designed to allure and attract. We also use a room freshener or candles to neutralize festering household odors. Smell can tell us where we are, create a mood, trigger behavior, mask, entice, and repel. It can denote social status: Does the person smell of a floral musk or rancid grease? There are natural smells (lilac), biological smells (urine), and manufactured or industrial by-product smells (sulfur).

In the exertions and activities of everyday life we generate odorants. Regardless of whether it is by design or by accident, these aromas fill our world. Theatre makes use of natural material, and in so doing, produces scent. As these fragrances drift their way to the nostrils of the attendants, they shape the ways in which the narrative is understood. Moist soil has a distinctive aroma, and its presence can immediately evoke the natural world. Fabulous Beast Dance Theatre Company exploits this is *Fragile* (2000), where they transform a theatre studio into a dirt promontory to give shape to movement images of the creation of man. It is a versatile loca- tion. On stage there are a giant aquarium sealed with tarnished brass, large enough for bodies to fight underwater; a giant rope; a giant wooden struc- ture, which looks rather like a lifeguard chair; an outdoor shower; and a bathtub filled with chalk. They use few props—some bottles of milk, many cans of Guinness, oranges, a saw, and a ladder.[56] Onstage movement guides the attendant through a series of episodes whose actions, movements, cor- poreal shapes, and interrelationship create an abstract narrative. We are guided as attendants by the smells, sounds, and movements. A woman emerges from the tank while a male and female creature fight over teach- ing and taking care of her, while a large blue male sits above, drinks beer, and watches. No definitive narrative is evident, but our reactions to the smells generated during the performance, such as perspiration mixed with makeup, lead to a deeply personal response. Hops remind me of Britain and the stench of the Tube on a weekend night. Fetid smells of sweating, alco- hol-drenched bodies and pheromones drift from couples cuddling in the corner. We search for meaning when it is not apparent and we are forced to scan our sensations to determine what stimuli fuels our perception of the experience. We pay attention to that which catches our attention, even if it was not intended to be meaningful to the performance.

The production team reported that they were fascinated by the range of descriptions of smells that attendants commented upon after the performance. People wanted to know how, for instance, the smell of crushed oranges was supposed to inform their interpretation of the dance. Although the smells that were generated during the course of a performance (including citrus, wet soil, barley hops, milk, and chalk) were such a pivotal part of my perception and experience, they were a by-product of the action. The choreographer, Michael Keegan-Dolan, insists that the smells were simply accidental, a by-product of the imagery. As he develops and the company tries to create it, smells accompany the media used. Even if he wanted to, he could not smell it because he suffers from anosmia.[57] Though not intentional, the smells were often the most concrete element in the narrative. The aroma of milk on flesh evoked seminal and amniotic qualities of the principle dancer's movement, transforming her into an iconic mother symbol. Other slimy, sticky bodies were visceral reminders of sex, birth, and primal desires—fluid mixed with dirt created an aroma that could not be ignored. No longer were the images that streamed in front of us fictional; the movement, texture, and color released long-forgotten memories of digging in the mud and playing in the bathroom cabinet. These writhing bodies dripping mud were visually arousing, but the added element of the mingled smells of milk, soil, and beer provoked memories of youthful sexual dalliances with lovers rolling in the leaves. These smells aroused me and made me hunger for the dancers. These memories and emotions created tangible narratives out of the dancers' movements. Our experiences of the composite sensation received over the duration of the event created the metaphor of sex and death as vividly as dialogue might in a traditional play. These physical moments trigger sense receptors that in turn activate memory. Our brains and our experiences predispose us to interpret the stimuli according to our own evoked memories. Past, present, and imaginary come together in the shared moments between performers and attendants. Though these memories were contingent and triggered by contingent stimuli, they contributed to the creation of atmosphere and narrative.

In a much more conventional production, olfaction and gustation are used for metaphorical effect. Taste and smell are intimately related. What we normally assume is taste is actually a combination of taste and smell sensory information, more properly defined as flavor. Researchers explain that about 80% of the tastes we describe are actually aromas.[58] Smell is more sensitive than taste; we inhale a greater volume of air than we taste of a liquid.[59] Along with texture and temperature, the perception of flavor comes from a combination of aroma and taste. Ben Brantley reports of Ivo van Hove's 2007 production of *The Misanthrope*:

> The edible look is all the rage—and I mean rage—in the fashionable circles of Paris this season. Head-to-toe layers of ketchup, chocolate syrup, watermelon pulp and crushed potato chips. . . . But if Alceste is applying his lunch externally to épater the aristos, he is also putting his insides on public display. The stench of his pain fills the air; it smells like ketchup and watermelon and chocolate. For the rest of the play, Alceste wears his food stains as if they were stigmata, and whenever he shows up onstage, you flinch for what he's feeling.[60]

The tactile quality of the spoiled food, as well as its stench, is used as a means to evoke the emotional morass the misanthrope experiences. His stench impinges itself on the unsuspecting noses of those in close proximity. Therefore, the production uses smell to evoke mood and trigger involuntary visceral responses within those attending to the production. Van Hove is able to break the fourth wall and make physical contact with his attendants, thereby making an audience listening to seventeenth-century verse attendant to twenty-first century actor–attendant interaction. To further understand the means by which practitioners are triggering visceral reactions, we must investigate the role of taste, as it is intimately entwined with our sense of smell.

ONE CANNIBAL TO ANOTHER WHILE EATING A CLOWN: "DOES THIS TASTE FUNNY TO YOU?"

Taste gives us the ability to evaluate what we eat and drink so that we are encouraged to eat substances that our body is able to use as fuel and prevented from consuming potential poisons or toxins that will damage our bodies. Whereas bitter and sour flavors cause aversive reactions because poisons are bitter, and spoilage is associated with sour, we appreciate the taste of sugar because we require carbohydrates, crave salt because we require sodium chloride, and have an appetite for fish sauce because we require protein. In other words, our taste preferences and cravings for certain types of food are conventionally tied to physiological needs: sweet (energy rich nutrients); umami (amino acids); salty (modulating electrolyte balance); sour (typically the taste of acids that cause stomachaches); and bitter (allows sensing of diverse natural toxins). None of these tastes are elicited by a single chemical. Taste perception also is influenced by thermal stimulation of the tongue. In some people, warming the front of the tongue produces a clear sweet sensation, whereas cooling leads to a salty or sour sensation.

Our sense of taste is mediated by taste receptor cells, which are bundled in clusters called taste buds. A pore at the top of our tongue makes contact with the fluid environment in the mouth. Some of the taste cells in each bud make contact with the primary taste nerves over a synaptic connection. When stimulated, neurotransmitter molecules will stimulate the primary afferent nerves. Taste receptor cells sample oral concentrations of chemical molecules and report a sensation of taste to the brain. When we take a bite of something flavorful our saliva dissolves its chemicals and our taste buds absorb its free-floating molecules. Once that molecule attaches to a receptor cell, transduction begins. Our tongues are the primary sense organs that collect gustation data through the gustatory pores. Nerve endings for the taste and touch/temperature/pain systems surround the base of the taste bud cells. Interwoven among the taste cells in a taste bud is a network of dendrites of sensory nerves called "taste nerves." These nerves (the facial nerve, the hypoglossal nerve, and the glossopharyngeal nerve) bring data from defined regions of the tongue to be compiled and analyzed before being sent to the brainstem. There, the signals are combined and trigger arousal. When taste cells are stimulated by the binding of chemicals to their receptors, they depolarize, and this depolarization is transmitted to the taste nerve fibers, resulting in an action potential that goes to the thalamus and then to the cerebral cortex. As they move through the brain, they combine with olfactory data to give form to flavor.[61]

Once taste signals are transmitted to the brainstem, several efferent neural pathways are activated that are important to digestive function. When we taste an apple, our mouths fill with saliva and our stomachs begin to secrete chemicals that start the digestive process. The sense of taste is equivalent to excitation of taste receptors, and there is substantial difference in taste sensitivity among individuals. Roughly one in four people are several times more sensitive to bitter and other tastes than standard tasters. We have receptors for a large number of specific chemicals that have been identified as contributors to the reception of taste. The large numbers of flavors that we perceive are due to airborne molecules sensed by olfaction. As we breathe, we bring smells into the mouth that mix with the flavor chemicals. What we do not realize is that what we think of lemon is not derived from sweet, sour, and bitter flavor compounds, but rather from terpene aroma compounds that are perceived when mixed with breath during the act of sniffing.

We taste with a mixture of input from taste buds, smell, pain, texture, and temperature. There is no one means to get the information to the brain, as olfaction and gustation are interwoven perceptions. Smell ties together several strands of data into one sensation. In addition to signal transduction by taste receptor cells, it is also clear that the sense of smell profoundly affects our sensation of taste. As we ingest food, it moves to the back of the throat, where there are olfactory nerves. When they respond, they send nerve impulses to the olfactory bulb, which in turn sends messages to the temporal lobe, which is involved in memories of place and to the part involved in speech. This is why smells can evoke powerful memories. Some researchers claim that smelling some aromas can inhibit language formation, thus leaving us with only visual memories. An important finding reported by Dana Small is that there is strong evidence that the final common pathways of taste and smell go to the non-verbal right brain.[62] Like information for smell, taste messages also end up in the limbic system. Arriving in the limbic system results in immediate preconscious associations that will trigger memories tied to the places and times that the flavors have been experienced previously. Taste sensation can be a form of virtual time travel.

One day, Helen, the title character in Barbara Hodgson's *The Sensualist*, begins to realize the book she has found is beginning to change her awareness of her physiological state. One by one, each sense becomes overwhelming and she cannot help but be conscious of it at a given moment. She uses her awareness and attentiveness to taste sensation to savor the flavor and textures of the food that she placed into her mouth. A simple lunch becomes a gustatory symphony:

> As she chewed it an overwhelming sensation flooded into her mouth and down her throat—the French fry felt incredible. . . . Grains of salt melted in provocating bursts upon her tongue, or hid in toothy crannies and slowly spread their bring magic, or better still, landed full square between incisors and exploded into intoxicating splinters.[63]

Hodgson demonstrates the potential of what sensorial-rich awareness of taste can do for emotional and mental state. This description of her meal takes on an orgasmic appreciation of the sensations she savors. Though taste and touch are at the heart of this experience, smell too is evoked. The chemical senses respond to the flavor and aroma together:

> Smell, like taste, is a concrete sense in which receptors respond to what are literally pieces of the thing perceived. When one tastes, however, the stimulus is known in that it is also seen, felt, and placed into the mouth, whereas smells often seem to come from nowhere—and to disappear into nothingness. It is, perhaps, the contrast in our olfactory experience between the compelling perception of a physical thing and its ambiguous source, often undetected by any other sense, that lends smell its peculiar mystery and contributes to the strong emotional responses it can evoke in humans, and to the significance frequently attached to it: the smell of life, the smell of death, the "odour of the soul."[64]

Taste, like smell, can evoke memories that are laden with emotional qualities that are often difficult to describe because their textures and flavors stimulate our limbic system and stir up our primitive responses to the world. Because food is essential to our survival, social rituals revolving around food are central parts of every culture on earth. To employ sensations that lead to taste is to tap into an intrinsically essential part of the human need for social contact.

Our experiences of taste are remembered by the brain and cataloged like every other stimulus we encounter. It enables us to identify new experiences and discern the value of the stimuli. As we make use of our knowledge of the world in the creation of an artistic experience, we mix and match elements to stimulate responses from our attendants. How will our particular recipe trigger response? How will our memories be connected together this time?

> Helen woke up with the taste of her life in her mouth. Not just the remains of memory but the complete archives, as if she had never ever throughout the years, brushed, scrubbed, rinsed, scraped, or picked. . . .

> The identity of this new taste, these new tastes rather, rushed through her suddenly like a hot flush through the cheeks, and once recognized, they overpowered everything else. She savored honeyed souvenirs of laughter and enchantment; where had they been all this time? She devoured ambrosial remnants of amity and intimacy, and dull substantial meals of contentment and tranquility.[65]

This recombination allows Helen to acknowledge her feelings and accept that she can feel again. Her experience recollects what it felt like to desire by evoking her memories and overpowering her conscious mind so that she could recognize what her feelings and emotions were trying to tell her. She needed her senses to direct her in an unfamiliar way back to the feelings that she had long ago repressed. Her world became alive again as she reclaimed the sensual world. A world connected to other bodies and textures, smells and flavors; a sensual world that, if lived in the moment, could offer the splendors of being alive. She demonstrates the potential of being sensitive to her sensations.

Taste sensitivity refers to the intensity with which we perceive tastes and flavors. Individuals who experience tastes and smells as being strong are said to have high taste sensitivity. They are able to distinguish individual flavors in a mixture with some accuracy, such as the flavor of grasses and mango in a fruity wine, whereas for individuals with low taste sensitivity, tastes, smells, and flavors are not as strong, and they cannot discern individual flavors in a mixture and instead taste the wine as wine. Taste sensitivity depends on multiple factors, including the nature and number of taste receptors on taste bud cells and the number of taste buds a person has. The Taste Science Laboratory has found that people with different taste sensitivity approach decision-making in differing ways. Though they are not sure precisely why these tendencies are true, those who do not taste well have a less active orbitofrontal cortex and logic will dominate, whereas those who have moderate sensations or strong sensations have a more active orbitalfrontal cortex and are likely improvise, or to weigh values and contingencies.[66] There is likely a direct correlation to how sensitive we are to sensation and the manner in which we make conscious our perceptions of the world. Our biological subjectivism shapes who we are and what we think of the world. Although there is no absolute for how taste affects those who experience a stimuli, the excitation of different regions of the brain as a result of flavor point to its potency in shaping an attendant's experience of a theatrical event.

Likewise, it is difficult to detach our gustatory sensation from those of our olfactory sensations. An active tasting of food engages smell and touch, as well as involuntary motor responses generated during mastication and swallowing. Whereas taste is oral, smell is nasal. Taste molecules are dissolved in a carrier like saliva, and temperature and tactile stimuli modulate the responses of taste nerves, whereas smell molecules respond to chemicals in the vapor phase. Our web of sensory awareness activates by default. Our attention, however, can be manipulated by consciousness. If we actively pay attention to the sensations of taste and smell, we can enhance our experience of them. Our appreciation of what we experience takes effort. When we become inured to sensation, we lose the joy and wonder of living. There is an important aspect to using food to create a mood and an atmosphere that encourages social rites.

FEASTING AS A THEATRICAL EVENT

The use of food as a component in theatrical entertainments has a long history. Numerous critics have charted this use, most notably Barbara Kirsenblatt-Gimblett, who describes a range of food performances from the early modern through modern period in an attempt to unpack the aesthetic uses of food by the futurists and the surrealists in the creation of meaning. By evoking sumptuous feasts, power and social hierarchy reasserts itself. Food has been used as both a social lubricant and a means of displaying munificence. Denise Cole claims:

> Today, audiences often attend ... entertainments, which serve food during the course of the performance or at least before the show and during intermission. However, during the lavish feasts of the Middle Ages, food did not just *accompany* a performance; food *was* a performance exhibited on special occasions when wealthy nobles shared their bounty with strangers, tenants, and guests. Feasting and festivity were inextricably fused in medieval hospitality; the one did not exist without the other. ... it also gave aristocrats an opportunity for an elaborate and costly display of their power in an age that communicated not only through ocular but also through tactile and gustatory media.[67]

One way that traditional theatre practitioners have tried to make the transition to activating the gustatory sense to make a connection to the play being performed on stage was in a production in Cork, Ireland, where the company laid out bowls of gummy worms and other nauseatingly sweet foods that the characters—smack addicts—were going to be consuming on stage during Mark Ravenhill's *Some Explicit Photographs* (2001). The effect was to give the attendants a sugar-shock as we watched the action, perhaps, metaphorically, the energy crash that resulted could be in aid of the crash the characters were encountering on stage.

However, activating taste sensations can become an event in itself, leading us on a journey flavor by flavor. Cole continues: "Although the theatricalization of medieval and early Renaissance feasts is widely known, the presentation of food that made up these feasts was more than a mere accompaniment to human performance. Food *was* performance."[68] As we know from Kirsenblatt-Gimblett, modernist performances made explicit use of food as a stimulant of theatrical experience. These tactics still are in use today in cutting-edge experiments in the food world. Homaro Cantu is an experimental chef that has transformed a night dining at his restaurant Moto into a gustatory event. Although he does not in any way think of it as theatre, it is certainly performative. His food challenges conventional assumptions about what food should taste, look, and feel like. His adaptation of a conventional dining room into a set prepares the diner's expectation of something different; his creation of food products that resemble props more than an entrée and his manipulation of what constitutes food set the stage for a novel experience. Jennifer Reingold declares:

> Even before the session begins, there are a few clues that this is not your average fine-dining establishment. Start with the Class IV laser, normally used for surgery, on a prominent display in the dinning room. At Moto, it's the huge tank of industrial-use liquid nitrogen in the backyard, used to freeze things that are normally hot and to mold foods into wholly unnatural shapes. Finally, there's the huge photo of Salvador Dali, mounted prominently above the stairs leading into the basement kitchen. Printed on the photo is a quote: "The only difference between a madman and me is that I am not mad."[69]

Cantu has crafted an artistic response to challenge a participant's notions of food and food production. Whereas unsuspecting customers expecting sushi instead get a "degustation menu" would leave exasperated, others willing to experiment would be dazzled. He makes use of food replicators (a dispenser that sprays vegetable inks on edible paper), aromatic utensils, and lasers to enhance the participant's gustatory and olfactory sensations. Diners are aided by the props used to serve the food, and are thus able to monitor how they should perceive this food. Reingold describes the response of José Andrés, another experimental chef:

> his brow furrowed as he tastes bison with the aid of Cantu's aromatic utensils—forks and spoons with corkscrew handles that hold sprigs of thyme and rosemary—and watches him use his laser to burn a hole in a vanilla bean, whose fumes are used to enhance the flavor of the beef dish he is serving.[70]

Cantu's creations include "the edible menu, a soy-based concoction with vegetable ink spread out to resemble a soft piece of parchment; synthetic champagne injected into your glass with a giant black medical syringe; and flapjacks sizzling on a 'griddle' frozen to–273 degrees."[71] His carbonized fruit lets a taster feel fizzy explosions of pineapple or orange as they bite on the fruit stored in pressurized carbon dioxide. Reingold explains that food companies are thrilled by the prospect of taste dispensers or mass market potentials of the technology that Cantu experiments with. An evening at

Moto sets up an experience that allows us to have a new taste, touch, and smell experience where our instincts have precedence over experience. The possibility of the ways that the theatre can exploit these devices is interesting as well. Imagine eating food with the characters on stage, much the same way that you smelled the aromas of the scratch-and-sniff films.

ACTIVATING THE WEB OF SENSORIAL PERCEPTION

Can a sample taste of authentic "Cuban cuisine" (or is that "Latin American cuisine"?) actually be the same as sampling an authentic "Cuban Mamacita?" Coco Fusco and Nao Bustamante's *Stuff* (1996) intertwined food and sex as a way of displaying diverse identity through stereotypes. Fusco and Bustamante created multiple characters based on overt stereotypes and used them to show the ways in which the sex trade makes a commodity out of appetite. Attendants are put into contact with the performers, their props, and Cuban food. There was no escaping the smells, sounds, and touches of this performance. The premise of the evening is that "The Institute of Southern Hemispheric Wholeness" will transport attendants on a virtual tour of exotic Latin culture. Rosemary Weatherston describes the five sketches that make up the basic structure of the event:

> The Institute's spokesman, "Triple-E," . . . oversees the onstage actions of Institute employees, "Blanca" . . . and "Rosa," . . . via an enormous video screen. Combining the qualities of a used-car salesman and the Wizard of Oz, Triple-E uncannily reproduces the salvational tone of late-night infomercials as he relates the wonders of international consumerism.[72]

By conflating food and sex, they were attempting to communicate how easy it is to perpetuate the exploitation of others simply by innocently tasting *arroz con frijoles*. No matter how much we understood the intellectual arguments that the artists were making, we could not escape our own complicity in perpetuating the stereotypes that they were enacting. Intellectually, we could distance ourselves and say that we would never buy into the sex trade and exploit the women that these stereotypes represent. However, by participating in the event itself we were forced to acknowledge that our responses were based on our assumptions, which are the same assumptions that are chaining these women to prostitution. Direct interaction between the attendants and performers guided the event. Participants were chosen at random from the bank of seating. The actors would climb over people to drag unsuspecting participants onto the stage. We were asked to share food, or be tested on our bilingual ability. Others were invited down for rumba lessons. One fortunate young man was given a crash course on learning the basic phrases necessary to bed a Latino woman. By the end, participants had been dressed up, given lines to speak and food to eat, and taught to dance and sing.[73] Although we might not buy the services of a prostitute, we might still sample the rice and beans that the performers were serving us. Like tourists consuming authentic Cuban food walking down the street as we spend our dollars visiting Havana, we tasted this so-called authentic food in the theatre. If there is a market for services, vendors will debase themselves to satisfy it because they need money to survive. When we saw the performance, we wanted to make a statement to the artists and not participate. When we were chosen, we refused to eat and we left. However, whether we partook in the food or not, our emotional and intellectual responses contributed the energy and exchange between the performers and the attendants. There is no escape—we were all contributing, even if inadvertently, to the perpetuation of the sex trade that the event was calling attention to. We made sense of the event based on our experiences and (mis)perceptions of the content of the scenes.

Fusco and Bustamante tried several strategies to convey the complex arguments they were presenting about third-world exploitation and post-colonial complicity. The performance used food to highlight the relationship between western appetites for sex and daily consumer practice. Fusco and Bustamante explain, "If food here serves as a metaphor for sex, then eating represents consumption in its crudest form. We are dealing with how cultural consumption in our current moment involves the trafficking of that which is most dear to us all—our identities, our myths and our bodies."[74] By creating stereotyped characters that interacted with attendants, they gave us intimate exposure to the exploitive tourist experience. Choosing men in the audience to join them on stage and learn key phrases in Spanish to pick up prostitutes, they were mimicking the salesmanship of the actual pimping of women, as well as the tourist's willingness to be led into a prepackaged experience that conforms to their notion of what the Spanish-speaking Caribbean Latin world should be like. Preparing food in our proximity allowed us to smell the ingredients and involuntarily be drawn into the experience. Multiple strategies were used to activate our involvement and therefore activate our complicity within the event. Regardless of our resistance, Fusco and Bustamante used song, dance, dialogue, image, smell, and taste to seduce us into buying into their message. They were determined that we participate and be entertained so that they in turn could turn around and implicate us in the behavior that they were showing to be reprehensible. Active participation is garnered by a conscious strategy by an artist to activate and make us aware of our sensations, emotions, feelings, and thoughts. They are training us to think in a different way via visceral stimulation. In this way, the web of the senses is harnessed by the theatre to make new neuronal connections and change us at our electrical core.

WHERE DO THE CHEMICAL SENSES LEAD US?

Taste and smell can be used as a means to activate attendants' awareness of the ways in which the web of sensorial perception stimulates their experiences and comprehension of a theatrical event. Elsewhere, I described a performance of *La Baraque* (1999) that was part of *Le Campement*, a group of performances in spaces situated together outside the Industrial Palace, Prague consisting of *La Baraque* (the hut), *La Tente* (the tent), and *Le Tonneau* (the barrel).[75] *Le Campement* was designed to establish a shared space where attendants and performers would interact intimately. As we gathered at the entrance, we were directed to one of three performance spaces. Because the event sought to activate the attendant's web of sensorial perception, every aspect of our experience—from gathering at the gate and entering the tent, to our trips to the toilet as the hours droned on—became a meaningful part of the event.

Though we were led into the performance space and told that we could sit anywhere at any of the long, wooden communal tables, we had to negotiate the space and figure out on our own what our function was in this event. Those who were lucky enough were able to keep warm because of their proximity to a large wood-burning stove with a large black cauldron of soup simmering. The smell of the soup made our stomachs growl and our mouths water. Because the show did not seem to start, we began chatting with the strangers around us as if we were in a pub. Bottles of wine could be bought, and bread was passed out to each of the tables. We sat, ate, and chatted with those around us, while some others smoked. When was the event going to start? Our eyes began to tear from the cigarette and wood smoke. Little by little, we began to realize that this was the event and that there were actors moving through the room, leading each table in small actions; an actor might play a word game, or do a slight-of-hand magic trick. The smells and the sounds of the environment led us to respond in culturally conditioned ways. Our actions helped create the atmosphere. We might be annoyed by the close proximity of others smoking, or by the endless chatter from the tourists sitting at the other end of the table. The actors would use sound, light, props, or movement to capture our attention. Someone might peek in through a window and shout, or a bird may run free through the crowd with someone chasing it; a puppet may peek in and swing across the ceiling, or a woman might sing a ballad. Movement, sound, or light captured our attention. The performers were creating a mood, a rhythm, and a tempo for the evening, which required that each of us had to be attendant to our perceptions to catch the act. Did something move in the corners of our eyes? Was there a light on outside that window across the way? It cajoled us into paying attention to the small details of the environment and actions of the crowd around us.

The troupe aimed to heighten our awareness and interaction with the world around us by paying attention. They sought to create a shared experience between performers and attendants by disrupting the mediation of theatrical conventions, relying instead on everyday skills of negotiating social interaction. Where should we focus? What environmental sounds, smells, and actions are significant? The program articulates this as:

A conscious demolition of the barrier between the audience and the stage liberates both spectators and actors and offers a possibility of a joint experience. The hut has long wooden tables where as many as 150 people can be seated, walls of Canadian cedar, a ceiling of sail cloth, an old dance floor, music, wine and soup.[76]

Because we could smell the cedar, hear the wind flapping in the sail cloths, feel the warmth of the body next to us on the bench, and share a meal with a stranger, everyone in the space of the hut was forced to engage in social activity. The event was shaped so that we would have to actively interact with others to participate. We were all piled in on top of one another on long benches; if one person were to move or get up, five others would have to shift. If we wanted some bread, others would have to pass it down the table; we might have to collaborate with others at the table to interact with the performers. We had to be sensitive to the needs of others—smoke in the eyes from cigarettes, being too loud so others could not pay attention to what might be going around them. The troupe created an artistically mediated experience that called upon us to monitor the sounds, smells, and bodies of others, and to imagine what might be chance and what might be staged. As the hours rolled on, and the crowd grew restless, drunk, or bored, the performers surprised us with the smallest things, such as an engine revving outside and headlights streaking through the window, or shouting. Toward midnight, the simmering soup was ladled out of the cauldron and each table was invited to break bread and share soup. The performance had a flavor and smell, and it encouraged us to be human and social.

If we were to ignore the small sounds, little acts, or to shut out the atmosphere, there would be nothing left to distinguish it from a boring night out in a strange place. There were few words spoken, little spectacle, and no conventional structure. All we had to comprehend the event were our wits and perceptions of the changes in atmosphere, tone, and temperature. The heat of the stove, the stinging of the cigarette smoke in our eyes, and the sounds of the crowd chatting away were all the stimuli we had to experience. Its structure encouraged the use of the senses to explore its mediated world; the installation activated taste, touch, smell, sound, and sight.

Many of the sensory performances that I have mentioned encourage conversation and social exposure. Rather than sitting passively in the dark, we are required to participate and explore. We were invited to share food, cut open clothing, or inhale the fragrance of simmering food, thus forcing us to become social animals and break free from the constraints of social decorum. Ultimately, due to the stimulation of a multi-sensory experience, the participants in any event are forced to use their bodies to explore and seek out input that will lead them to consider the way in which we interact with others, situate ourselves in an environment, and survive. If we are encouraged to use the full range of our sense perception, we become active attendants rather than passive, isolated viewers detached from the artistic experience.

Our senses are systems that our organism uses to negotiate and move through the world; by their very nature they orchestrate our interaction with others and our environment. Thus we do not only attend the event, but also are attendant to the event and participate in it. We become actors responding within the constraints of an artistically mediated structure designed to trigger behavior or sensorial memory. By activating all senses or senses that are beyond words or sight, we can break through the constraints and patterns offered by conventional theatrical invitations. Performances that harness more than our eyes and ears to perceive the world encourage us to wake up, to be alert to the world around us, and to actively interact with the objects and creatures around us. It is an invitation to live, to feel, and to be a part of a shared experience.

There is such a pervasive influx of technology in today's society that the senses, while always present, get muddled, confused, and reconfigured until what we consider reality becomes blurred with an advertiser's desire to sell the latest Apple iPhone. By calling attention to the range of sensory stimulation available to practitioners during a live event, we can begin to chart the instances when smell and taste are used deliberately as meaning-laden elements within a theatrical composition, even when technology is involved. Though it is a written narrative rather than live event, Patrick Süskind's *Perfume* is an example of the possibilities becoming attendant to one's sensory experience can offer in the enrichment of one's interpretation of the experience of a theatrical event.[77] Set in eighteenth-century Paris, the novel's protagonist, Jean-Baptiste Grenouille, is a man born without a smell to identify him. Those around him despise him and distrust him inexplicably. As we have learned from basic olfactory neurology, as humans we make judgments about the world around us by smell. Whether we are drawn by pheromones or we are repelled by the smell of disease, those scents color our assumptions about those we come in contact with long before we are conscious of our judgments. Süskind uses this man without scent to reveal a world that has created a hierarchy of scent. The rich use expensive perfume whereas the poor reek of the smells of their professions—for example, a tanner smells of the acids used to treat the leather. Ultimately, Grenouille creates a scent so powerful—the distilled essence of a pubescent virgin beauty—that he can control the masses. The idea of the book is evocative of how smell is used, and it also calls attention to the uses of perfume in society and the ways of creating moods and drawing people to us for political, sexual, and financial gains. Now imagine if the scents were a part of his arsenal to manipulate the viewers in an artistic situation.

Grenouille has the extraordinary ability to discriminate aroma like no other human. As a result, he has an amazing capacity to treat scent like a catalog of ingredients that he can summon at will to identify, locate, and dissect anything as if he had a spectroscopic nose:

> at first awake, and then in his dreams, he inspected the vast rubble of his memory. He examined the millions and millions of building blocks of odor and arranged them systematically: good with good, bad with bad, fine with fine, coarse with coarse, fetid with fetid, ambrosial with ambrosial. In the course of the next week, this system grew ever more refined, the catalog of odors ever more comprehensive and differentiated, the hierarchy ever clearer. And soon he could erect the first carefully planned structures of odor: houses, walls, stairways, towers, cellars, rooms, secret chambers . . . an inner fortress built of the most magnificent odors, that each day grew larger, that each day grew more beautiful and more perfectly framed.[78]

He created an association for each smell, knowing full well what potential evocations each could summon within a human. As a perfumer, he could create complex aromas to shape encounters. Although only a dream for contemporary theatre practitioners, the potential for experimentation is great if this philosophy were to be followed.

Whereas ordinary humans are unable to be conscious of what they smell, Grenouille could:

> And he did not merely smell the mixture of odors in the aggregate, but he dissected it analytically into its smallest and most remote parts and pieces. His discerning nose unraveled the knot of vapor and stench into single strands of unitary odors that could not be unthreaded further. Unwinding and spinning out these threads gave him unspeakable joy.[79]

Inhalation could be an orgasmic indulgence for him. By being denied the tactile and social comforts of human society, he fostered his ability to savor human contact through our smells. At one point, he retreats to a cave on a high mountain peak to escape from the stench of humanity he despised. However, when he was happy:

> He would often just stand there, leaning against a wall or crouching in a dark corner, his eyes closed, his mouth half open and nostrils flaring wide, quick as a feeding pike in a great, dark, slowly moving current. And when at last a puff of air would toss a delicate thread of scent his way, he would lunge at it and not let go. Then he would smell at only this one odor, holding it tight, pulling it into himself and preserving it for all time. The odor might be an old acquaintance, or a variation on one; it could be a brand-new one as well, with hardly any similarity to anything he had ever smelled, let alone seen, till that moment: the odor of pressed silk, for example, the odor of a wild-thyme tea, the odor of

brocade embroidered with silver thread, the odor of cork from a bottle of vintage wine, the odor of a tortoiseshell comb. Grenouille was out to find such odors still unknown to him; he hunted them down with the passion and patience of an angler and stored them up inside him.[80]

Grenouille's experience of the world placed highest emphasis on olfaction over vision, hearing, or touch. By accessing and cataloging a part of him that no other could, the resulting narrative descriptions of his conscious experience reveal an unfamiliar side of life to us. In fact, he reveals a side of life that we have been taught to be ashamed of and mask with perfumes and soaps. By training himself and creating neuronal connections between stimulants and their evocations, he was able to master the art of perfume.

This is the aim of becoming aware of gustatory and olfactory sensations in the context of theatrical performance. We will exercise our brain and stimulate our capacity to remain flexible and liberal thinkers. To broaden our sensorial repertoire is to train us to rearrange our sensations so that they are meaningful. In some ways, this can suggest that theatrical stimulation of the senses is cathartic in that it exercises our biologically evolved alert system, helping us prevent short-circuits of stress that the constant influx of a new way of technological life that our bodies have not adapted to yet. Following on from taste and smell, which are tangible chemical senses that sample the world outside our bodies, is sound. Sounds impinge themselves upon our eardrums and invade our bodies. Aural stimuli will complete the web of sensorial perception that guide us through life and create our subjective responses to the world.

5 Aural Landscapes
Voices, Noises, Vibrations,
and Other Quivering Stimulators
of Cochlear Perception

As John Cage taught us, there is no such thing as silence. We are constantly surrounded by sound. Sound originates from the motion or vibration of an object, and it does not matter whether it is the scratch of a field mouse scurrying along the beams inside the wall barely audible late at night, or the boom of an exploding chemical plant heard for twelve miles across a busy city; thousands of the single tones processed by the human ear are heard by a mechanism known as air conduction. Sounds fill our lives and communicate to us about the world around us. Theatre that makes use of these sounds captures our attention and has the potential to evoke emotions and feelings. Beyond the obvious use of language in theatre, how is sound used in theatrical performance? There are many types of sound productions during a performance beyond the spoken word, such as sound that is generated by voice or musical instruments and environmental sound. The uses of these sounds demonstrate how sound triggers visceral sensations, which in turn evoke mood in the context of performance. How do these sound experiences capture our brain's attention and trigger visceral reactions that can be analyzed? How do aural landscapes affect our perception of the physical landscape and keep our brains alert for the introduction of new elements?

THE ANATOMY AND PHYSIOLOGY
OF THE AUDITORY SYSTEM

The ear acts as a receiver for sound, as well as plays a major role in our sense of balance and body position. The auditory system is comprised of three components: the outer, middle, and inner ear, all of which work together to transfer sounds from the environment to the brain. It can discriminate a small difference of sound frequency, and it can identify the location of a sound source with precision. The process of hearing begins with pressure changes that result from objects vibrating and travelling through some medium, such as air or water. Brian Moore categorizes two types of sound:

Those for which the pressure changes have a random or irregular quality are perceived as noise-like; examples are the sound of a waterfall, or the consonants "s" or "f". Those which repeat regularly as a function of time are called periodic sounds, and generally have a well-defined tone or pitch: for example a note played on a musical instrument.[1]

Whether it is a noise-like sound, such as the hissing of a train's smokestack in Kneehigh's *Brief Encounter* (2008), or a periodic beating sound, such as Leonardo's wooden heels at the opening of Carlos Saura's version of Lorca's *Bodas de Sangre* (1981), sound is initiated when an event moves and causes a motion or vibration in air that our ears perceive. Diane Ackerman describes this process as "an onrushing, cresting, and withdrawing wave of air molecules that begins with the movement of object, however large or small and ripples out in all directions."[2]

In our ears, a sound wave is transmitted through four separate mediums along the auditory system before a sound is perceived: air in the outer ear; bones in the middle ear; liquid in the inner ear; and neurons to the brain. When a dancer brings two garbage pail lids together, as is done in *Stomp* (1991), the resulting sound waves cause the eardrum and then the three tiny bones of the middle ear to vibrate. The same thing happens as Angela Lansbury expels air across her larynx to sing the open bars of *Sweeney Todd*. Once the bones begin to vibrate, the pressure sends waves along the basilar membrane, thus stimulating some of its hair cells.[3] Air-transmitted sound waves are directed toward the delicate hearing mechanisms with the help of the outer ear, which gently funnels sound waves into the ear canal. When air movement strikes the tympanic membrane, the energy generated through a sound wave is transferred from a medium of air to that which is solid in the middle ear. The ossicular chain connects to the eardrum via the malleus, so that any motion of the eardrum sets the three little bones of the ossicular chain into motion. It then transfers energy from a solid medium to the fluid medium of the inner ear via the stapes. In this process, sound waves vibrate at different speeds. The function of the inner ear is to transduce vibration into nervous impulses. While doing so, these rapid-fire electrical impulses analyze the sound for frequency/pitch and intensity/loudness, as well as duration. The inner ear is made up of the cochlea, the sensory organ for hearing, as well as the vestibular system for balance. These systems are separate, yet both are encased in the same bony capsule and share the same fluid systems. The vestibular system helps to maintain balance, regardless of head position or gravity, in conjunction with eye movement and somatosensory input. The stapes is attached to the oval window. Movement of the oval window creates motion in the cochlear fluid and along the basilar membrane. Motion along the basilar membrane excites frequency specific areas of the organ of Corti, which in turn stimulates a series of nerve endings. The central auditory nerve, also known as the eighth cranial nerve, carries an electrical signal from the cochlea via the brainstem to the cerebral cortex in the temporal lobes of the brain. The auditory cortex in the temporal lobe of the brain perceives and analyzes sound, and creates a thought, picture, or other recognized symbol.[4] Our response to that sound depends upon the nature of that sound. Speech sounds, however, may be processed differently from others. Our auditory system processes all the signals that it receives in the same way until they reach the primary auditory cortex in the temporal lobe of the brain. When the messages finally reach the cerebral cortex, they are processed and interpreted into whatever it may be, such as raindrops, musical notes, or a telephone ring.[5] Sound level information is conveyed to the brain by the rate of nerve firing, and when speech sound is perceived, the neural signal is funneled to the left hemisphere for processing in language centers.

We are able to determine the location and source of sound as a result of binaural hearing; that is to say, the ability to hear in both ears. A sound that we hear in the left ear first will be louder than sound reaching the right ear a split second later. When the brain compares the information from both ears, it can distinguish whether the sound originated from the right or left. Furthermore, the brain is able to discriminate between the sound we want to hear and noises in the background, thus we can hear our companion speaking at crowded party. Furthermore, this enables us to determine our location within space.

Hearing functions as an alert system. When we hear a siren coming from the cross-street at an intersection, it captures our spotlight of attention and we turn our heads to watch for danger. There are brain cells in the midbrain that only respond to the introduction of a sound, and others that only respond to the switching off of the sound, i.e., a change. For example, when sitting in an air-conditioned room, when the air conditioner turns on, we notice the change. After a while, our brains accommodate to the noise and it blends into the background and is ignored. When it switches off, again we notice it for a short time. These cells allow the ear to respond to acoustic change—we adjust to constant sound, and we note change immediately. Peter Alberti explains the interaction of sound stimuli with other parts of the brain:

> Sound stimuli produce interaction with other parts of the brain to provide appropriate responses. Thus, a warning signal will produce an immediate general reaction leading to escape, a quickening of the heart rate, a tensing of the muscle and a readiness to move. A baby's cry will alert the mother in a way it does not alert others. The sound of martial music may lead to bracing movement of those to whom it is being played and induce fear and cowering in the hearts and minds of those at whom it is being played. Certain sounds can evoke anger, others pleasure. The point is that the sensations produced by hearing are blended into the body mechanism in the central nervous system to make them part of the whole milieu in which we live.[6]

It is through these changes that we can begin to chart the effects of sound on the individual who is listening. As we shape a soundscape within performance, we are providing stimuli to keep the attendant attuned to the action transpiring on the stage. These stimuli keep our neurons firing and our attention focused. In the same sense, the sounds can divert and direct our attention away from action as well.

ALERTS, NEURONAL FIRING, AND THE AURAL FABRIC OF EVERYDAY EXISTENCE

An alert will capture our attention, causing us to monitor for significant stimuli. We live in what Jim Drobnick calls a noisy ball, registering creaking floorboards, neighbors' coughs, airplanes overhead, and humming light bulbs.[7] Our bodies stand on alert for significant changes that may affect our well-being. In 1913, Luigi Russolo called attention to the cacophony we live in as a call to make use of noise as an artistic element:

> To convince you of the surprising variety of noises, I will mention thunder, wind, cascades, rivers, streams, leaves, a horse trotting away, the starts and jumps of a carriage on the pavement, and the white solemn breathing of a city at night, all the noises made by feline and domestic animals and all those man's mouth can make without talking or singing.[8]

The sounds of modernity that surround us affect us to the core. They impinge upon us constantly and our brains are confronted with the choice of whether to consider the stimuli as meaningful. Those of us who have adapted to the noise and are able to tune out the noise are lucky, for there are many who are prone to monitor aural stimulation constantly and are made crazy by the din. Douglas Kahn muses on the nature of noise and its significance:

> Noise is the forest of everything. The existence of noise implies a mutable world through an unruly intrusion of an other, an other that attracts difference, heterogeneity, and productive confusion; moreover, it implies a genesis of mutability itself. Noise is a world where anything can happen. . . . In a predictable world noise promises something out of the ordinary, and in a world in frantic pursuit of the extraordinary noise can promise the banal and quotidian. In a predictable world it can generate possibility and then obligingly self-destruct. Yet noise has also been an occasion for hearing loss and loss of hearing, psychic malaise, and psychological warfare.[9]

The nature of aural interpretation has changed as a result of the modern world's din. It has taken on a myriad of functions. Much thought has been put into its potential meaning, but its biological effects are undeniable.

Experimentation with sound has led artists to make use of ambient noise to stimulate our bodies in meaningful ways. Cage explains:

> Wherever we are, what we hear is mostly noise. When we ignore it, it disturbs us. When we listen to it, we find it fascinating. The sound of a truck at fifty miles per hour. Static between the stations. Rain. We want to capture and control these sounds, to use them not as sound effects but as musical instruments.[10]

We are familiar with noise being used as a sound effect to create a sense of mimesis in a play, but it can also be used for an embodied effect as a means of creating an atmosphere or as a means of conveying mood or feeling. Like the changing qualities of light harnessed by Appia and Craig to create a moment-to-moment manifestation of mood, sound is used to influence embodied experience in creative expression. Beyond verbal communication, sound offers us a means of situating ourselves in space, and provides us with a means to protect ourselves from oncoming danger. For example, the sound of an oncoming truck tells us to not to step onto the pavement. Although we can distinguish several qualities from the impulses it detects, unlike vision, hearing cannot blend different sounds. Conflicting sounds do not blur into a brown mess as color might, but rather the cacophony we hear is channeled into different pathways that monitor, perceive, and interpret these sounds into meaningful data. We can follow a conversation, hear the footsteps of someone approaching from behind, and note the helicopter passing overhead simultaneously. Likewise, we can hear different musical tones weaving their way through a song. This simultaneous reception enables our brains to become invigorated aurally in myriad ways.

Even when we do not see what object is making a noise, we endeavor to create a semblance of the object in our mind. After all, we need to know whether we should run away from the large bear or ignore the rabbit running in our direction. Our bodies prime for action when sound vibrations are perceived. Georgina Kleege explains:

> When you imagine a sound—a voice reciting a line of verse, a phrase of music, a jackhammer pulverizing pavement—blood rushes to the auditory centres of your brain, as if the sound were outside rather than inside your head. When you read, perhaps this is what's going on. Neurons fire. Juices flow. Electrochemical changes occur. You begin to "hear" something, not quite a voice, but a shadow of a voice. You might even feel something, a tickle in your throat, a twitching in your tongue and jaw muscles, as if that interior voice were really on the verge of pressing outward, down through larynx and lips, to make itself heard.[11]

We begin to make concrete what we hear. Our attention focuses on identifying the sound and situating where it is located. We begin to imagine its size and mass to give shape to it. Stephen Connor describes this as making a semblance of the vocalic body, which is to say to make manifest the origin of the sound by imagining the object that made the sound.[12] Thus, when we hear the crunching of leaves outside our window, we dissect the sound to identify the weight of the step and classify the sound to determine whether it is an animal or a human. If we determine it is a small body, then we relax again. The same follows with a cry in the night: Is it a fox cub or is it a human baby? Is the sound's origin close or distant? Should we ignore it or run to the creature's aid?

Kleege describes giving form to the voices that narrate books to the blind. She explores the vocalic body to interrogate the ways that sounds influence our perception. Kleege imagines:

> I sense that sighted people are much quicker to create mental images from voice, because images matter so much more to them. What assumptions I make about people whose voices I hear are rather rudimentary and general. Older voices, both male and female, tend to be deeper than young voices, and vice versa. So when I start listening to a tape, I may think, 'female over fifty from the Midwest.' But I'm conscious I may be wrong on all counts.[13]

To some extent, it does not matter whether she is right about the person reading. What is most important is that she has given the reader definable human characteristics. In that way, the content of the aural stimulation will be colored by her associations with the sounds. Her description articulates the process that our brains go through as we gain experience in the world to make judgments about what we hear. In the same way, it suggests how perception is prejudiced long before we are conscious of what we think about the stimuli. If the voice has a thick Southern drawl, and I am a Northern-educated individual who associates the drawl with a corrupt politician, I might be skeptical of the content of the words that the speaker intones. In the same sense, making manifest the origin of the sound helps us understand what the sound may be trying to communicate to us.

We are also affected by the cultural habits of listening. What we pay attention to and what sounds we find meaningful are influenced culturally and experientially. What is familiar is also meaningful and enjoyable to our bodies, so as we listen, we develop the social discipline of listening, and that affects our perception. Drobnick asserts:

> Listening, as well as performing, involves the materiality, the culture, and the politics of the human body. The semantic content of music registers through the body (and the five senses that incorporate the very foundation of embodiment), as well as the mind, its rational powers mediated by emotional reactions. The experience and meaning of

music is physical, intellectual (in the broad notion of the word), and spiritual; and it is deeply and fundamentally social.[14]

The act of listening is a means to provoke the embodied mind and invigorate sensorial perception. As we listen and focus our attention on the aural stimulation, we allow our body to feel emotion and respond preconsciously. The power of music to communicate by way of preconscious articulation is often a satisfying release from rational thought. Drobnick notes:

> music's pleasure is produced in part by aural stimulations which in turn trigger physiological and emotional responses that result in some sense, inevitably temporary, of well-being. This pleasure is embodied; it may be simultaneously of body and mind and as such the sonoric simulacrum of an organic totality absent from an otherwise fractured reality. Nonetheless, music's organicism can only be imagined to the extent that it is lost as soon as it is gained, inevitably lost the moment sound ceases.[15]

Sound is fleeting in duration and, like information garnered from the chemical senses, it is consciously frustrated. We often rely on our brain's ability to predict a sound and fire off in an expected way rather than to fire in new ways. As we have discussed previously, once we begin to consciously perceive smell, taste, or music, our organism has already shaped their reception. Only by disrupting the brain's expectations can we begin to learn.

Daniel Levitin theorized that music impels us to tap our feet because the mind seeks out patterns in sounds and forecasts the next probable sound.[16] He explains that we take pleasure in figuring out the puzzle and are frustrated when patterns are violated. Jonah Lehrer demonstrates this when he argues that we become fascinated when those patterns are violated, leaving our brain to struggle to find coherence. He explains:

> The emotions generated by musical tension—a tension taken to grotesque heights by Stravinsky—throb throughout the body. As soon as the orchestra starts to play, the flesh undergoes a range of changes. The pupils dilate, pulse and blood pressure rise, the electrical conductance of the skin lowers, and the cerebellum, a brain region associated with bodily movement, becomes unusually active. Blood is redirected to the leg muscles. (As a result, we begin tapping our feet in time with the beat.) Sound stirs us at our biological roots.[17]

As we encounter the sounds of the symphony, our bodies fire off neurons to our brains, triggering a sequence of physiological responses to the music. Our bodies respond to the aural stimulation of the symphony in a similar manner to the ways in which they react when riding the flight simulator in an amusement park. Lehrer uses Stravinsky's *The Rite of Spring* (1913) to demonstrate how audiences unfamiliar with a new style and sound in music rioted:

> The brainstem contains a network of neurons that responds *only* to surprising sounds. When the musical pattern we know is violated, these cells begin the neural process that ends with the release of dopamine, the same neurotransmitter that reorganizes the auditory cortex. (Dopamine is also the chemical source of our most intense emotions, which helps to explain the strange emotional power of music, especially when it confronts us with newness and dissonance.) By tempting us with fragile patterns, music taps into the most basic brain circuitry.[18]

As we encounter the unfamiliar melodies, our brains begin to go haywire, searching frantically for some sense within the unfamiliar. Our sense of well-being has been violated, so we must struggle to find an explanation for the new stimuli. This is part of the same system that makes us so flexible and adaptable to the changing circumstances of surviving in a chaotic world. Stravinsky had control over this physiological mechanism and therefore could guide his attendant's response. Because his structures mimicked that of the firing of neurons, he gave us an experience of the chaos that ensues as the phoenix burns in its ashes:

> If dopamine neurons can't correlate their firing with outside events, the brain is unable to make cogent associations. Schizophrenics have elaborate auditory hallucinations precisely because their sensations do not match their mental predictions. As a result they invent patterns where there are none and can't see the patterns that actually do exist. The premier of *The Rite*, with its methodological dismantling of the audience's musical expectations, literally stimulated madness. By subverting the listener's dopamine neurons, it also subverted their sanity. Everything about it felt wrong.[19]

These new stimulations help forge new pathways to adapt to new embodied responses. The greater the exposure we have to a particular stimulus, the more pleasurable it will become; its familiarity forges habitual pathways within our brains. As we become attendant to listening, our aural awareness will aid in our reception of stimuli.

Our ability to listen actively greatly enriches our experience of theatrical events. The goal of an embodied experience of theatrical events is dynamic engagement with stimuli beyond language and action. Andra McCartney explains:

> Hearing is done not only with the ears, but also with every fibre of our beings as vibrations of sound move into our bodies. Sound touches us, inside and out. And this feeling of being touched by sound is heightened

by technology: when microphones amplify and record sounds, they not only involve the ears, but also every other part of the body.[20]

When sounds are amplified the vibrations shake our bones. In SRS's *Il Buchettino*, the ogre's voice shakes our cots and causes us to tremble. For we know from experience only huge masses have the ability to shake the ground in that way. The rhythmic beats of the bass in techno music will recalibrate our hearts, speeding it up to match its tempo. Sound shapes our physiological responses through its beats and rhythms. A sonically composed piece will attempt to shape the soundscape to influence the listener's perception.

As a performance is built, the collaborators will consider who is listening and the potential for shaping an embodied experience. Matthew Goulish writes to a hypothetical listener:

> I have tried to compose some of your most particular experiences . . . I realize that you are not a typical, but very particular, listener. . . . I realize that I have imagined you. Nevertheless, you have one invaluable advantage; you are the one listener about whom I really know something . . . You are absolutely necessary for me—since it would be impossible for me to imagine this process other than in conjunction with a constantly imagined percipient. In this way creation and perception intermingle and are elements of the same complex phenomenon.[21]

If there is no listener, then there is no artwork. It is no better than a book buried deep within a library. To make the composition written in the past speak in the present and become a part of present experience we must have a receiver to pick up the stimuli. We deliberately create compositions that will stimulate embodied experiences. We are all trained to function by our senses as we negotiate the world. As we call attention to the senses in relation to performance, then we can better understand that conscious comprehension is not the only aim. The indistinct feeling and emotions that are evoked and elicited make real theatrical experience forever changing the attendant's memories.

SIGNIFICANT NOISES: JOHN CAGE'S SILENCES

Noise is ubiquitous. Sonic waves are cresting through us always, most often at frequencies that our ears cannot detect. We cannot avoid these waves. Therefore, all sounds can be considered as significant noise if we consider the act of listening as a means of perceiving our place in the world. In the creation of theatrical representation, sound and speech are critical to the creation of mood and atmosphere. Attendants rely on sound to shape the details of what they see. Jonathan Sterne argues that sounds are defined by our hearing, and thus that sounds are part of us:

> You can take the sound out of the human, but you can take the human out of the sound only through an exercise in imagination ... As part of a larger physical phenomenon of vibration, sound is a product of the human senses and not a thing in the world apart from humans. Sound is a little piece of the vibrating world.[22]

Whether the reproduction of sound is achieved to create mimesis or to manipulate the attendant's feelings, humanness is intimately connected to sound generation. Even when early movies had no sound there was the sound of the projector, but music was added to make sound significant for the movie-goer.

John Cage explored the musicality of noise as a means of harnessing sound to create music out of everyday life. The creaks and hisses of the house can become a symphony. Michael Zwerun describes silence in relation to Cage's work: "Silence is all of the sound we don't intend. There is no such thing as absolute silence. Therefore silence may very well include loud sounds and more and more in the twentieth century does. The sound of jet planes, of sirens, et cetera."[23] Our silences are punctuated by noise; we cannot escape. How we pay attention to those noises and how we perceive them depends on our awareness of them and the meanings that we ascribe to them. We often cannot describe the qualities of a sound. As we sit and watch SRS' *Tragedia Endogonidia*, we hear and feel the low-level vibrations that shake our seats and listen to something that sounds like feedback pierce our ears, but we lack a means to determine what it is. What we do know is how the sound makes us feel.

This leaves us in a quandary as we try and reconstruct our experiences of a noise-rich production. Bernard Schultz explains the tactics that we resort to in order to describe our fleeting experiences:

> For many of the states that occur with the context of our phenomenal experience, particularly in the area of acoustics, we lack terminology. Direct demonstration and experience are thus the only adequate means of communicating such states. The unnamable and indescribable in this experience of art does not have a metaphysical cause, but is to be described instead to the objective circumstances of our perception.[24]

We must chart and describe our perceptions as a result of sensorial stimulation. After we become conscious of the source of our feelings, then we can trace them back to the sensations that resulted from aural stimulation. Cage's early collaborations with Robert Rauschenberg and Merce Cunningham demonstrate the practicality of using noise to shape the aural components of dance performance. His best-known work was 4'33" (1952), which challenges conventional notions of listening and musical composition. In it, a performer sits at the piano playing four minutes and thirty-three seconds of rests. By pushing back the responsibility of the audience to understand the music of silence, he asked us to become aware of our sense of hearing. One of the largest frustrations with performances that force us to sit back and monitor our sensations is that we are not trained to, or know how to, do this. Kahn articulates this:

> An unsuspecting audience . . . might attempt to reconcile the silence with its expectations before discovering, perhaps, what the piece might be. The initial absence of music might be taken as an expressive or theatrical device preceding a sound. When that sound is not forthcoming, it might become evident that listening can still go on if one's attention (and this is Cage's desire) is shifted to the surrounding sounds, including the sound of the growing agitation of certain audience members.[25]

Without the traditional cues as to what to expect, the audience is at a loss. It does not matter that generations have passed since the shock of the first performance; our brains expect instruments as mechanically produced generators of sound. Violating this frustrates our brain's prediction system and risks alienating the attendant.

In effect, Cage challenges us to become attendant to the social disciplines of listening, as well as our physiological mechanisms for hearing. We have to find a means of hearing the sounds around us to be able to appreciate how they are shaped in musical composition. The ways in which sound is perceived are as important to reception as they are important to the processes of musical composition. Kahn explains the effect of his theory and practice:

> Cage set out to tilt the balance in favor of the ear, and many people have heard the world differently because of his efforts. Yet they may not have heard all he had hoped to hear, for he wanted to hear all. His attempt began with adopting the avant-garde strategy of noise, prefigured in phonography and latent within percussion and other forms of resident noise, whereby all sounds were fair game for musical materiality, given certain conditions for their incorporation. He then followed with another tactic, associated most notably with his composition 4'33", which entailed rejecting the importance of whether a musical sound was present or absent within a composition and, in the process, extending the field of artistic materiality to all the nonintentional sounds surrounding the performance—that is, by shifting the production of music from the site of utterance to that of audition.[26]

His experimentation led to awareness that there is more to listen to than the sounds generated by musical or vocal instruments. Like Russolo, the sounds of the world around us are a likely palette to create a composition.

Our inability to escape sound requires that we acknowledge its place in perception and conceive of the ways in which we can understand ambient sound as affecting listening. Cage was as interested in the processes of listening as he was in challenging notions of what is necessary to make music. Kahn observes:

> This musicalization was then extended to all sounds, inside and outside the performance space, since the ability and willingness to listen were the only requirements, and these abilities in turn were extended, with the aid of amplification and other technological devices, to small sounds and hitherto inaudible sounds. The latter move was associated with his famous visit to the anechoic chamber, where he heard the ever-present sounds of his body, the low sound of his blood circulating, and the high-pitched sound of his nervous system in operation. This was a very important moment since it was here that *all sound* was joined to *always sound*.[27]

Sound is ever present, and as a result, "always sound" must be embroidered into any aural composition. This is important for theatrical composition as well because, beyond the text, the atmosphere of the performance space plays a role in our reception of the piece. Sound can disrupt a performance as well. For example, in the late 1980s I saw a production of a Moliere play where the beating of Kodo drummers playing in a nearby auditorium overwhelmed the vocal projections of the actors. Those actors tried to keep the rhythm of the verse, but the rhythm worked in opposition to the rapid deep booms of the drummers that bled through ceiling. As a result, the vibrations infected the performers' physiological response to the world and the timing of the verse. Whereas aural stimuli can affect us physically, it also can have an unconscious irritating quality. There is a cross between deliberate stimulation and the ambient sounds of the location of performance. All these contribute to the overall embodied social experience of attendance.

Incorporation of multiple strands of noise, speech, and music in Cage's *Roaratorio: An Irish Circus on Finnegans Wake* (1979) creates a sound collage that challenges our listening practices. Cage determined that thousands of sounds that depicted locations and noises appear in James Joyce's *Finnegans Wake* (1939). Robert Bean reports:

> In his pursuit of Joycean sounds, Cage researched the place names mentioned in *Finnegans Wake* and conceived of travelling to and recording ambient sounds from each site. He selected 626 places, corresponding to the number of pages in the book, but due to the extensiveness of such a project, ultimately solicited recordings from the locations instead. *Roaratorio*'s resulting sound collage is an excessive cacophony of voice, Irish music, and vernacular sounds including radios, televisions, automobiles, barking dogs, and crying babies.[28]

The prerecorded sounds are mixed with Cage's barely audible recitation of the text. Thunderclaps, rumbling earth, laughing and crying, farts, bells, and whistles blend together to evoke a place through its ambient local sounds. We know this world because we experience it, seek out what is recognizable, and conceive a plausible mental picture of reality.

The experience of *Roaratorio* is fleeting, as if we are walking through a large crowd in a foreign city where we are inundated with information and overwhelmed. Allen Ruch describes the piece in much the same way that I would describe my experience of sitting in Stephen's Green in Dublin's city center on a Saturday afternoon. If I close my eyes I would not only hear the sounds of the lake, children playing, and birds, but also the sounds of commerce on Grafton Street. I would focus for a moment a conversation from a shop entrance, or hear buskers hustle some money playing the fiddle. However, my pleasant afternoon is interrupted by this crazy old homeless man muttering or singing in almost intelligible phrases. When he gets worked up, he is loud, but he calms down again, mutters sotto voce, and disappears. Ruch imagines that he grabs a quick pint before being cast back out on the street.[29] Our brain does not discriminate between the city around us and recorded sounds of the city; it processes the information in the same way. How the material is understood will not be augmented by the web of our other sensations, but our embodied experience will make sense of the stimuli and attempt to identify and locate the origin of the sound. Our organism chooses how to envision what this world looks like. This fictional work elicits real experience. Sorting it all is a challenge that can be off-putting. Bean contends:

> Hearing, listening, and sonority can be difficult pleasures. More so in the case of a piece like ... *Roaratotio* ... in which the challenge to listening is intentional, and apprehension in a conventional, linear sense is impossible. ... It engages such a heterogeneity of sounds and noises that disruption and disorientation are paramount. This piece exemplifies a complex, radicalized form of listening that to come to terms with it requires a distinct mode of auditory experience—what I call *polyphonic aurality.* This term, implying simultaneously the opening of numerous ears and the production of an incomprehensible sound collage, also alludes to a renewal of the collective act of hearing.[30]

Attendants must be prepared to listen and trust that the onrushing wave of sound will make sense to our feelings regardless of the inability of our mind to make conscious sense out of it. Noise is a compositional device that channels the perceivers to pay close attention until they are sure of what the sounds may mean.

Bean continues by describing Cage's practice as a means to challenge conventional listening practices:

> *Roaratorio* can be best described as sixty minutes of *prepared noise.* This creates an aesthetic of both anxiety and pleasure. Clamour often

generates an atmosphere of discomfort, and Cage was accustomed to audiences leaving his performances because of boredom or irritation. He attributed this to a lack of understanding and a refusal to allow unfamiliar sounds into the experience of a composition. At the same time, the openness to listening that Cage offers can also be experienced as pleasure and astonishment. Our ears are invited to wander freely through the complexity of aural textures. It is possible at one moment to focus on the overall din, and then perhaps hear the drone of Cage's voice reciting mesostics. The next moment one may hear fiddles, Bodhran drums, Uillean pipes, or a recording of a dog barking, glass breaking, or a child crying. This may eventually lead to a daydream that will displace the presence of sound entirely. The audience is encouraged to inhabit the invented racket of *Finnegans Wake*, perhaps to be inside of HCE's head as his dreams unfold in the night. Our ears are provoked long enough to re-experience the act of listening and to witness the "activity of sounds."[31]

Cage provokes us to inhabit the spaces of Ireland by way of ambient noise. Our perception of these sounds will provide information of the spatial location of the sound generator in relation to where our body would be in that space if we were there in that environment experiencing the sounds. We will perceive the animals and drums and the other indications that other humans inhabit this place. We will fill in the details based on our experiences. This reconstruction allows us to be geographically located within the places of *Finnegan's Wake*. Mere sound transports our awareness to far away lands, whether real or imagined.

Performances that activate sight and sound engage even more sensorial avenues to make concrete the experience of the world of the composition. Cunningham and Cage have collaborated on adaptations several times. Here, movement and sound collage together to trigger impressions for the attendant. We can feel it both aurally and sympathetically through movement. Anna Kisselgoff describes a 1986 adaptation of the radio piece for dance:

> *Roaratorio* is very much an oratorio of sound and movement—but it does not quite roar. . . . It is, above all, an exercise in perception, as are so many Cunningham dance works. . . . At its best, *Roaratorio* is pure atmosphere, a cacophony that affects us aurally and visually. The thicker the soup the better it tastes.[32]

Cunningham and Cage added vision and movement to the piece as a means of more fully engaging the web of the senses. Although poorly received, the piece served to dynamically engage an audience in the notion that sensorial awareness is the means by which we understand the world. To understand the act of listening is to gain experience and understand the world from the perspective of active engagement. Unfortunately, to find significance in the

message, attendants had to make a perceptual jump, which
successful.

USING SOUND TO CREATE ATMOSPHERE

Whom do you let hear your farts? Expelling gas is one of the more intimate sounds we make, often made in the privacy of the toilet and certainly
only deliberately expelled without shame amongst our closest confidants.
Even when noxious smells do not accompany the sound, a loud fart can be
embarrassing. Inconvenient sounds escape from our bodies all of the time,
and burps, slurps, grumbles, and wheezes reveal the state of our internal
systems. Christof Mignoe exclaims:

> The body is a noisy place. It emits and transmits, it cannot contain
> itself, it has no built-in muffler. Its only silencer is willed, and . . . to
> retain a fart is sometimes just as ill-advised as to expel it. The orches-
> tral renderings of our innards are rarely appreciated for their musical-
> ity. Rather, they are consistently considered as an affront or offense in
> Western mores.[33]

Bodily noise is an intimacy borne by proximity and familiarity. Rarely,
except in comedy, does a fart find articulation in theatre. However, Joseph
Pujol, otherwise known as Le Petomane, was the toast of Paris at the turn
of the twentieth century. Dressed in top hat and tails, delivering his lines in
a monotone deadpan, he would tell a story and fart to illustrate his tale. For
example, the monologue of the Chanticleer demonstrates:

> Now tonight, my dear public, I'd like to present
> Some friends from the barnyard, each one an event.
> I'd like to start up—with an eight day old pup.
> *Imitation*
> Now dogs of all kinds I can do by the score
> We next hear the watchdog—his tail caught in the door.
> *Imitation*
> Patau, his old father wants to help him be freed.
> But alas and alack, why! He's still on the lead.
> *Imitation.*[34]

His emanations were used to characterize a whole host of personality types
and activities. More often than not the sounds satirized human foible. Paul
Spinrad describes a typical performance, wherein he

> performed some imitations, using the simple, honest format of announc-
> ing and then demonstrating. He displayed his wide sonic range with tenor,

baritone, and bass fart sounds. He imitated the farts of a little girl, a mother-in-law, a bride on her wedding night (tiny), the same bride the day after (loud), and a mason (dry—"no cement"). He imitated thunder, cannons ("Gunners stand by your guns! Ready—fire!!"), and even the sound of a dressmaker tearing two yards of calico (a full 10-second rip).[35]

A maestro of sound and vibration, Le Petomane used his tonality for comic effect. Sounds from the body evoke images of the bodies they came from. We relate to something that is not appropriate socially and culturally because we share the same physicality. By playing his sphincter, Pujol was able to imitate the most revealing details of characterizations. Kahn's notion of perception points to reasons why we relate to Pujol's medium. He states:

> Humans perceive the world while being within the world; they are implicated within it and are not somehow outside looking in or on. The object does not extend itself to the waiting individual: the individual finds it. And if meaning and feeling resides there, it is because the individual finds a piece of himself or herself.[36]

Pujol's sounds impinged upon attendants, and they were able to recognize the sounds their own bodies emitted. As they were implicated in the act of farting, they were able to understand by experience the bodies that the farts evoked.

His hugely popular and lucrative act was performed first at the Moulin Rouge, and drew attacks from critics for its poor taste. A lambaste mocks his performance:

> All my life I shall never forget the first time I saw him or the second time I heard him . . . astonishing . . . marvelous . . . sublime! Never had I been carried so high into the ether of art . . . never, never, never [. . . .] the Master [. . .] put his hands on his knees and with the nonchalance of a lord, smilingly opened his—erhum! . . . and began. [. . . .] Impetuously it growls, thunders, explodes, groans—cyclone—hurricane—tempest! Lightning strikes in the tortured firmament and whilst in the distance a warning gun is fired, distractedly under our very eyes the thunder growls to excess . . . it was terrifying . . . never have I seen such a storm.[37]

Though making a mockery of the performance, the monologue makes use of an evocatively descriptive vocabulary to capture the sounds and sensations experienced as an attendant of a performance. This level of awareness of the role of sound is useful to explain how sensations of sound can be described and charted in the perception and interpretation of a theatrical event.

Perpetual noise envelopes us at all times, creating an atmosphere that affects our bodies before our minds become fully conscious of the ways that the ambient sounds are coloring our perception. Gabor Csepregi points out the dramatic potential of the introduction of sound by comparing it to odor. By pointing out that different places from barns to churches have peculiar odors associated with them, he is able to describe spatial atmosphere as tonal. He explains:

> Odours, like sounds, detach themselves from their sources, permeate the lived space, and induce a reaction. There is, however, a difference in the way we are affected by odour and sound. Whereas the former encompasses us rather gently, discreetly, without inducing a shock or a significant resonance, the latter—sound—exerts a more compelling influence and elicits a more marked response.[38]

Sound calls attention to itself, and as a result, is an effective manipulation of our response. We need only think of a horror movie when our heart beats quicken to the pace of the soundtrack. Despite our anticipation of a surprise we will still startle when the music changes regardless of whether what we see is scary. Likewise, we can always discriminate between the sounds of trains running along the London Underground and that of trains running along the Paris Metro because each has a distinctive cadence as it bumps along the tracks, and the ambient chatter of the other riders has different rhythms and tones.

We become attuned to our surroundings because we share the reception of the atmospheric conditions. The energy of those chattering around us affects our conversational patterns and volume. When we ride the subway in Tokyo, we dare not speak despite the size of the crowds because human voices are silent, and to speak would upset the tranquil state of the other riders. While in New York, we can yammer on as loud as we would like without concern for our neighbors. Our vocal energies can affect those around us. Csepregi explains:

> Since we apprehend, often unconsciously, sounds with their affective meanings, the choice of certain phonetic elements already elicits a particular atmosphere. . . . Pauses, coughs, stammers, hesitations, and silences are also integral and necessary parts of every "conversational music."[39]

The stresses and emphasis of our patterns of speech create a rapport between speakers, and this give and take is similar to the empathetic responses generated with mirror neurons. Csepregi calls this "phonetic empathy," which is a result of sharing a moment. The emotional qualities of the rhythms and the silences are as meaningful as the words spoken is known as "atmospheric togetherness."[40] To be attendant to those around us and to understand and communicate with them, we must attend to how we hear what we hear and attend to what we do not hear. This act of listening is active. Without active listening we become inured to the aural stimulation around us and retreat into ourselves. Conscious attentiveness to our hearing changes the nature of what we hear. Perception and interpretation is dependent upon our context.

Our understanding of sound must expand so that we may consciously attune our sensibilities to the broad range of vibrations that constitute meaningful sound. Sound atmospheres exist, according to Csepregi, even without music or other noise. We detect them all of the time in our day-to-day conversations with friends. Take for instance our interaction with our boss. We attune ourselves to more than the words he speaks, but also his tone of voice and the rhythms and cadences of his speech to discern what is really being said.[41] Our knowledge and understanding of musical pattern help us decode the intonation of speech and other sounds when we encounter them in the world. As these sounds are manipulated in theatrical practice, an active listener in a shared atmosphere will be able to engage in the work. Like Cage's audience for *4'33"*, we must work to apprehend the ambient sounds in the auditorium to appreciate the marking of time.

As more and more artists explore the use of sound in visual art as a physiological trigger, we are starting to see the importance of teasing out the differences between physiological responses to lived and mediated experience. Bernd Schulz considers:

> This phenomenological-esthetic approach has been and is intended to counter the increasing fictionalization of our environment, in which direct physical experience is becoming more and more impossible. We may consider the ear to be closer to the world of the dream and the unconscious than the eye. Yet as the most sensitive organ for the exploration of reality, it connects our inner experience with the world around us.[42]

Rather than calling attention to the body's ability to appreciate music and manipulated sounds, the capabilities of the brain to perceive the whole range of audible vibrations points to the human ability to negotiate the world through sound as well as vision. By paying attention to the phenomenal reception of sound, we can deemphasize the bias we have for sight.

Hearing is not as easy to describe and classify as we often assume. We are as inarticulate about sound as we are of the chemical senses once we move beyond musical sound. Schulz believes that sound artists condition our brains to hear beyond the conventional taxonomies of music. He states, "In terms of the psychology of perception, the installations of sound artists appeal to the phenomenal consciousness in that we perceive for more differences than we can identify and label according to certain categories."[43] Considering the works of sound artists with this in mind will help define the potential range of noises and sounds that can be harnessed to create a shared atmosphere of aural influence.

Susan Hiller's *Monument* (1980) is based on the experimental recordings of Konstatin Raudive, who amplified silence and found that it was sonorous. Attendants sat on a bench and listened to recorded voices. Hiller explains that, "On one level, *Monument* is a *momento mori*, like all of Raudive's work. In order to hear the soundtrack, you need to participate in the work by listening privately in public."[44] She found that the act of listening to a recorded voice funneled into attendants' ears was a kind of sensual enticement. She continues:

> The intimacy of my voice speaking in your ear was a direct physical approach to viewers, a kind of seduction. At the time of *Monument*, this was really an unusual way for an artist to work, but I had been thinking a lot about the so-called tyranny of the visual and was looking for a more physical way to approach my work. If you sit on the park bench to listen to the *Monument* tape, in fact you can't really see the visual part of the work very well or at all, and that was deliberate. Touching someone's ears with your voice is actually a very intimate contact. In this sense, voice is physical, voice is body. Body is evoked and transmitted by voice, and not represented—this was one of the radical, political underpinnings of *Monument*, which was positioned "against" representation as some kind of fake immortality.[45]

The embodied physicality of the recorded voices gave body to the words of the dead. Recorded voices resonate inside our heads and sound as if they are our voices. These voices become a part of us, as if the speaker shares our space, intimately breathing into our ears. That which is supposedly inaudible is conveyed through sensation, giving shape to an absent body. The act of listening to a voice in the installation becomes significant. As Csepregi argues:

> We know how much sound, colour, and light can modify the way we experience living spaces. A cathedral appears handsomer when organ music is heard: we sense the music's harmonizing influence as the resonating tones of a chorale penetrate the transepts and the nave. Likewise, in a theatre we notice a change as the lights are turned off and people suddenly cease to talk with each other. To be sure, the sounds or lights do not modify the material aspects of these spaces; they merely evoke a momentary and later significance that we experience as atmosphere. . . . They are affective qualities that we detect in our immediate surroundings. Because they touch and move us, in the deepest senses of these terms, atmospheres are . . . stirring emotional powers.[46]

The moment-to-moment stimuli become material and can be described as the shared atmosphere of the artwork. These sounds, tastes, and smells of the world are shared between attendants and we are able to sample the past. While we need not be present in the event at the same time, its experience will color each of us and become incorporated in the fabric of our life's experience. The ways that we respond on a given day will differ, but our sensorial response will have made the experience tangible for us. Performance that activates the sensorial web makes tangible the intangible by making present the fleeting perceptions of bodies that have preceded us.

Part of the importance of a shared atmosphere in theatrical representation is the corporeal means by which representation is evoked. To evoke other bodies is to create a shared moment where communication is possible. By engaging the web of our sensations, the event becomes accessible to our consciousness by both physical and intellectual means. The use of sound is a useful example because we can both listen to dialogue as well as monitor the ambient noises of the space that we share with the performers or their proxies. We are able to understand alternative performances that use aural means as a central communication medium because we know how to apprehend the world using our senses. We do not need to understand the words being spoken to get a sense of what is meant. We evoke bodies while we perceive to make sense of the barrage of stimuli we encounter on a moment-to-moment basis. Sound artists may challenge conventional modes of listening and hearing, but aural stimulation becomes significant because it evokes other bodies. Being attendant to those stimulations will enrich our experience of what we see, taste, smell, touch, and hear.

FORAYS INTO THEATRICALIZED NOISE: MOVING TOWARDS AURAL VISCERALITY

Once the technologies of photography freed painters from painting mimetic portraits, painters were able to experiment with the elements of composition and produce abstract works. As Thomas Edison introduced new recording technologies for cinema and phonography, these technologies enabled artists to experiment and to break free from conventional aural and visual mimetic techniques. This led to the manipulation of sound as something more than the creation of music or dialogue. Kahn argues that:

> When the principles of montage were applied within the context of asynchronous sound film, sound—once it was no longer tied directly to visual images, speech, and story—was able to exist in a more complex relationship with them. In turn, once sound was no longer tied to cinema, a radical form of sound and radio art was implied. Sound also became radical once it was tightly tied to cinema in the form of animated cartoons. Not only could sound and image exist in a pronounced one-to-one relationship, but sound came first in the production process instead of being secondary or tertiary to the primacy of visual image and the limited sounds of dialogue.[47]

The potential for sound to be shaped as something other than music provided an opportunity for artists to attempt to shape noise into an artistic expression. As Artaud advocated making use of sound as a means of evoking feeling, the futurists and Dadaists sampled sounds to create illogical compositions; that is to say, compositions that used the logic of preconscious not conscious perception. Sensation provided the spine for their dramaturgical compositions. The creation of sculptures that became automatons spewing nonsense or noise machines punctuating performances—these avant-garde experimentations broke free from using sound in a mimetic manner and used it as a means of creating an atmosphere, evoking a mood, or accentuating a feeling.

Like the symbolists, the futurists experimented with the stimulation of the senses for visceral effect. Russolo's manifesto advocates using the ambient sounds of the mechanized world to create compositions of the everyday. He challenges us to break free from our inherited tradition of making music with symphonies made up of violins, trumpets, and cellos and instead make music with car horns, printing presses, and hissing radiators. He proclaims:

> **We must break at all cost from this restrictive circle of pure sounds and conquer the infinite variety of noise-sounds.** Each sound carries with it a nucleus of foreknown and forgone sensations predisposing the auditor to boredom, in spite of all the efforts of innovating composers. All of us have liked and enjoyed the harmonies of the great masters. For years, Beethoven and Wagner have deliciously shaken our hearts. Now we fed up with them. **This is why we get infinitely more pleasure imaging combinations of the sounds of trolleys, autos and other vehicles, and loud crowds than listening once more, for instance, to the heroic or pastoral symphonies.**[48]

Like the birds today that have learned to mimic car alarms as their mating songs, Russolo speaks of making use of the sounds that surround us to make a new music suited to our familiar circumstances. He was not far off, as neuroscience has taught us that if we are repeatedly exposed to the same sounds and rhythms, they will become pleasurable. Russolo asks us to harness the sounds that have been encoded into our neuronal firings to speak to our pleasure centers. He suggests:

> Let's walk together through a great modern capital, with the ear more attentive than the eye, and we will vary the pleasures of our sensibilities by distinguishing among the gurgling of water, air and gas inside metallic pipes, the rumblings and rattlings of engines breathing with obvious animal spirits, the rising and falling of pistons, the stridency of mechanical saws, the loud jumping of trolleys on their rails, the snapping of whips, the whipping of flags. We will have fun imagining our orchestrations of department stores' sliding doors. The hubbub of the crowds, the different roars of railroad stations, iron foundries, textile mills, printing houses, power plants and subways.[49]

We can harness the everyday to make use of learned behavior and reception patterns and evoke the experience of the new rather than dig up the experiences of the past, for new technology will promise a new life freed from the baggage of the past. Our embodied experiences will guide us in an intuitive way past the corruption of the logical mind.

Noises are never just noise in artistic representation. They take on meaning because they are meant to be perceived in the context of a theatricalized event. These noises are manifested in the atmosphere of the event and are meant to be significant. In a recent movie imagining the making of Hogarth's satirical paintings, *The Harlot's Progress* (2006), the din of eighteenth-century London accompanies every scene. Whether we are in Hogarth's studio, where we hear the neighbors arguing, or in a brothel, where we hear the grunting sounds of copulation, the bustling of everyday life accompanies the characters' dialogue. Sound is more than sound; it is a means of creating the atmosphere of the harsh conditions of eighteenth-century life. Noise is used as a means of making real the sensations of life in London. Kahn discusses the implication of noise in art making:

> Wherever they might occur among the arts, noises—interchangeably soundful and figurative, loud, disruptive, confusing, inconsistent, turbulent, chaotic, unwanted, nauseous, injurious—and noises silenced, suppressed, sought after, and celebrated always pertain to a complex of sources, motives, strategies, gestures, grammars, contexts, and so on. As such, they become significant.[50]

What we make of the din that accompanies production has as much to do with our expectation that noise and sound should mean something in the context of performance. If we associate sounds with smells and activities, the mere suggestion of one strand of that sensation will trigger the brain to elicit all the strands of sensation. We hope that all we experience is significant in relation to communication, and seek to commune with the world around us.

Stimulation need not be concrete in relation to the theatrical event. As with the hallucinatory quality of the attendant's experience at Burning Man, all sensations in the auditory context can be understood as having significance. Harnessing the sounds of the desert into a spiritual evocation is the same as harnessing high pitch screeching as communication between machines. Though we do not understand the tones that our fax machine communicates to other fax machines, we know that information is being exchanged. Noise takes on many forms:

> The sense of an immersion in noise is guaranteed by the ease through which so much can be perceived within it. There was a proliferation of acts and techniques within the avant-garde for interpolating noise, most of them related to seeing images within visual noise, as innocently as children see animals and faces within the clouds, just a little more

intoxicated. Nowhere was this more pronounced than in Surrealism, where such interpolation became elevated through its psychological, psychic, and psychotic associations. While much of the avant-garde was concerned with processes of abstraction, it was exactly the opposite for Surrealism. The interpolation of noise was a means by which meaning was generated from abstraction project and thus corresponded directly to Surrealism's larger project of bringing realms of reality hitherto guarded or unknown into mimetic practice.[51]

Harnessing the abstract, indescribable qualities of noise to communicate what is beyond rational comprehension was a brilliant strategy to make use of sensation as a means of expression. As our understanding of the ways in which the brain processes sound and other sensations grows, the more applicable the avant-garde experimentations become. Intuitively, attendants of Burning Man found a way to communicate imprecision precisely through imprecise means. Our unarticulated neuronal firing became significant as embodied experience and understanding.

Our presence is integral to artistic expression, and sound artists Ryoji Ikeda and Hans Peter Kuhn make use of more traditional museum space to set up a context in which to consider the sound as the generator of experience. This sonic isolation foregrounds the potential of theatrical sound as something more than dialogue or music. Cowan describes Ikeda's work as

> a sound, light, and architecture installation in which the artist . . . uses strobe lights, lasers, and high frequency sound waves in a long, narrow corridor to make viewers, who may only enter one at a time, dizzy with the oncoming, sudden light. The concept is that the movement and presence of the person walking through the hallway disrupts the sound waves, setting off the discomforting effects.[52]

As we move through the space our senses are deranged. This disruption triggers us to become attentive to the stimuli that perplex us. By activating the brain in this way, Ikeda is playing with attendants, pushing us to pay attention to the ways that the sound waves interact with the architecture and the lighting. Charles Stankievech argues that Ikeda's work uses sound to mimic light:

> Ikeda describes his work as having a particular sonority whose quality is determined by one's listening point in relation to the loudspeakers. Furthermore, the listener can experience a particular difference between speaker playback and headphone listening. The sound signals can be thought of in the same way as spot-lights.[53]

This description can be furthered by suggesting that the sound waves are mimicking the processes of the consciousness' spotlight of attention. The sound stimulates us to perceive and be attentive to the aural stimulation.

Ikeda does not only work as an installation artist. His opus includes dance performance with Dumb Type (a Japanese dance company), cinema, and solo audio work highlighting the specific qualities of binaural hearing. Stankievech observes:

> Almost all Ikeda's work could be described as metric, with beats and blips piercing space–time at consistent intervals. However, the psychoacoustic effect is anything but the metric or striated space that Deleuze and Guattari problematize. Like that of the American Minimalists who preceded Ikeda, his work generates a topological space that is constantly in flux—even if the sequencing of the music is more precise than a quartz pulse. In fact the sound's exceedingly meticulous interval forces the mind to react with a paradoxically increased intensity. The point of course is to modulate one type of space with the other.[54]

Our perception of the installation spaces are affected by the pulsing beats of the sound, and our physiological responses color our conscious perception and analysis of the spaces. By manipulating the sound to stimulate binaural processes, he is able to call attention to the listener's perception of spatialization within the gallery space. When Ikeda works within the context of dance performance, the sound becomes intertwined with the bodies of the human figures as they move through the space, the changing qualities of the light score, and the spatial constraints of the theatre. It is the sound that provides an emotional context and narrative to the movements of the performers. The performance's tempo and duration are made visceral to the attendant:

> "C7: Continuum," from the album *0°C*, does exactly this. Underlying the piece is an organic heartbeat—a rare choice for Ikeda—but the heart's natural sound is contrasted with his typical high-frequency oscillating pulse, and the normal repetitive metric matrix is created. Laying down a meditative framework, an unusual sample opens a wormhole between the history and the future of listening. . . . At first "Continuum" simply repeats the spatial remapping established by the stethoscope: the internal heartbeat sample from someone else's chest mapped into one's own cranium. This subtle and classic bodily exchange is further supported when halfway through the track.[55]

Ikeda's fascination with the body and medicine is made physical by the heartbeat that punctuates the narrative. Our bodies are tuned to the movement of the performers, as we are influenced by the vibrations of the soundscape. We cannot help but be tied to the performers and the other attendants. For its duration, the social body is made one with the others within the shared atmosphere.

By using a highly social experience of live performance, Ikeda's work with Dumb Type is able to comment upon the loss of sociality that is a result of technological advancement. *Voyage* (2006) is typical of the way in which sound is used with dance and video to create a commentary of technology's alienating qualities. A press release describes the performance:

> *Voyage* examines the uncertainty and dislocation of the modern world through a combination of intense sound, movement, text and projected images. Using movement and motion, speed and stillness, nature and illusion, this multimedia performance pricks the skin of anxiety and leads us to question where we are and where we may be going. *Voyage* portrays a dark and lonely, yet humorous world in which technology driven communication, speed and shifting locations are a way of life—if not necessarily a welcome one.[56]

Performances are often described by charting the effect of the sounds, and the feelings and emotions that the performances provoked. Like Ikeda's installations, sound and noise are used to create an aural atmosphere that serves as the context within which to understand the collage of movements and images that occur over the duration of the event.

From its first moments, the piece is hypnotic, coaxing attendants to be attentive to the images in front of them. The sound regulates our breathing and guides our perception of what transpires in front of us. Alison Croggon describes the opening moments of the performance:

> Darkness. After a time, the faintest of illuminations; at first you are not certain whether it is a trick of the eyes. An electronic roar that sounds disconcertingly at once like an amplified organic sound—perhaps the rushing of blood through the body—and machine-like begins to swell up from silence. As your eyes adjust and the lights slowly brighten, you begin to make out the edges of three huge silver spheres on stage, and a human form moving in the shadows against the wall of electronic sound. The dancer's movements are like flight, like swimming; her body is reflected in the polished floor beneath her. She returns to darkness.[57]

Movement can only be understood in relation to the sound. Croggon struggles to find a descriptive vocabulary to encapsulate what the sound was like. What is clear are the feelings that were evoked in her. She goes on in her review of the performance to describe how perception of the images, sounds, and effects led her to an intellectual interpretation of the action:

> A particularly beautiful vignette features a voiceover that lists a long sequence of wishes, beginning with "I wish I were an angel." A woman lies prone on a circular mat in the middle of the stage, surrounded by gorgeous images of the natural world which transform to a giant

doubling of herself, projected on the back wall of the stage and reflected on the stage floor. The projected image, with its actual grass, dominates the physically present woman, a manifestation of the hyperrality of the virtual image. At first benign and fanciful, the vague banality of the wishes become more and more suggestive of human disaster, until the words dissolve into an earsplitting shriek of white noise, while the image becomes a matrix-like flow of digital numbers and letters, before resolving again into sense. But now the seemingly childlike "I wish I were an angel" is more sinister; it is a deathwish, an inability to cope with the pain of loss.[58]

Words and other types of sound worked together to influence the attendant's interpretations of the dancers' movements. The sounds insinuate themselves into the brain. They seem to become part of our thought processes, as our tympanic membrane and ossiclar chain vibrate sympathetically. Its vibrations are recreated in our eardrum, and we live the sound.

SOUND, IMAGE, SPACE, AND TEXT

As Ackerman reminds us, "Sounds have to be located in space, identified by type, intensity, and other features. There is a geographical quality to listening."[59] I exemplify the ways in which sound can capture an attendant's attention and define space in a description of Wilson's *H.G.* (1995):

> The sound drew me into a chamber that I had to negotiate a maze-like turn to find. . . . It attracted me because of its seemingly human presence, as if someone walking back and forth were dragging something over the length of the ceiling. The nature of the room above was defined by the echoes of these sounds, and gave it a depth that could not be perceived in the near-dark conditions of the space. The only visual stimulation within the chamber was a brightly-lit square opening in the ceiling, in side which a globe hung against a white background. The sounds made the chamber seem spooky: Who was up there? Why was the person there? How did it all relate to space?[60]

As we negotiated our way through the underground cavern of the Clink, the echoes of our footsteps, dripping water, and the rumbling trains overhead gave us a sense of how large a cavern we were in and how close we were to the walls. We could tell if the ground was soft (it absorbed sound) and the walls were stone (sound bounced off them). The environmental noise and ambient sound drew our attention and became significant to situating ourselves in the environment. We wanted reassurance that, though we were feeling uneasy, we were safe.

More abstract noises created a mood that stimulated emotional responses to the space. The quality and volume of other sounds set the tone of how we responded to the information that our other senses were charting. We also encountered sounds that indicated humans were present, though not seen. Other human-generated sounds that were encountered were designed by Hans Peter Kuhn:

> There were mysterious and eerily human whistling sounds, characteristic of Kuhn's work with Wilson. There were also garbled, half-whispered German voices coming over the reams of paper in the doctor's office in the typhus ward. These give an eerie, hospital-like, almost concentration-camp feel to the cavern, perhaps associated with the images of the room filled with tagged shoes in another part of the installation.[61]

These sounds created a context for identifying and understanding what the space and sculptures might mean. There was an unmistakable connection between the images and sounds that indicated that this installation was making a comment upon Nazi extermination camps and scientific experimentation. As a result, we knew where we were in time, in what type of space, and the environmental conditions of that space.

Recent scientific experimentation has charted the brain activity and thus the emotional response of listeners of music.[62] Scientists have attached sensors to volunteers to chart their physiological responses. They were able to image the effect of music on brain activity and show the direct correlation between sound and rhythm upon mood and emotion. Ackerman, writing of similar experiments, concludes:

> Regardless of their cultural background (Japanese and American businessmen, Australian aboriginals, and others), all responded to the same passages of Bach in the same way. Next [scientists] measured hand-muscle responses when they felt joy, anger, and other strong emotions. The graphs plotted for the emotional states correspond to those for the passages of Bach. Music seems to produce specific emotional states that all people share, and as a result, it allows us to communicate our most intimate emotions without having to talk about or define them in a loose net of words.[63]

Music and abstract sound are able to communicate specific emotional states without engaging the conscious workings of the brain. Thus, music can quell the savage beast because it communicates in a pre-linguistic manner directly with the limbic system.

This phenomenon is particularly potent when we consider it in relation to the stimulation of more than one sensory system. When all of our senses are invigorated, the data they receive is cross-fertilized and influences our perceptions of all the senses. As our bodies transfer attention from one sense to the next, we begin to form a picture of the event. As we untangle that weave of sensations we can become more precise in our physical responses and our conscious understanding of the event. Drobnick tells us that:

> Representation and interpretation, for example, are issues in which sound shares with pictures and text, yet sound reconfigures these very issues by inflecting representation with affect, and interpretation with embodiment. The act of listening is not an activity done remotely; it inevitably invokes corporeality, it envelops listeners, and . . . it resounds within the body. The types of "literacy" involved with listening are strikingly complex; they not only exceed but challenge the conventions of visual and textual models.[64]

Our embodied response to the stimuli simultaneously resonates and responds. A demonstration of this can be seen in the work of Maria Chavez, who describes herself as a turntablist. She uses a phonograph and vinyl records to produce sound by scratching the stylus across the record, and then she manipulates the sound by way of a mixer. She collaborates with other artists by responding to their artworks in real time. For example, she has created works that are inspired by spaces built by architects and works that are inspired by paintings, sculptures, or other mixed-media. At DiverseWorks in 2003, she performed her sound manipulations in concert with a visual artist. As the collagist worked, Chavez created a sound composition in response to his creation of a collage, and he was creating a collage in response to her sound composition. They were improvising together in relation to each other's work. He created line adhesions on plates of glass with colored tape. Each was layering according to their own work over the duration of the performance. The activity of producing the visual art was combined with Chavez's scratching sounds. He was hidden from direct view and we saw his images through the mediation of video imagery, as well as through of the aural soundscape. They were calling attention to the processes of creation by asking us to listen and to see the creation of the composition. Its shape was the performance itself rather than the object that was created as a result of the actions that were performed visually and aurally. Chavez was describing through sound the process of an artist creating an image. She described what she saw and, in turn, her aural description affected his process. There is the ability to receive the stimuli; then there is the action of the process of reception of the physical stimulus; and then there is the third part, which is the attentiveness to the stimuli where our reactions become evident to consciousness, where we make an effort to understand the stimuli.

Kathleen Forde describes another audiovisual event by Granular-Synthesis that stimulated a physiological response to the fusing of image and sound:

Their installation *LUX* consists of a dark room with an abstract single-channel video projection of various mutating color fields that constitute the only light source in the room. The accompanying rumbling, pulsing soundscape appears to be intrinsic to the vast moving image, and vice versa. Any motion, change, or reorganization of the visual and sonic formations functions as a unified field; any modulations of the video in light and color cause equal modulations in the sound. The image completely suffuses our field of vision, and the low sound frequencies can be "felt" as they invade and pulse through our bodies. The overpowering sound and image, received by our senses as one unified medium, penetrate the interior of the body. It is nothing short of devastating, and yet also strangely serene. *LUX* induces a psychological state in which our consciousness of the interface between body and machine disappears—at which point the work becomes sublime.[65]

The immediate physical impact of the work led to a conscious analysis of the work by its attendants. This strategy of coaxing us to be an active partner in working out the cognitive process is also at play. The experience of the event wakes up our awareness of sound by turning our logical relationship with our senses on its head. Forde goes on to explain why these events are evocative and what they may demonstrate about contemporary society:

Whether they are shocking, soothing, or confusing our sense, contemporary media artists who conflate sound and vision are responding to the "numbing down" of our society by directly affecting our cognition. . . . These artists remind us that our consumption of seemingly impersonal new technologies is by definition subjective and personal. Technological interfaces are filtered—by way of our sense—through our intellect, emotions, imagination, and memories every minute of every day.[66]

Regardless of our intellectual analysis, it is impossible to ignore sensation in the articulation of why these events have an effect on attendants. It calls attention to the live, social nature of the act of creation and the means by which we understand that communication.

In a more traditional theatrical presentation, sound can be used to create authenticity and help attendants imagine the conditions within which the characters are suffering. Types of sound production used during the performance of Baraka's *Slave Ship* included sound generation by voice, environmental sound, and sound generation by musical instruments. As a means of mimetic realism, sound can transport us to the time and place of the action and elicit an emotional response. The keening of the characters wore attendants down. Harold Clurman's review of the original production stated that the performance was "full of raucous sound." Sounds create an atmosphere in *Slave Ship* to immerse attendants into the cramped quarters of the hold of the ship. Kimberly Benston observes:

> Every effect of feeling and every physical condition is portrayed through sound. The props call for ship "noises," ship "bells," sea "splashing," whip and chain "sounds." The slave-characters evoke the state of misery with constant moans, cries, curses—all bare intonations which, rather than describing a condition, become its essence.[67]

Baraka's awareness of atmospheric din is made manifest in the play, suggesting that attending the event is an aural experience. The ambient noises of life aboard the slave ship conveyed the misery of the captives. Not only were the moans and voices of the passengers aboard the ship an integral part of the sound design, there was music as well as pregnant pauses that called attention to the way in which sound could become significant noise. One of the more interesting discussions of sound work in the play involved the instances where sound effects were absent. Gil Moses described his use in production of what he termed "emotional space" to make Baraka's text physical.[68] Emotional space was used during the production to encourage an active shared experience between actor and attendant. Moses explains that:

> Emotional space connoted the distance between the notes of a song, two lines of dialogue, or two bars of music. These moments of silence were taut, filled with anticipation for the attendants. Effective orchestration of emotional space, manipulating the silences and pauses, could create a feeling of anxiousness and tension.[69]

Sound that was elicited directly embodied experiences that evoked emotion. The production made the attendants active participants in the experience of being on a slave ship.

WALKING AROUND WITH SOMEONE ELSE'S VOICE IN YOUR HEAD

Directing attendants' attention outside of a conventional theatre space is challenging. It is as if the artist needs to teach us how to pay attention to the surrounding environment and to note details as significant that might ordinarily be disregarded. Janet Cardiff and George Bures Miller's audio sound walks demonstrate the ways that sonic attentiveness can be harnessed to make sense of abstract experiences. Andra McCartney describes the genre's importance:

> A soundwalker's engagement with the landscape is at once sonic, tactile, and kinaesthetic. It is defined through what is heard of others' sounds,

through interactions with the surroundings, and by the recordist's own movements. Amplification translates the subtlety of touch into an audible play with surfaces and textures. In soundscape works, traces of tactility are embedded that help to link distant and everyday places. They explore auditory experiences and memories of natural and urban environments, and attend to and reflect upon the depth of daily rituals.[70]

By being attentive to aural stimulation, attendants can begin to ascribe meaning to the experience of engaging with their environment. In much the same way, we might begin to make sense of an installation; the kinetic experience of an audio tour gives shape to our interpretations of the elements of composition that we experience in three-dimensional space.

Cardiff and Miller shape aural worlds for participants to sample as they move along pre-determined routes in the various cities where these works are conceived to nurture the participant's attentiveness to aural reception. What is striking about the worlds that they manipulate is that they call attention to lived experience by way of a recorded fiction, thereby blurring the line between the mediated and lived experience. While immersed in the same environment where the artists previously recorded their composition, participants monitor someone else's thoughts. We experience the environment in real time, thereby activating two different aural monitoring regions within our brains. This calls attention to the ways that we perceive and construct the world aurally.

In a manner inspired by audio tours of museum collections, Cardiff and Miller record a tour that takes walkers on journeys that move through galleries, crowed streets, or parks. They record ambient sounds, as well as narratives describing what the participants are seeing. At once informative and discombobulating, the recording leads participants to unfamiliar places, where we are able to listen to the world around us, as well as an artist's mediation of that world. Our brains will not discriminate between art and reality because the aural stimulation mimics a three-dimensional soundscape. As a result, their experience blurs into the fictive experience:

> In their art, they combine image, video, and sound, as well as architectural and sculptural installations that take the viewer on a confusing and fascinating journey. Sound and a special binaural recording and playback technology are key components in their installations, producing a highly sensitive and spatial audio and sensory experience. Their work evokes thoughts and associations that become inextricably interwoven with personal experiences, thus creating a constantly changing new fiction.[71]

Breaking free from the passivity of looking in a gallery or sitting and watching in a theatre allows Cardiff and Miller to reconfigure our relationship to the artwork. Our active spatial navigation invigorates our sensory systems. In describing Cardiff and Miller's *Chiaroscuro* (1997), Jennifer Fisher explains that "Cardiff's audiotours use sound to impel the proprioceptive sense: the feeling of moving through the exhibition and encountering various presences. The focus of this piece is not objects or people, but the affective significance of spatial practices."[72] We actively engage in the piece as we choose to navigate through different spaces and place ourselves in relation to buildings and objects while our perceptions are being colored by audio recordings. Thus we are experiencing the work and perceiving it in the way that we navigate the world while running through Paddington Station to catch the train.

Cardiff and Miller aid us in the transition from passive viewer to active participant by setting up the rules of the experience. Gregory Williams describes the process that begins once you hit play on the recorder:

> the instructions primarily took the form of a series of commands, delivered by Cardiff in a voice that alternated between sensuous and sinister. . . . Cardiff quickly compelled the spectator to fall in line with the sound of her footsteps, which periodically could be heard in order to set the proper pace.[73]

In the same way that an actor may take instruction from a director, we are commanded to discover the blocking of the scene. Though unwittingly, we are the protagonists in this situation. We experience the event as an actor moving through the spaces, and it is our perspective that ultimately determines the finial narrative set up in the script. Cardiff and Miller provide the script and the scenography, but our participation conflates that of the art object and the audience.

As the experience unfolds, they use the form of the event to stimulate our proprioceptive responses to the journey. Williams suggests:

> By supplementing the voice-over with a complex web of ambient sounds, disjointed narrative fragments and aural effects, Cardiff acts as hypnotist, keeping the visitor off-balance and conjuring up a steady stream of associations that are as diverse as the participants' memories. Her low, soft voice brings about a sensation not unlike the hypnopompic state, the period immediately preceding awakening when consciousness and the dream world vie for dominance. Suspended in this liminal moment, the tour winds its way among buildings, down paths and along a canal, drawing attention to hidden corners and narrow passageways that ordinarily receive scant recognition.[74]

We have to rely on our senses to make sense of the narrative that we are hearing and seeing. We need to use our consciousness to sort out the experience. Experiencing Munster in this manner will forever color our perception of the city. Our memories are shaped by the stimuli, and as we seek out patterns, our brains are actively working to figure out what is happening. Fisher elaborates a similar response to her experience:

> the participant is asked: "Try to walk with the sound of my footsteps, so we can stay together." The sense of proprioception is central to this piece in that the motion of the speaker directly parallels that of the listener. As Cardiff's footsteps mark time for the participant, they trace a route through the virtual soundscape that blends with the actual proximate space of the museum. The binaurial recording technique gives a three-dimensional sonic presence and the sense that the recorded sound is inside you, sharing your own interoceptive processes. As Cardiff inhales deeply in the elevator, you are inevitably reminded of your own breathing.[75]

As a result, we are living in the moment, paying attention to every detail that we hear and see as if it were significant. They have led us into a situation where paying attention to our senses is the means by which we will make sense of the event.

Another event points to the ways that their work uses the attendant's body to make tangible evocations of the past. Cardiff and Miller's *Her Long Black Hair* (2004) takes place in New York's Central Park. Although there is no resolution to the provocative mystery, attendants are offered an actor-less theatrical experience of resurrecting long-lost memories. We follow Cardiff's directions on a meandering exploration, retracing the footsteps of a mysterious dark-haired woman from the past. At various points we are instructed to pull old photographs from the 1970s out of a packet that we were provided. The Public Art fund describes the piece as:

> a complex sensory investigation of location, time, sound, and physicality, interweaving stream-of-consciousness observations with fact and fiction, local history, opera and gospel music, and other atmospheric and cultural elements. At once cinematic and non-linear, *Her Long Black Hair* uses binaural technology—a means of recording that achieves incredibly precise three-dimensional sound—to create an experience of startling physical immediacy and complexity. As Cardiff's soundtrack overlaps with the actual sounds surrounding the listener, past and present intertwine to form a multilayered, open-ended reality. The walk echoes the visual world as well, using photographs to reflect upon the relationship between images and notions of possession, loss, history, and beauty. . . . These images link the speaker and the listener within their shared physical surroundings of Central Park, shifting between the present, the recent past, and the more distant past.[76]

Sights and sounds allow participants to follow in the footsteps of those who have walked before them. By conflating their experiences with those who have been there in the past, the artists are passing on lived experience and knowledge. In our active engagement with the photos and our attempt to make sense of the clues, we create an embodied theatrical experience.

Only through our engagement will the work become theatre. We must willingly enter into the contract with Cardiff, who wants her audience to participate:

> In the formation of her semi-fictitious environments, Cardiff lays out the parameters of a short-term collaboration between artist and viewer. She encourages a certain co-dependency between creator and observer, not unlike the relationship between the dog and the inventor in the old RCA logo.[77]

The creators set up the parameters of the event, providing us with instructions and stimulation, and we respond to the work by paying attention. Active listening engages our perceptual faculties, immersing us in an experience of the artwork. Paige McGinley describes *Cabin Fever* (2004), where once she puts on the headphones and sticks her head in the diorama box she is immersed in:

> a miniature representation of a familiar rural scene: a trailer home, leaves on the ground, trees, a gravel driveway. It is night. Someone is home. The lights are on inside and there is the unmistakable blue flicker of a television screen. As I watch intently, the sound score begins to intrude, interrupting my looking. The sounds of a quiet summer night: crickets, leaves rustling, the murmur of activity in the house. The sound of car wheels on gravel draws my eye into the diorama, to the driveway. A car door slams, followed by footsteps, followed by a screen door opening and closing. I hear murmurs, conversation. A man and a woman. The volume rises. They are shouting now, but I can't make out what they are saying.[78]

McGinley describes where she is and what she is experiencing so that she may be able to sort out the action of the narrative. It is the relationship between what she sees and what she hears that affects how she perceives the experience. Her reception of the event and eventual conscious interpretation is dependent upon charting her sensory awareness of the triggers set up by the artists. What occurs over the course of the audio cues is not immediately understandable by purely rational means. McGinley continues:

> And then, horrible sounds: things being thrown, objects hitting walls—are those bodies hitting walls, hitting each other? The violence is viscerally unbearable, I want to take the headphones off, when, suddenly, a shot. A gunshot that makes me jump. And then, chilling silence. The screen door opens, slams, feet running on gravel, falling, getting up, running toward the car door, which slams shut, louder and more urgently than before. The car wheels dig into the gravel, throwing it into

the air, speeding away. And then, crickets, and the blue flicker of the tube. . . . It takes me several minutes to realize that we are back where we started, the tape has looped.[79]

Aural clues provide the means to trigger the attendant to question the action. Once that process has begun, both her body and her brain are engaged in the action.

What interpretations can we take away from this abstract and conceptual stimulation? If we rely on sensation, for which it is difficult to make these enigmatic and fleeting feelings tangible because we lack a precise language for sensation, then in what way can the interrelationship of these sensations and fragments of language take on a comprehensible meaning? In *Opera for a Small Room* (2005), Cardiff and Miller created an installation that houses the record collection of R. Dennehy, who lived in Salmon Arm, Canada. They proclaim it "a small room for the opera of his life."[80] There are close to two thousand records stacked around a wooden cabin built in the center of a large room, eight record players, and twenty-four antique speakers. These record players are mixing sound by sampling lines from opera arias to a cacophony of voices and rhythms, speeding up and slowing down. You have to peek into the cabin through cracks in the wood and through a large window. Cowan describes what she perceives:

> Here there is a clutter of old records, all marked "R. Dennehy," filling bookcases, scattered on the floor, on tables and chairs. Some turntables and speakers sit among the tiny "studio" and bare light bulbs, along with a vintage chandelier, and old speakers. The lights go down and surround sound booms around the outside room, the music of just before a concert, when the orchestra is tuning and people take their seats, finally applauding, and the show begins. The room outside of the cabin remains dark, save for lightning that strikes when an opera singer hits his highest note, but the cabin's light changes, synchronized with the music of a Tom Waits sounding narrator, the effect of a shadow moving around a room, the sounds of shuffling, coughing, the pulling out of a chair, and the record player starting and stopping on its own. The music is a medley of opera, *When a Man Loves a Woman,* a train careening around a corner, the deafening sound of crickets, thunder and rain, a hypnotist's coaxing, all as a Heinz tomato ketchup can hanging from the ceiling glows red with light.[81]

Cardiff and Miller describe this man's shadow as a back-projection that moves as if he is a DJ. Who he is talking to is never clear, and what his relationship to the objects in the space or the sounds is up to the attendant to determine. Acting as voyeurs, we are left to piece together the data to try and conceive of a rational narrative to connect the elements together. Once again our sensations are there to guide us.

The elements of composition are put together by the artists to create a live context in which we can piece together for ourselves what the sounds, lights, movements, and words elicit. By creating a context to actively engage in, we are led to ask questions of the material, and through these questions experience the thought processes of the artists. Cardiff and Miller state that they

> are interested in the extreme cultural juxtaposition of opera and the small western town in which R. Dennehy lived/lives. What did he think about while listening to these records recorded in foreign cities half way around the world. Was he a trained singer? Did he want to have a career in opera? Did he lose a lover and find solace in the music? Did he always imagine traveling one day to these faraway opera houses? We imagine that he sings along to the records creating his own opera of displaced time and space.[82]

Although we may never be able to recreate this exact line of questioning, we are involved in our own questioning, where we imagine why these images and sounds are given to us. We wonder who this character is, where he is from, and what he thinks about the world. We make judgments about him because of the sounds that we hear and the rhythms that we feel. We relate to him as a live person. Though all we know of him is that the records were once owned by him, his traces evoke a living presence that we can see. It is like when we climb up a medieval church spire and wonder at our ability to walk in the same spot that generations have walked before us. It is a tangible connection to the past, although there is never a direct experience of what they heard, smelled, felt, or saw.

Rather than follow the action of a traditional drama, these works compel us to follow the aural cues of the recordings and the environment. Fisher explains what this does for our experience of these tours:

> They function as artworks that can be neither seen nor touched, but impel the beholder to see and move in particular ways. Each audioguide provides a distinct atmosphere that frames the experience of viewing with the sense of sound and felt space. The tensions between the visual, aural, and proprioceptive senses are vital to understanding how exhibition scripts pertain to the body in space, and thus how exhibition codes are incorporated (or resisted) by beholders. Specifically, tactile and aural resonances have the potential to challenge the hegemony of visuality in exhibition aesthetics and politics.[83]

Cardiff and Miller create an atmosphere that we understand by monitoring what it does to us physiologically. These bodily responses allow us to focus on our responses to the physical world, thereby developing our neural plasticity. Fisher points to atmosphere as an essential quality of the activation of sound in an artistic creation. Soundscapes impinge upon attendants and immediately prejudice their perception of all that comes after.

CULTIVATING LISTENING

To cultivate attentiveness to the sounds that make up the web of sensory stimuli that are offered to attendants during a theatrical event is to condition a way of listening that takes advantage of perceptual functioning. Drobnick terms becoming conscious of cultural conditioned manners of listening to hear anew to find meaning in the cacophonous world as "listening awry." Attendants who are able to listen awry are offered another pathway to access the potential meaning-rich content of a theatrical event. Breaking free from the assumptions of what aural stimulation is offered during performance requires that we consider noise as meaningful. A deliberate activation of the spotlight of attention requires us to savor sound. As Drobnick reminds us:

> When harkening to the clamour of the noisy ball, it must be remembered that listening is as much a learned behaviour as it is a perceptual function. We exist in a noisy ball, and we contribute to its racket; by listening awry we may also reflect upon the myriad meanings of murmurs and cacophony, and how the act of hearing is itself conscious, implicated, and subject to cultivation.[84]

Becoming conscious of the significance of the sounds that we make as a part of our daily life helps us ascribe meaning to theatrical sound design. As I sit here, I hear the clicking of domino bones characteristic of the ex-pat Cuban population in Miami impinging upon my concentration. We can identify the sound as culturally significant, reassuring to my neighbors, but also as a form of noise that distracts my attention. How I respond to the clacking sounds becomes significant. To a third party looking on, the contrast between the convivial party at the neighbors and my solitary apoplexies could become meaningful in the context of performance. The characters depicted and their responses become a rich narrative. Likewise, if, as listeners, we were trying to be attentive to a meditative chant at the same time, our experience of the chant would be affected.

We cannot ignore sounds as they vibrate inside our ear canals. We may miss the moment-to-moment changes in light quality projected on stage, but the tones activate our physiology regardless of our attentiveness to the sound. Gabor Csepregi observes:

> Sounds, as I have said, detach themselves from their source and pursue us. We are able to turn away from visible objects, but unable to preserve a distance between ourselves and the sounds. Colours "cling" to objects; sounds "move away" from them and "enjoy" an autonomous

existence. We see clearly the red light in front of us, but are at a loss as we try to figure out from where the ambulance is coming. We can easily impose our will onto the visible, but not onto the audible; we can close our eyes at any time, but not our ears.[85]

As a result of our inability to escape sound, artists have a particular opportunity to play with our aural involvement in a production. Sounds can be split and divorced from their source, as in Wilson's *Hamlet*. Hamlet may speak on stage, but his voice is amplified and projected from a speaker at the rear of the house. Sound can be distorted, as the storyteller in SRS' *Il Buchattino* speaks center stage and her voice is run through a mixer, deepened, tone lowered and amplified, transforming her from being tiny Thumbkin to the giant ogre.

The success of playing with sounds comes from the creation of a shared atmosphere. As our brains become used to the patterns of meaning-making through soundscape, then variation can be used to challenge our assumptions about what should come next. The artist establishes a pattern that we learn and then deviates from that pattern to keep us attentive and invigorated. We begin to savor the aural stimulation as a complement to the information that we receive from the web of our senses. Csepregi confirms the aesthetic implications:

> Our auditory sensibility cannot be reduced to a unidirectional attunement. Certainly, sounds come to us, press upon us, and resonate in us. But, just as we like to approach flowers and smell their pleasant perfumes, so, in the same manner, we like to focus actively on some sounds and reinforce their effect. . . . With all our being, we are able to detect and "breathe in" a particular sensory or moral atmosphere without, of course, taking, literally, a larger quantity of air into our lungs.[86]

Savoring sound is akin to savoring a smell or taste and taking note of sensations to remember and make part of our experience. In the same manner that we breathe in the flowers that we encounter, we breathe in aesthetic stimulation and savor the experience, thus stimulating our brains and making it a part of ourselves.

SRS takes advantage of our common experience of savoring our mothers' voices as they read us to sleep as children. They stimulate the web of our sensations when we attend *Il Buchettino*, choosing elements that coax us into relaxing and approximating the feeling of well being that we had as children snuggled into our beds listening to a bedtime tale. As I recount, the web of sensations during performance create for the attendant feelings that, in childhood, triggered our imaginations:

> The cedar and the safety of the warm beds enticed us to enter our imaginations and take on a dreamlike state—not in an alien proscenium

theatre, but enveloped in our own body heat. . . . The storyteller had only her voice and the story to draw us into this world. Yet, as she began to describe Thumbkin and his brothers, the house they lived in and the forest around them, faint sounds of the household, including the weight of footsteps in the ceiling above us, as Mom began to walk across the floorboards, began to creep into our consciousness. . . . we could feel the vibrations from the axe chopping the wood, the bristles of the broom on the floor and the slamming and bolting of the window shutters. Our beds shook and trembled giving substance and form to the environment of the woodsman's house.[87]

Here, the Proust effect is triggered by the company, thus allowing us access to our childhood memories. By savoring the storyteller's tale, we can be transported in time back to our beds as we listened to the activities of the house after our bedtimes. We can remember the crickets' maddening chirping, and the rustling of leaves outside our window as we clutched our blankets around our bodies, protecting our necks from vampires. Savoring the sounds of the performance seduces us into fantasy. Csepregi reminds us that this sensual quality to savoring creates an act of intimacy:

Once again, here the act of savouring denotes more than just a particular mode of sensory contact; it also implies a fundamental human attitude in which intimacy, calmness, presence, serenity, and liveability predominate. Thus, when we savour the charm and mystery of fog, or the sadness and melancholy of the requiem, we respond, with relaxed or rapt attentiveness, to a singular event. . . . Although the music of a requiem is carefully studied and rehearsed, we do not have the impression of being subjected to a constrained or artificial atmosphere. In spite of our sorrow, we may find a deep satisfaction in the markedly suggestive and enriching music that discloses a specific atmospheric colouration. We come to an altogether different awareness of the atmosphere when, in a state of passive reception, we hear music not as a unique aesthetic event, but as a background and in the background.[88]

SRS promotes an intimate atmosphere to induce and encourage the appropriate mood and behavior to listen awry and temper what we see on stage with the feelings and emotions that are evoked through all of our sensations.

In this manner, SRS is able to make manifest the past through lived experience by passing on vicarious experience, and thereby changing our embodied response to the world. As the old cliché states, the difference between history and art is that history is about what happened and art-making is about what it felt like to experience what happened. Live performance, by making use of the attendants' experiences of the world, makes real the past to pass on its lessons. As our brains make only small distinctions between reality and imagined reality, our neural networks can be conditioned by the experience of art-making and other empathetic imaginary exercises. The power of art becomes evident when we take this into account.

Shakespeare's rhetorical eloquence is well-known; generation after generation of American high school students have been taught to recite by rote Mark Anthony's "Friends, Romans, Countryman" speech from *Julius Caesar*, although it is debatable how many of them conceive what Mark Anthony was saying about politics and the effects of war. Can we empathize with him as he mourned for his friend and found the energy to channel his anger into political action? Romeo Castellucci's production of *Giulio Cesare* (1997) deranged the attendant's knowledge and experience of this speech by using an actor with a tracheotomy to play Mark Anthony. Each time the actor took in a breath we could hear the effort it took to form the words. Those of us unaccustomed to sound production in this manner may have felt squeamish with the new sensation. As we imagine what this actor's body may be feeling, we may shift in our seats or our hearts may beat faster. The sound of inhalation and speech through the tracheal incision made strange our familiarity with the text and, thereby, deranged our expectations of this speech. Consequently, the aural strain of listening to unfamiliar vocal qualities allowed us to consider the words more closely, and understand the difficulty of the rhetorical qualities of the funeral oration for Mark Anthony given his friend's death. It is another means to transmit and make concrete this experience in our bones. This artistically mediated experience points to the ways in which exploitation of our bodies' experiences can be a powerful means of artistic expression that can make our participation in the theatrical event more active. Similarly, this speech was accompanied by a performance by a machine. As Mark Anthony stood atop a crate, a machine resembling a candelabrum with large illuminated light bulbs crushed each bulb as he made rhetorical swipes at Brutus. Each time he gave Brutus praise, a bulb lit up, and then as he ripped down Brutus' character, a light bulb was crushed, exploding with a large pop. The props were a means of conveying the effect the words were meant to have on Brutus and the rest. Our involuntary responses to the sounds, similar to that of nails scratching a chalkboard, made us react physically, causing us to cringe in our seats. Therefore, visuals, abstract sounds, and text make concrete the purpose and effect of the speech.

Some of the most piercing moments in any SRS composition are Scott Gibbon's soundscapes. There is the play of real sounds, manufactured sounds, and sound generated by voice. Sound, unlike other stimuli, is as effective when mechanically reproduced because the vibrations stimulate the brain in the same way, whether mimetic or actual. In this instance, technology can be a useful instigator of stimulus regardless of its mediated qualities. In *Tragedia Endogonidia, A.#2* (2002), a pneumatic crossbow shot arrows into metal sheets, and there was a scene with a harlequin figure climbing a ladder and breaking glass, and electronic feedback waves shook the seating area. The arrow machine, when fired, released of burst of air, then the release of the arrow made a sound, followed by the sound the arrow made as it was puncturing the metal skein of the set. The effect of these sounds was eerie. After watching a performance of *Giulio Cesare* in Chicago, I overheard several young women talking about the performance as we walked toward the subway. The first woman exclaimed, "I don't understand what that was about, but I am too creeped out to go home on the subway right now." The second responded, "Yeah, I am going to have nightmares for a month. Who the hell imagines these things?" While they may not have consciously made sense of Shakespeare's verse, or identified the images created onstage that reference canonical images from art history, they understood the play emotionally and physically. None of the attendants, myself included, could escape the intrusiveness of the experiences, and the amplified sounds enveloped our whole bodies and shook us to our cores. The sounds became embroidered within our complete experiences of the performance, thus shaping an emotional response to the work as a whole. The physical world that the sounds are tied to give me the structure with which to imagine the emotional journey that the experience is triggering. These women understood the devastation of war that is loosed upon the populace, as depicted by Shakespeare and interpreted by Castellucci. Though we were attentive to the performance we were not in control, because the reptilian part of the brain that took over and allowed our overwhelmed senses to respond unencumbered by mental and social constraints.

Like amusement park thrill rides, these experiences allow us to participate in group activities relatively free from social constraints and restrictions. Think about raves or sporting events, where mass hysteria and mass rule are the way of the event. These techniques are breaking in below the cultural surface. We do not have to know anything about the specific culture. We do not have to read a culturally specific image subtly; the visceral nature leads us to the experience. It is a truly democratic experience. We all have our body with our innate physical sensations, and these types of experiences harness that, and do not leave us out even if we are undereducated and not culturally savvy. To reach larger audiences we have to reach the lowest common denominator between cultures—that which is visceral. The avant-garde is experimenting with more sophisticated uses of physical manipulation to give us an aesthetic of the visceral, thereby making these experiences more than superficial diversion.

6   The Sentient Body
Guiding Somatic Responses
Within Performative Structures

Steven Pinker argues that we need a theory of the ways in which the subjective qualities of sentience emerge out of mundane information access.[1] The processing of data collected by the senses allows the body and brain to perceive and then interpret the theatrical event through subjective conscious judgment. One presumption about the theatrical event is that it is an intimate act, where the interface between actor and audience provides a type of experience that no other mediated experience in life does. What are the implications of sense (perception) theories for actors, directors, designers, and attendants? In this chapter, I set up a brief explanation of the ways in which human physiology is attendant to both sensory stimulation within an artistically mediated event and the direction of non-verbal thinking and analysis; furthermore, I explore the implications that an increased understanding of the role of the senses in performance has for theatre artists.

Peter Carruthers posits that in the pursuit of a theory of phenomenal consciousness we describe the information that we access in the everyday. There is an underlying assumption of

> Naturalism [that is,] . . . the belief that all of the events and processes which occur in the world are natural ones, happening in accordance with causal laws. So there are no miracles, and everything that happens can in principle be provided with a causal explanation, or is subsumable under laws (albeit probabilistic ones).[2]

When that is a guiding assumption, then when we create fantastical worlds that will be perceived as natural and processed accordingly. Therefore, I am not suggesting that Naturalism is preferable in theatrical performance, but rather that we have the ability to accept mimesis as natural. If we can describe how information is accessed, then we can describe what caused that information to be received by the body. By being attentive, we can hone our abilities to identify what is causing our bodies to respond and, in turn, identify how our bodies are being stimulated. Awareness enriches our ability to interpret the form and function of the theatrical event. We process the sights, sounds, feelings, tastes, and smells that we experience in a web of sensation, our sensory apparatus sorting through the data to sift out the most relevant and significant facets to send to the brain. The better we understand how our bodies do this, the better able we are as artists to shape the attendant's experience of a given event. We arrange the components of composition to provoke the attendant's experience, making unfamiliar the familiar to attract their attention and imbed the experience in the memory. Each new experience stimulates neuronal pathways that change the way we perceive the world. It is the artist's task to attract and direct attentive attendants' attention, and in so doing, stimulate their brains to make new discoveries about the world.

We receive stimuli as a patchwork quilt of sensation, and "The confluence of sight, hearing, and movement affects memory."[3] Such confluence is important because when we remember a theatrical experience, we do not merely remember the words spoken. Whereas we can access drips and drabs of fleeting sensations for a few moments after experiencing them, what we remember long term are the sights and smells of the evening and the emotional journey that we took. We remember how the performance felt, and the pain in our backsides as we attend to Forced Entertainment in a frigid warehouse in Dublin the evening after a trans-Atlantic flight. The physical surroundings of performances remain in our minds as much as anything else. However, our memories can metamorphose into idealized representations that can stray from the actual experience. Like the attendants who dozed off watching a Wilson piece and reported to him that they liked elements that were not there—extensions of their dreams—our memories play tricks on us. But there were stimuli that promoted these feelings and emotions. We can identify some of them, like the dripping water in the medical ward of the Clink during *H.G.*; whereas in another, we can only give a sense of the vibrations in the seating area during SRS' *Tragedia Endogonidia, A.#02*. All of those sights, smells, and touches shaped our embodied experiences.

I have trouble watching conventional theatre, and I have little desire to sit through yet another national tour of *Death of a Salesman*. Yet, I learned what good theatre was by attending such shows. I was enraptured as I went on that journey. It passed something on to me that provides me with new knowledge about theatre that changes my perceptive awareness. A piece of the past was passed on and changed the way that I experienced the world and theatre, thus leading me to novel events. The sights and smells are different each time we see a performance, but we respond in set ways because we have deeply engrained habits of response. However, when we encounter an event that provokes us to go beyond our comfort level, it pushes us to new places and we become enraptured once again. Innovative theatre practice is potent because it helps our brains retain their adaptability, and introduces us to new paths of reception. To remain healthy and alert we need more and more complex and different experiences to keep our brains changing and flexible. Theater, sport, and innovative theatre practices that engage all of our senses provide that.

Western tradition has always been suspicious of sensuous thinking because it is nearly impossible for our conscious brain to untangle the web of sensation that informs our organism before conscious perception. However, becoming aware of different approaches to processing perception can help assuage some of that distrust. Linda Bartoshuk describes the usefulness of attentiveness to somatic perception:

> Early approaches to the perception of complex stimuli identified two types of sensory mixtures: analytic and synthetic. In analytic mixtures, the identity of the components is retained in the mixture. Playing a high, medium, and low note on a piano provides an example of an analytic auditory mixture. All three frequencies can be identified. In synthetic mixtures the identity of the components fuse into a qualitatively new sensation. Mixing color with a color wheel (or by mixing lights) provides an example of a synthetic mixture. The identity of the components is lost and the color of the resulting mixture is qualitatively distinct from the component colors.[4]

We need to approach the physiological reception of any live performance through a combination of the analytic and synthetic means. As we become attentive to the different stimuli, we need to be analytic to a point, identifying the tastes, touches, sounds, smells, flavors, and sights of the stimuli presented by the event one by one. However, we are cognizant that the senses do not easily unravel from the web of perception, so we also have to consider the confluence of the senses in a synthetic way, experiencing the new sensation offered by the different blending that the artist offers to the attendant. Whereas we might not be able to articulate the data that our bodies are interpreting unconsciously, we can try to be attendant to the different elements within the composition that trigger our reactions. There is a logical progression from the notes that the artists play on our sensorial biology. Through their pokes, whiffs, and screeches they are shaping our sensuous experience of the world. The end point is that these events become a part of our neurological make-up in the form of neuronal connections, memories, and images. The pieces live inside of us.

The theatrical event uses social experience to keep alive the events of the past, making real the imaginary, or making present the past. Each time we pick up Shakespeare and recite his verses, we are giving shape and form to a ghost. Though that ghost has been infected by the baggage of time (the distortions resulting from the passage of time, the influences of culture, etc.), it passes on some component part of the moment in time it was composed. Its recitation connects us to the past and gives us a shared moment with others who have experienced the performance of that moment. I will always remember that actor intoning Othello's repetition of the word "handkerchief" at Yale Rep while I was in high school. His voice merges with Ira Aldridge's voice, with my voice, and I recall it when my heart is broken and paranoia rules my thoughts as it did Othello's, in a similar way to someone else hearing that word in another era. These performances are a means of transmitting those inarticulate moments where our souls cry out, and to share its sensation with those in the future. In other words, through experience we understand, and through shared experience of art works we share an experiential vocabulary. Though I cannot describe what my heartbeat felt like, why my insides needed to be cut from my stomach, and all the thoughts that rushed through my head, through our experience of the world and its representations, our brains have experienced similar physiological and emotional states. Furthermore, through empathy, our brains will respond and together we understand.

Theatrical performance can be a form of travel in time and/or space. I remember a performance at a Northwestern University theatre of an Italian and Canadian collaboration. These performers created a piece about the earth and human development. The performance used basic theatrical techniques to show one place on earth and one stone in that place, thus showing the passage of time. The only thing that changed was the people that made use of the space and the ways that they made use of the stone. There was little if any text. The history of the world was expressed through emblematic actions. The stone was where cavemen ground their wheat; what a soldier used as a weapon to kill; where a sailor anchored his craft; and what people had fun throwing in the water and retrieving while scuba diving. From the first moment where a handful of earth fell from a curtain a few feet off the ground, to the first footsteps of man, to the end of the world, this space connected the attendant to a seaside location as it transformed over time. These basic elements kept my senses invigorated and showed a narrative. They showed the transformation through physical actions, the sounds of dirt and feet hitting the ground, though smell and touch were not necessarily essential, but we could connect to smells and other triggers that would be present in the location. They could be evoked through association. These shows are a part of me. Through remembering them, I remember a specific moment in my life out of the eighteen million minutes of my experience so far. It is a way of evoking specifics about long ago times that hardly seem real. In another way, they are not necessarily accurate memories. They are affected by sentiment and mood, and by what I have forgotten as well. Perhaps the accuracy of interpretation disappears as senses and memories fade, but they have already affected me and changed me. I have adapted because the stimuli have entered into my experience.

More recently I remember having a conversation with an actor that I had seen perform years earlier in a Forced Entertainment production at the ICA, London. The night I saw it, I was absorbed in the experience. It was a slow piece that lulled us into those experiences we have when it is 3 AM and the party is still going on, but we are all bored, waiting for something to happen.

Then suddenly, the actors changed their tempo and volume and turned on us. They began yelling at us to stop watching. That sudden explosion of sound woke up an old man who was sleeping at the end of one row. He jolted awake and fell out of his seat. The people next to him helped him up, for at first we thought he may have been having a heart attack. We also suspected that he may have been a plant in the audience. Because the show went on, we figured out he was not. The show had changed for us. We were mad at the theatre company. We were hostile, though in the end most still admired the piece. A few years later, I was outside the Becket Centre in Dublin chatting with one of the actors from that night and I brought up that moment. We remembered together that specific night, for it was noteworthy in its uniqueness. We recovered a moment in time and bonded. We shared that moment in time— one experience of the world. It gave us a way to connect to each other. This is an intrinsic value of the theatrical event as imagined through the senses.

Theatre by its nature is intensely social. Its live quality brings us together. Although it is fictional, it is cathartic because it takes us through the trials and tribulations of other humans and finds resolution through the compressed form of the experience that artists offer up to us as they shape performances that stimulate our embodied responses to the artworks. This makes the theatre an extremely powerful medium that is intrinsic to human survival. It passes down the experiences that we cannot know without help. The theatre makes us like the protagonists in Shaw's *Back to Methuselah*. Theatre imagines an evolution where the past can find embodiment and be passed down as an experience to help the adolescent humans who cannot help their lack of experience in surviving the harsh climate of earth. We learn in theatre, in real time, the thoughts as they felt for Aeschylus. We may not understand rationally, but it is up to us with our flexible brain connections to adapt and figure out what to do with the fragments of the past. We make them a part of us. We are all little Frankensteins running around, a patchwork of all those dead people infecting the way we act. The way I sound when I am annoyed passed to me from my father from his father, uncle, or grandfather (it doesn't matter), this trait has survived because we have mimicked the behaviors of those who have come before us. Some of it is biology, whereas some of it is the plastic mind adapting to the world. Theatrical experience that harnesses the senses sets out to shape a malleable mind so that its attendants can face the future and pass on their experiences to those in the future. Theatre fulfills one of our basic survival mechanisms: to pass on our traits. The more we keep our brains plastic, the more vital we become. Theatrical events influence and reconfigure those who are attentive, and thereby can be transgressive because it hopes to change humans to their core. Performance is often thought of as dangerous and transgressive because it induces change in its attendants' brains. Regardless of whether or not we are attentive to the event, it seeps into our consciousness and affects us down to our electrical and chemical essence. If artists pay attention to the power that they have in reconfiguring the physiological experiences of the attendants that come to be a part of a theatrical experience, then these creations can be seen as dynamic and powerful.

The form of the stimuli is important in the activation of the neurons that tell us what is real in perceived experience. Watching cinema and reading novels are different types of experiences that stimulate different parts of the brain than attending theatrical events. Recent research testing McLuhan's notions of "the medium as the message" demonstrates the differences in the media. Erica Michael and Marcel Just performed brain scans to show that hearing and reading prose are processed in different areas in the brain. Just explains:

> The brain constructs the message, and it does so differently for reading and listening. The pragmatic implication is that the medium is part of the message. Listening to an audio book leaves a different set of memories than reading does. A newscast heard on the radio is processed differently from the same words read in a newspaper.[5]

How we receive input affects where the brain processes the input and the different ways that we comprehend its significance. As Doidge concludes from this experiment, "each medium creates a different sensory and semantic experience—and, we might add, develops different circuits in the brain."[6] Because each form of media stimulates our brains differently, our brains process the stimuli in different regions, and as a result, the different arts have different physiological effects. While we read in *Perfume* about the protagonist inhaling the perfect scent, different parts of the brain light up from when we smell the cigar smoke in *American Buffalo*. Theatre's live qualities affect mimesis, and as a result of multi-sensory stimulation, our involvement and attention with mimetic representation process the experience as lived. This makes a different set of memories from watching a movie or looking at a painting. Though we use the same aesthetic concepts and make use of similar strategies to capture the attention of the audience, how we stimulate them and to what effect are drastically different.

When dealing with a multivalent medium, the brain is continually sorting stimuli and augmenting its perception according to probable interpretations. We are in a state of flux. Doidge explains:

> In complex activities several sectors must interact. When we read, the meaning of a word is stored or "mapped" in one sector of the brain; the visual appearance of the letters is stored in another, and its sound in yet another. Each sector is bound together in a network, so that when we encounter the word, we can see it, hear it, and understand it. Neurons from each sector have to be activated at the same time—coactivated—for us to see, hear, and understand at once.[7]

These networks are developed over time as our brains become experienced. Theatre that manipulates our sensorial experiences as a component of performance challenges our brains to make new associations. Doidge continues, "While we have yet to understand *how* thoughts actually change brain structure, it is now clear that they do, and the firm line that Descartes drew between mind and brain is increasingly a dotted line."[8] Our sensory systems think as much as our rational consciousness. What does it mean for us if we start thinking about the mechanisms of theatre as agents of brain reconfiguration? Performance can make familiar the unfamiliar and forge connections between experiences that the attendants may not have had before. We are forging the future and preparing individuals in the audience for the future by remaking their brains in our social and cultural patterns.

Our attention directs our sensory apparatus to the stimuli it wants to focus on, unless a new input supersedes directed attention. As it focuses on stimuli, it begins to perceive and form predications about the world according to our assumptions about the world. We know before thinking. Paying attention to what makes us respond can enrich our experience of the world and, in turn, enrich our experience of mimetic representation. Anne Bogart describes the value of attention in relation to artistic practice and audience reception. She separates attention from consciousness to describe the mental focus of the practitioner at work, as well as the attendant:

> Attention is not the same as consciousness. Physiologically, attention is the ability to consciously select certain features from the vast array of sensory signals presented to the brain. Sensation, awareness, past experience, and reflection (self-awareness) all participate in the phenomenon of attention. This integrated consciousness modulates conscious states and directs them, finally arriving at mental focus and interest.[9]

An integrated consciousness allows the attendant to receive the stimuli and interpret it according to pre-conscious and conscious mechanisms without distraction. As directors guide our attention through blocking, coordination of effect, and tempo and duration, they create an atmosphere conducive to focusing. Bogart believes it is essential to be able to create evocative theatre:

> Attention is a powerful tool. It can be used and misused, consciously or unconsciously. The quality and depth of one's attention is ultimately what counts most in every situation. Attention is, after all, one of the few aspects of life that one can control. The only gift we can give to a situation is the force of our attention. We can control attention and we can control the quality of our attention. When attention is compromised, the outcome is weaker.[10]

Continually finding means to keep the attendants responding to the stimuli as they unfold for consumption is a daunting task, as we become inured to conventional tactics. As tactics become familiar, they lose their ability to captivate in the same powerful way that they did before. New times demand innovative ways to capture and captivate our attention; otherwise we are doomed to falling into a rote response to the familiar.

As a means of immersing attendants in experience, several entertainment venues have found ways to use sites of disaster as a means to promote experiences that aim to create a social means of promoting understanding and empathy through embodied experience. Proponents of these "dark tourist" destinations claim that these events are a means to create a humane society by making real the effects of our history. By capturing attendants' attention, they hope to convey what it was like to be a part of the events that transpired at these locations.

SOMATIC ADVENTURES FOR THE PERCIPIENT ATTENDANT

There are myriad tourist destinations at disaster sites that attract a certain authenticity of experience. We can have an entertaining day visiting the London dungeon, or get locked in a cell at Alcatraz to feel the confines of the space. Whether we visit the killing fields of Cambodia or the gas chambers of Auschwitz, we are present in the space of destruction. John Lennon and Malcolm Foley define visits to these types of destinations as "dark tourism."[11] Currently, there is a frenzy of debate about the ethical side of these tourist sites, but I am more interested in how a live experience of history is attractive to us. An example of the performative nature of these sites is a visit to the Cu Chi tunnels in Vietnam, where visitors can crawl through maze of tunnels and experience the heat, dust, and claustrophobia of living underground. Attendants can sample foods that the subterranean guerrilla fighters ate, and can fire AK-47s into the jungle. The theatricality is apparent as attendants hear the sounds of machine gun fire and interact with former soldiers/actors dressed as Vietcong (VC). Seth Mydans explains, "At Cu Chi, the visitor is greeted by a sign reading: 'Please try to be a Cu Chi guerrilla. Wear these uniforms before entering tunnel'."[12] Attendants are invited to don the uniform consisting of black pajamas, pith helmets, rubber sandals, and a rifle. As we don VC costumes, we become actors in a narrative of war. We can crawl around, but to suit the larger girth of western tourists, the tunnels have been made larger, lest we should get stuck. Meanwhile, we see the booby traps, hear the propagandistic slogans of the VC, and experience a taste of their life at the compound. How we respond relies on cultural connections to the events. My mother-in-law, Vy Tran, responds in revulsion, trying to forget the beatings that the VC gave her husband and son, and the bullets she hid from as she and her children fled into the ocean. However, we can watch gleeful American tourists too young to remember the war firing $1 rounds off into the jungle on the Cu Chi gun range. This environment provokes both responses from the same sounds, smell, foods and temperatures. Context shapes understanding.

An event that takes this embodied experience even further by creating an extended narrative takes place in Parque Alberto, Mexico, and is offered by the Hnahnu tribe. All of the actors have had experience crossing the boarder themselves, and are familiar with the tactics of the smugglers and border-patrol agents. Whereas the event in question is a group theme park attraction rather than a site of desecration, its premise is macabre. As a participatory theme park, tourists can become migrants attempting to cross to *El Norte*. You are led across a rough landscape by a guide with no food or water and hunted down. The walk is an all-night affair that takes attendants on a long trek through the mountains. Once night falls, participants are loaded into a pick-up truck and driven deep into the desert to wait for their guides to come to lead them to the United States. Poncho, the guide, eventually arrives and tells everyone to do as they are told and keep their mouths shut. He is a part of a gang of ski-masked *polleros,* or chicken herders, who smuggle migrants into the United States. These men have made the journey across the deserts and rivers and over the boarder when they worked in the United States. We embark on our journey, running past cacti, up hills, and over anthills, slipping and sliding down embankments and running until we are out of breath and pushed to run some more until we are past the point of exhaustion. The *polleros* move quickly through the treacherous terrain, barking orders at us to stay put in the bushes and not move a muscle. We are trying to avoid the *migra,* or border-patrol agents, who are never far behind. Finally, after what seems an eternity, the order to sprint is given.[13] This activity goes on as the group escapes in pick-up trucks with sirens and searchlights. During the chase, the group slips into a tunnel to avoid capture. Ioan Grillo describes:

> At one point the group walks through a nest of giant ants that bite people's legs. One girl starts screaming after injuring herself on the trip and has to be supported by friends as she hops along. The group slides down a steep ravine, a particularly hard task in the middle of the night, and many come through with cuts and bruises.[14]

We feel the sand in our boots, scratch at the ant bites, and wipe away the sweat from our brows. Every ounce of our stamina is necessary to keep up after five miles, and our hearts race at each rumble of a truck engine and whine of the sirens. Eventually, most of the migrants are captured, and border guards tackle a man to the ground, yelling for him to surrender his papers. The agents are violent and yank his arms back, probably tearing his shoulder blade.[15]

In the end, this is just a taste of the experience of a migrant sneaking across the border. We will not be processed by homeland security and will not have lost the thousands of dollars that would be paid the *polleros* to guide us across. The Hnahnu have crafted an experience to get the participants to feel the trials of the border crossing. They get us to slip and slide, increase our heart rates, sweat, fear, ache, and long for water. They confuse us, exhaust us, and use the sounds of the landscape, the border guards, and the lights to make sure that we go through the stimuli that we would encounter in a real attempt to cross the border to the United States. The light of the moon and the stars are their light design, and the beams of the searchlights and the sirens are the triggers to stimulate our reptilian responses. The sounds of the landscapes and the orders of the *polleros* and the border patrol are the dialogue. We listen intently to each other's exertions and breath and try and remain silent to evade detection. This proximal experience of what it is like to cross the border for tourists is an example of how experience is constructed and exploited. As participants we have all of our senses invigorated. We are able to exercise our reptilian senses as we try to avoid capture, negotiate the rocky terrain, feel the sweat of toil, and the pain of lack of water. We are asked to become aware of the physical conditions of the journey and are given a run-through of what the experience is like when nothing is at stake.

From a more conventional live art experience, we can see the ways that artists can create structures that demand attendants use their senses to respond to the artwork. Here we move from visiting an actual site recreating an experience to one that uses a site as a setting for the recreation of historical practices. For *Two Undiscovered Amerindians* (1992), Guillermo Gómez-Peña and Coco Fusco lived for three days in a gilded cage in Columbus Plaza in Madrid, then in Covent Garden in London, and also in various locations in Australia and the United States, masquerading as newly discovered aboriginal inhabitants of an island that Columbus missed. Intending to satirize the display of "discovered" peoples, the artists were unprepared to find that many attendants took the "Couple in a Cage" as "authentic." Gómez-Peña and Fusco re-imagine the anthropological shows featuring natives that regularly toured the courts of Europe. The premise was for the couple to spend their time engaged in ritualistic tasks. Fusco explains:

> We performed our "traditional tasks," which ranged from sewing voodoo dolls and lifting weights to watching television and working on a laptop computer. A donation box in front of the cage indicated that for a small fee, I would dance (to rap music), Guillermo would tell authentic Amerindian stories (in a nonsensical language) and we would pose for polaroids with visitors. Two "zoo guards" would be on hand to speak to visitors (since we could not understand them), take us to the bathroom on leashes, and feed us sandwiches and fruit.[16]

Whereas we might think that a couple dressed in outlandish costumes such as a leopard-print facemask, studded leather, and trendy sunglasses might immediately be identified as fictional, they were considered as authentic aboriginals by many who stopped to interact with them. In fact, some of the attendants became agitated by the inhuman practices that they believed were being perpetuated.

What did the experience mean to passersby? Diana Taylor, in a cultural reading of the piece, attempts to give a plausible analysis of attendant responses:

> Many viewers, much to Fusco and Gomez-Peña's surprise, believed the show was "real" and that the Guatinauis came from that far-off world of National Geographic-land. For all the parodic staging and acting, many in the audience believed the performance. They spotted traces of ritual action and other signs of primitivism that they recognized but didn't exactly understand. Others showed more skepticism. One woman, who looked Mayan in origin and expressed an interest in and knowledge about Guatemala, refused to fall for a simplistic "is it or isn't it?" approach to the issue of native identity. Her somewhat defensive and defiant pose suggested that she knew better than to comment on whether "undiscovered" people exist, saying only that if you're willing to pay people to travel around in a cage, you'll probably find candidates.[17]

Regardless of whether we as attendants took the event as real or fictional, we become engaged in the situation. We were forced to confront our feelings about, and response to, these two in a cage, as we congregated around them in a large public space. We could hear the comments of those around us and monitor the sounds of the traffic on the side streets. Those of us who believed that these two were incarcerated knew what the hot sun felt like beating down on them. We could smell the aromas of the square wafting in the air and recognize the unpleasant odors of city life, such as rancid garbage and urine, as well as the sweet odors of the cafes. How frustrating it would be to have to ask the guards for a banana. Like Rizzolatti's monkeys, we could mirror the feelings of the people that we could see and reach out and touch.

Reactions to *Two Undiscovered Amerindians* ranged from outrage to mockery. Some believed, whereas others did not. The ways that attendants responded and interacted surprised the artists. Fusco explains:

> Other's self-presentation; and even those who saw our performance as art rather than artifact appeared to take great pleasure in engaging in the fiction, by paying money to see us enact completely nonsensical or humiliating tasks. A middle-aged man . . . insisted on feeding me a banana. The zoo guard told him he would have to pay $10 to do

so, which he quickly paid, insisting that he be photographed in the act. After the initial surprise of encountering caged beings, audiences invariably revealed their familiarity with the scenario to which we alluded. We did not anticipate that our self-conscious commentary on this practice could be believable. We underestimated public faith in museums as bastions of truth and institutional investment in that role. Furthermore, we did not anticipate that literalism would dominate the interpretation of our work. Consistently from city to city, more than half of our visitors believed our fiction and thought we were "real."[18]

In addition to feeding the male, there were often attempts to get even more intimate. Taste, smell, touch, sound, and vision were all activated by placing two figures in a public space. In the United States, there was a certain amount of reticence in responding, whereas Fusco and Gómez-Peña report that, in Europe, businessmen would approach the cage and start hooting like jungle animals. Fusco reports that:

> Interestingly, women have been consistently more physical in their reactions, while men have been more verbally abusive. In Irvine, a white woman asked for plastic gloves to be able to touch the male specimen, began to stroke his legs, and soon moved toward his crotch. He stepped back, and the woman stopped.[19]

Attendants were left to respond as their instincts dictated. Youths in Madrid would taunt the couple and offer them "delicacies," as Fusco termed them, of beer cans filled with urine. There were some shocking and violent responses to the male figure as well. In London, a group of skinheads attacked and had to be restrained by onlookers; and in Brazil, acid was thrown at Gómez-Peña's leg.

Encountering new and unfamiliar events is difficult for us. We need some sort of guide to dictate for us how we ought to respond, because we try and predict appropriate responses according to experience. Perhaps because children are used to the unfamiliar and are comfortable accumulating new experiences, Fusco reasons that they offered the most humane responses:

> Young children invariably have gotten the closest to the cage; they would seek direct contact, offer to shake our hands, and try to catch our eyes and smile. Little girls gave me barrettes for my hair and offered me their own food. Boys and girls often asked their parents excellent questions about us, prompting ethical discussions about racism and treatment of indigenous peoples. Not all parents were prepared to provide answers, and some looked very nervous. A woman in London sat her child down and explained how we were just like the people in the displays at the Commonwealth Institute.[20]

Children engaged with the performers as human and attempted to make contact with them through their familiar tactics of touch, speech, and sharing. They process the experience as any other and attempt to understand why these people look different and are treated as caged animals are. This is the essence of an attendant awareness of a theatrically constructed event. We need to become aware of the triggers that are making us respond. As we become aware of those triggers, we can then try and process what the situation is making us feel and why it is making us feel this way. Gómez-Peña and Fusco are placing the attendants in proximity to a practice of the past and calling attention to the notion that the world really has not changed much. It thrusts in our face what our social prejudices and biases are based on our reactions—it stirs up a hornet's nest within us. Perhaps being in proximity to others as they respond to the exhibit shows us as much about ourselves as it does about our own reactions—can seeing others respond bring the focus back on ourselves and get us to monitor and question how we are responding to the live humans encaged? It is a surprising revelation.

Fusco uses experience to shape her pieces. For a recent production, she went to a training camp for Prisoner of War Interrogation Resistance run by Team Delta, where she was trained to withstand interrogation. These camps make use of torture techniques to prepare attendants for a hostage situation. This is the type of training journalists and contract workers attend before shipping out to war zones. Attendants are given a glimpse into what torture is like so that their embodied responses will be familiar with the sensations and not experience as much shock. In that situation our bodies can filter out more unnecessary stimulation because those sensations will be familiar and already be a part of our memories, allowing our brains to keep focusing on our rational thoughts. For example, in a lecture about *Operation Atropos* (2006), a video she made about torture techniques, Fusco talked about the experience of hearing the "fictional" torture of a companion in the next room as a tactic to get you to talk, because, out of empathy, you do not want your partner to suffer because of your actions. It is the most effective technique that torturers have once they have worn down, deprived, defamiliarized, and deranged the torture victims' experience. These rehearsals of torture enable participants to prepare for possible abduction, increasing their chances for survival. Mimetic circumstances that stimulate a wide array of sensory triggers can accustom us to new situations, preparing us for the future. Fusco engaged in this research for *A Room of One's Own* (2006), a performance piece about women in the military. She takes her experience of the torture techniques to craft a performance that will guide the attendant's responses to the material. By creating an experience for attendants, she is making sure that they have an embodied reaction that will communicate through the senses on both the unconscious and conscious levels. These artists are constructing events that actively seek to involve attendant participation, and thus are making flexible our brains' capacity to make events that have never been encountered familiar. As a result, theatrical composition has a tremendous power to shape and transform experience by transmitting knowledge from host to host—sometimes transgressing accepted social bounds.

TRANSGRESSION, PERFORMANCE, AND HUMAN EXPERIENCE

Artaud tells us, "One does not separate the mind from the body nor the senses from intelligence, especially in a domain where the endlessly renewed fatigue of the organs requires intense and sudden shocks to revive our understanding."[21] Miami is a tropical paradise where, most days, it is warm and the sky is blue. While pleasant, the only time that we become aware of our surroundings is when nature, in a move that Artaud would be proud of, wreaks havoc upon the city. In 2005, three hurricanes (Rita, Katrina, and Wilma) set the city into a ritual of chaos. We had to fight the crowds at the market scrambling to get the last loaves of bread, and scrounge for water and charcoal. Fighting for precious resources, aggressive residents cut into lines at the gas station. This was before the storm unleashed its power, disrupting the rituals of our privileged, comfortable lives. Alone, huddled in our homes, with boarded windows and no electricity, we weathered the storm listening to the howling wind, the cracking trees, and thuds of flying debris. The flood waters rushed down the streets like newly formed rivers. Sleep was difficult; with each crash, our reptilian awareness kept us on our toes. Afterwards, with roofs ripped off, trees and electrical lines covering streets, we emerged from our sealed boxes and assessed the damage. New communities emerged as neighbors helped each other clear their yards, pooled their resources and shared meals, played games, and chatted with each other to pass the time. It took a mass disruption to stimulate interaction with our neighbors, who live feet from us. That everyday complacency returned relatively quickly once the electricity came back on. In New Orleans we saw something far more drastic, closer to Artaud's description of the plague, unfold with the looting, murder, and corpses left in the hallways of abandoned hospitals. It took mass disruption to bring renewed awareness to the social structures that we take for granted. Transgression in performance is the artist's impulse to test the limits of social contracts by disrupting sensibilities, whether physical or mental, to release them from their complacency, even if for just a moment.

By its nature, live art is necessarily an intimate act whose performance relies on subjective response. This human contact—one that we do not always get in other modes of everyday experience—creates an interaction between attendant and performer in a live environment. In that way, its practices demonstrate an intrinsic strategy that makes use of physiological sensations to make the capacity of the human to feel tangible to attendants. Its liveness invites the activation of our sensorial engagement. As we enter into an agreed contract of expectations in the attendance of a performance, it carries with it a moral and ethical responsibility on the part of the performer not to do damage to us; we do not want to be electrocuted, or physically assaulted by robots. It is by pushing the boundaries of what is expected or conventional that some performances remove the safety net between performer and attendant and commit many violent acts on the psyche, the intellect, the aesthetic, or even the body.

Are these strategies necessary? Lydia Lunch describes the potential effect or draw of performative structures:

> Took up too much time servicing one john at a time. Had to crank it up another notch. Manipulation elevated to Art Form. Put it on the stage. In front of an audience, who like johns, pay by the hour, the half hour, or in this case, every ten minutes. Instead of pleasure, sell them pain. My pain. Their own pain. Regurgitated and spat back at them . . . Make them pay to be tortured. Assaulted. Abused.[22]

The notion of performative transgression is the evolution of the means by which performance, through the stimulation of a multi-sensory experience, strives to viscerally jolt the attendant's understanding and experience of what it is to be human. Can going too far be the only way to break free from the habitual complacency of conventional modes of theatrical response?

Contemporary artists such as Lunch exploit these concepts to create sensory-rich experience. We are familiar with the strategy used to take the event out of the traditional passive stage/auditorium configuration of the proscenium theatre, to work in intimate galleries or in site-specific locations to encourage a different relationship between attendant and actor. We have set expectations of what a performance will be like when we walk into a Shubert theatre; we will sit in the dark quietly and passively absorb the distant spectacle. Meanwhile, if we should walk into a dockland's warehouse, we would expect to move about and actively engage with the artwork. Taking performative acts outside of the theatre encourages a more active participation, where one must be attendant to the performance.

The proximity to the performers and their bodily exertions adds to the level of information that the attendant picks up about the performance. As Franko B wants his performance work to be like the active experience of going to a museum to see an image they can smell and touch, his attendants will have a range of sensorial experiences that encourage active participation.[23] Perhaps the particulars of the performance will fade from memory, but a semblance of the experience will remain within the sense memory. That memory is embodied thinking, and only through an active awareness of sensorial stimuli can the experience begin to be spoken about, using language and cultural models of interpretation. By trying to touch our senses, he asks attendants to embrace being human and to recover our contact with other humans.

However, what are the bounds by which these events can transgress the conventional assumption about the rights and responsibilities of the performers to the attendants? The configuration of intimate live art performances encourages the active participation of attendants to the event. The dominant subject of live art has been to the discussion of the body and its various coding. It follows that the body as a subject and a medium begs us to examine from a rational standpoint our own bodily response to these events. In that way, the live artist is in a unique position to stimulate our bodies. That stimulation gives us an experience of one or more of the component parts of the performance.

The first concern, however, is to try to ascertain to what extent transgression is really a concept in the strict sense. To transgress is to go beyond the bounds or limits prescribed by an edict, or to break, violate, infringe, contravene, or trespass against. It also can imply an offense against someone, or disobedience. Anthony Julius outlines the ways in which transgressive practices have been evident within the visual arts; transgression as a concept emerges from modernist practices. We can use these definitions to extrapolate the ways in which live-art practices employ these tactics in contemporary performance. Julius argues that:

> The modern period may be characterized in part by three distinct kinds, or versions, of transgressive art: an art that breaks art's own rules; an art of taboo-breaking; a politically resistant art. That is to say, there is an art that repudiates established art practices, an art that violates certain beliefs and sentiments of its audience, and an art that challenges the rules of the state.[24]

I would like to concentrate on the taboo-breaking art for a moment. Although it may be

> entirely conventional in its execution, its violence is directed more at its audience than at the art canon. It does not so much wish to extend or challenge art as to extend or challenge the attendant. Just as the art canon is in a certain sense the subject of the art rule-breaking artist, so the attendant is the subject of the taboo-breaking artist.[25]

To imagine a sensuous theatrical event in the future, we must go back to the early experiments that attempted to arouse attendant response. On the evening of February 5, 1920, in France, six Dadaist speakers assaulted an audience with G. Ribemont-Dessaignes' manifesto recited simultaneously. A critic described this as an "indescribable racket made worse by the protestations of the audience."[26] The performers attacked:

Before descending amongst you in order to eradicate your decayed teeth, your scabby ears, your canker-ridden tongues./ Before breaking your rotting bones—Opening your bilious stomach and removing, for use as livestock feed, your swollen liver, your filthy spleen and your diabetic kidneys [. . . .] We shall take an enormous antiseptic bath.[27]

Then the attendants taunted them back. Although Ribemont-Dessaignes repudiated this event later, it cannot be denied that he was lashing out against the audience, transgressing the accepted social limits of decorum. This impulse to do damage has not disappeared. It is not a haphazard occurrence, but one designed to shock and offend us morally.

Julius contends that "Politically resistant artworks have divided audiences: those against whom they are directed, and those whose morale they are intended to lift. The stance of the artist is thus both oppositional and representative."[28] This transgressive lashing out against society is a means by which we are able to appreciate the fragile social structure that guides our interactions. An example of these types brutal psychic abuses are Lunch's performances. She is self-proclaimed as ranting, screaming, and hostile, and is always on the forefront of the underground, exploring various forms of expression, such as spoken word performances, writing, acting, film making, sculpture, and photography. Her artwork is fraught with anger and scathing wit that assaults attendants in a sadomasochistic onslaught.

Lunch's work is a hybrid of gritty sex and violence that appears honest, allowing for self-identification, yet its bitter attitudes are unsettling and alienating. In Houston, Texas, in 2005, standing with a drink at her feet, Lunch launched into monologue that began with the current political situation, touching upon the economy and, of course, the war in Iraq. In her view, we are all victims of an oppressive fascist state. At first we were vocal and it felt as if she were preaching to the converted, but as her dissenting view of global politics became increasingly radical, angrier, and more militant, she alienated a sympathetic audience. She seemed cut off from us, refusing to interact, talking at us hostilely, rather than merely talking to us. It was not that we did not agree that the current colonialist attitudes of our foreign policy are bulldozing the rights of the entire world, but rather that her proclamations attacked our core political beliefs without offering perspective on changing or coping with the socio-political tides that are larger than any one of us.

Lunch next moved into more familiar territory, recounting autobiographical intrigues with dysfunctional love affairs. Here, in graphic detail, she reminisced on her co-dependence upon her paranoid and violent lover, whose drug-induced insomnia led him to believe that an unseen force was creeping on the roof waiting to get him. At its best, her language describing their intimacies was sensual, and the rhythms of her speech mimicked the sexual passion and ecstasy of the experiences. As the images of her violent relationship and her writhing images of beatings and lust streamed by, we became exhausted by its onslaught. It was as if she been at this too long and we were forced to take in her coke-ridden, violent sexual escapades. Her trauma was being transferred to us. Her hostility overpowered the experience. Why were we listening to someone who wanted to lash out and hurt us? What were we meant to leave her performance with? She attacked everything in her sights without any perspective as to how things might be different, or even whether they should be different. Lunch offers no perspective on life and seems to wallow in the self-destructive abyss of substance abuse and dysfunctional interactions. It is a pessimistic outpouring of an individual trapped in living death. The only interactions she seems to describe or demonstrate through performance are hurtful, violent, and without hope. However, Artaud's view that "Perhaps the theatre's poison, injected into the social body, disintegrates it" is more to Lunch's taste.[29] By injecting her poison into attendants, she will spread her disease and destroy the world that she does not fit into. It is not about creation, but destruction.

How can annihilation instigate change? A few years back I was chatting with a friend, lamenting our inability to escape overexposure to violence and profanity, and the question came up of what shocked us. Our responses had become so habitual, making violence humdrum that even shocking content has a hard time piercing through our cynical shells and actually affecting us. It was not until, while flipping though some images days later, I came across photos from the 1930s in China that recorded the flaying of living humans tied to poles by Japanese soldiers. I found that I still could be shocked—in fact, even terrified—by a print image. These images, while reminiscent of Goya's *Disasters of War*, were different. Whereas Goya's prints were aesthecisized, these images seemed unmediated. Such was the shock of seeing something so unimaginable, so horrifying, and so painful that, to this day, thinking about it can send my flesh crawling. Seeing human skin being pulled away from the muscle with a machete—I know that to an eighteenth- or nineteenth-century human who may have been accustomed to witnessing lynching, hanging, and other public executions this may seem weak, but to my twenty-first century constitution, this brought home the death and destruction of war and human cruelty in a more direct way than Goya's prints. His viewers, familiar with this type of atrocity, needed only an aesthetic reminder, whereas we need more graphic detail to achieve the same effect. That is not to say that I was not affected by these artistically mediated images. Violence can be beautiful: Take, for instance, the dripping blood of Franko B against a white background during one of his performances. But aestheticification is a distancing effect. To see something that is real—that abuse struck home in a different way. Live artists often bring the aesthetics of art to bear on real events. Franko B's performance work is beautiful, but it is also proximate. Aesthetic performances orchestrate a visceral response from attendants so that they actually might experience the violence and abuse of the disturbing images, actions, or events that transpire in front of them.

Whether performance has a positive or negative effect upon the healthy body has as much to do with how we deal with the stress of encountering new experiences as it does with aesthetic taste. Jim Rose, a self-identified circus freak, describes a show in Montreal where hundreds of tattooed, pierced, hardcore fanatics dropped one by one as they saw the Human Pin Cushion spout blood. Though not physically assaulted, the proximity to self-mutilation, and the ingestion of worms, garbage, and light bulbs, triggered these attendants to faint. These attendants who had pierces and tattoos themselves may have been more inclined to such a radical reaction because of their familiarity with the pain associated with carving and piercing. Their neural networks fired sympathetically to the performer's pain because they knew how extreme his pain was. Artists who transgress formal boundaries of fiction, acceptable public behavior, and attempt to affect us viscerally, have found ways to make real the stimulus that might shock us into a new awareness or allow us to defamiliarize ourselves with the values and boundaries with which our societies have inculcated us. They do not create Realism, but rather use theatrical tricks to mimic experience. On top of this, they may use transgressive means to get those forms to go beyond our social and political norms. The act of breaking our fragile beliefs is a way to infuse our assumptions with alternative perspectives; that is to say, to allow us to experience the world from a different perspective.

Bodies and fluids, especially bodily fluids, carry their own history of meaning. We not only have built-in cultural aversions to bodily waste products, but we also have visceral reactions when we come in contact with them. They play such an important role in our lives that we do not confine our talk of them to clinical matters, but rather refer to them constantly in everyday conversation when we disparage objects as "crap," and accuse our friends of "taking the piss"—our idioms have their own colorful and offensive history. Furthermore, when these fluids are placed in public, offensive associations begin to pour out. Andre Sarrano, Ron Athey, Robert Mapplethorp, Karen Finley, Tim Miller, John Fleck, and Holly Huges even became targets of the U.S. Congress in 1989 for including these bodily fluids in their works. Residual prejudice against the sensuous and bodily makes it difficult for us to appreciate and acknowledge the positive attributes that these types of stimuli can offer us in a theatrical context.

Our bodies can sense and react to pungent smells, viscous textures, and colorful liquids. We have a natural, as well as culturally conditioned, response to these sensations. As a consequence, smell is an essential way for us to situate ourselves in the environment. Theatrical artists use our experiential knowledge of these substances as their sensorial scenario. Their script is in the order and presentation of substances, shapes, smells, or actions that will trigger some sort of contingent repose within attendants. Not only do the bodies on stage speak and express, but also our bodies have some sort of contingent response to these stimuli. There may not be a rational understanding of what is occurring on stage, but the visceral experience provides the body with a possible way of understanding and participating in the performance.

In *Mama, I Can't Sing (part III)* (1996), Franko B constructs the environment using light, his body, and props such as cages, gurneys, chairs, braces, and medical paraphernalia. He further adds texture and coloring to these images by coating his body with effluvia, thus his white body stands out starkly against the fine red mist sprayed in the air. There is no conventional narrative, but the sequence of images triggers a visceral response within the attendant of the event. He uses his body as a sculptural form to be manipulated, painted upon and bound. It is a hybrid of live performance, live art, and a theatre of sensation. As each object is attached or inserted, our bodies are made to feel his discomfort:

> Our reactions to seeing naked, mutilated bodies, bodily fluids not seen in public and procedures usually reserved for the doctor's office become the text of the performance. By the time Franko's [manacled] body is placed in a cage, we begin to formulate feelings of helplessness within this, our uncertain and ever changing world.[30]

When speaking about this type of performance, the inevitable question is whether anyone ever stops these shows because these performers are mentally unstable. To transgress social boundaries immediately elicits a discussion of sanity. But there is something more at stake, a spiritual and moral transgression evoking ancient religious imagery. Stuart Morgan describes an earlier work:

> In a deep, murky space a naked man . . . makes his way towards a spotlight. As onlookers realize that he is already bleeding from both arms simultaneously, the mixture of powerful reactions is overwhelming— disgust and compassion certainly, but most of all powerlessness and inability to prevent the inevitable: a quick death . . . Arms dangling by his side and pools of blood starting to form at his feet, Franco adopts a pose which has long been commonplace in the religious art of the West. With palms held upwards, a powerful spotlight shining from above and an artificial mist hanging around his naked body, he seems to be imitating an accepted posture of the risen Christ of the New Testament.[31]

The violating of principles, conventions, pieties, or taboos thus gives serious offense. It takes transgressing the normal conventions of propriety to trigger the attentiveness of an attendant's sensory systems in a way that stimulates the reptilian systems, priming the brain to make new neural connections, thereby reconfiguring neural pathways away from habitual paths.

Going too far is an ethical necessity in today's society, because it encourages our natural biological processes to trigger changes in behavior and perception. It is difficult to give weight and consequence to an image or a concept because we are too inured by the barrage of graphic imagery each day; we have become desensitized to the world around us. When it is necessary to rebroadcast images of the twin towers burning and kidnapped foreigners in Iraq being executed, we are in a position where we must find ways to make the world around us tangible. Perhaps the only way to make the world around us real, the world saturated with Hollywood fantasies and prurient gratuitous sex and violence, is to reach attendants in proximity, and engage both their minds and bodies within the modes of theatrical trickery.

Returning to Artaud,

> One of the reasons for the asphyxiating atmosphere in which we live without possible escape or remedy—and in which we all share, even the most revolutionary among us—is our respect for what has been written, formulated, or painted, what has been given form, as if all expression were not at least exhausted, were not at a point where things must break apart if they are to start anew and begin fresh.[32]

Having been inoculated by a world mediated through the screen and remote communication, we are in as much need for public interaction and stimulation as ever. We can see it everywhere, from Nintendo's new products, which allow our body movements rather than buttons to control the figures in their games, to amusement park rides that bounce us around in a flight simulator and spray water in our faces as a virtual space war unfolds in front of our eyes. We see these attempts to create a sensory-rich environment geared to stimulate and titillate us.

As we become socialized within our various cultures, we strive to find a way to construct a fragile balance between our beliefs and others to live with those around us. As Louis Aragon relates, "Laws, moralities, aesthetics, have been created to make you respect fragile things. What is fragile should be broken."[33] It is our responsibility to transgress so that, out of the ashes, we can respect the power of nature and social obligations. The senses allow immediate access to the psyche, enabling the insidious changes that transgression provokes.

PERFORMANCE DESIGN AND SOCÌETAS RAFFAELLO SANZIO

Recent scientific research demonstrates that the fears of religious organizations and governments are warranted, for when audiences are presented with messages to which they are sympathetic, electrical activity within their brains becomes increasingly active. Familiar experiences strengthen our perception that our conception of the world is correct. Even more insidious are the means by which theatre practice can make use of our perceptual experience to shape our brain processes. Ironically, each time theatre practice has been forced to find ways around censorship and repression, we have honed the ways in which performance makes use of non-linguistic means to shape an attendant's perception of an event. Transgressive artists are able to speak to us through our senses, our emotions, and our pre-conscious experiences of the world, thus deranging the boundaries of monitored expression.

The scenographic elements of the theatrical event are the means by which the physical presence of the actor is shaped and given focus. The interplay of space, time, movement and light provide the actor with a playing space as well as affect the experience of attendants to a performance. In other words, the scenographic elements trigger visceral experiences by stimulating the five senses of the attendant. It is through this sensorial stimulation that embodied communication occurs and is available to the attentive attendant. What are the ways in which the elements and principles of design are made use of, through invisible and intangible ways, to convey that which cannot be uttered? SRS' *Tragedia Endogonidia* demonstrates the ways in which the non-verbal elements of design transgress conventions to affect us. By confounding our expectations of how we respond to theatrical expression, SRS speaks to our preconscious minds by manipulating our experience before we can make sense of what is occurring.

Performance design is an active conception of design, replacing the notion of static art with "the dynamic principle of embodied spatio-temporal event."[34] The fabrication of a theatrical event is more than the analysis of a dramatic text as executed by directors, designers, and actors; it is a dynamic blending of concept, performance, and reception. As Dorita Hannah and Olav Harslof define:

> As a loose and inclusive term Performance Design asserts the role of artists/ designers in the conception and realization of events, as well as their awareness of how design elements not only actively extend the performing body, but also perform without and in spite of the human body. . . . Acknowledging that places and things precede action—as action—is critical to performance design as an aesthetic practice and an event-based phenomenon. In harnessing the dynamic forces inherent to environments and objects, and insisting on co-creative audience as participatory players, it provides a critical tool to reflect, confront and realign worldviews.[35]

By broadening the definition of the elements of performance to include the places and use of space as intrinsic to creating a context within which to understand the performing body, we are able to consider performance design in the framework of action potential. In each situation in which we find ourselves, we look to the environment for ways to actively engage in it and respond. It is this context that allows the sights, sounds, smells, and other sensations we experience to have meaning, whether implicit or explicit. The performance design of the episodes of *Tragedia* makes apparent the space in between communication, where myriad silent transgressions beyond our conscious attention seep into our experience of the world. Founding members Claudia Castellucci, Romeo Castellucci, and Chiara Guidi work together with their production team to compose dynamic compositions that are a blend of image, sound, sculpture, and narrative that demand the collaboration of the attendants. Daniel Sacs describes their work as "a theatre of sensation, where lights, sound, and the entire theatrical apparatus become actors on the 'stage' of a spectator's body."[36] SRS stimulates the attendant's body and brain by way of the shapes, sounds, movements, and images that they present. Castellucci conceives of the design of his performances as an embodied spatio-temporal event: "Every sensible element is to be perceived and considered through the drastic mentality of the tragic: lights, voices, spaces and bodies are there, before us, and they show us all of the strangeness, all of the stupidity, all of the foreignness of the 'theatre' support."[37] The theatre is a medium whose conventions can be manipulated for rhetorical purposes of transforming representation into experience, thereby potentially affecting attendants from within.

Composed in various cities across Europe over a several year period, *Tragedia* is made up of eleven episodes that explore the nature of tragic conception. Few were able to witness the entire cycle, thereby calling into question whether any one episode could be defined as definitive. However, the event transformed over time as a result of the incorporation of local references, as well as the local reactions from attendants. Castellucci describes this as a form of pollination:

> A characteristic of this project on tragedy is that it changes from city to city, therefore it is in the process of becoming, but besides being in a process of becoming it's an organism in continual flux, so the performance is never the same; but that's no reason to call it a work in progress. Because it really appears to be the opposite; every time it opens for an audience, it's a finished and complete production that supplies, within itself, the mechanism of endogonidial reproduction, a division of itself, a sort of fall-out of spores, which provide for the future and successive growth.[38]

Each episode disseminated pollen in the form of the elements of production into the wind to find receptive hosts for the content's maturation. How we respond to the instigations of the event is dependent upon our active participation. Each segment is filled with often obscure references, such as texts objectively derived from the goat's body sign, or more recognizable stories, such as those from history. To those who are not part of the coterie, performances can appear to be deranged. However, cultural references aside, even uninitiated attendants have a way in. Castellucci explains, "Although *Tragedia* can also be seen by someone who knows absolutely nothing of this. The first level of involvement is cortical, in my opinion: it takes place in the cerebral cortex. You are there as a sentient being before an event." [39] By being attendant to the way the sights, sounds, vibrations, and air feel, we come away with a visceral understanding of what transpired, even if we cannot make conscious sense of it all. Guidi describes the ways in which attendant presence is evocative:

I think atmosphere is the radical dramaturgy, and, at root, it is about knowing where you are, in what atmosphere. The question of which atmosphere is the problem of light and the problem of sound which can (by means of either their absence or their presence) create this type of atmosphere. So, above everything, there is an inspired dramaturgy, of place, of where you are. [40]

It is the physical qualities of scenographic representation that carry the dramaturgical journey. The resulting performance is transgressive because it violates the boundaries between performance and attendance; the elements trigger our senses to resonate as if we are instruments being played by the performance.

In effect, what this means for attendants is that they must consider each episode on its own, dissecting its form, content, and barrage of stimulation according to its performance. What can I make sense of in this seemingly obscure presentation? For Guidi, the process begins with the attendant's active translation of the elements of performance into something sensible. She contends:

Each show inaugurates a language of its own. Each episode has its own narration, or reinvention of a narration. I can recount what I have seen on stage. This becomes a dramaturgical fact. The act of telling. I can write down what I saw. That is an act of dramaturgy. I can write a theatrical text after, or according to what I saw. This I count as a pure dramaturgical act, arising from the elimination of the chorus: work thus inaugurating a new dramaturgical language. Every show has its own dramaturgical language. I believe the rhythm may be, in *Tragedia Endognidia*, the dramaturgical language of each episode. Each episode has its rhythm. Each episode is recognizable by means of its rhythm. [41]

Sensibility comes from creating one's own through-line, whether it is a narrative in each episode or finding sense in the pace and rhythm of the images and sounds. Although this sounds rather abstract, the process is made concrete through the attentive monitoring of one's sensations and connecting those to the recognizable cultural referents to art, history, and literature. What are the signs that can be identified and how did the experience through time of searching for those signs make us feel? Whereas the overtly recognizable signs of a Pulcinella figure, mythical characters, and images drawn from art history can be readily grasped, the insidious feelings and emotions that are generated within the attendant during exposure to the theatrical event add another layer of fleeting communication not easily grasped or identified.

From Castellucci's perspective, he has to negotiate between what he produces on stage and the responses he gets from attendants. To do this, he takes advantage of the time element where bodies and objects move through space, and he has the literal expressive presence of the live body of the actor. He argues:

> Two "temperatures," two expressive registers, are present: on the one hand the logical structure of the movement principle and on the other the body and its truths, which is the most concise form of communication possible and also the most disconcerting, the most pointed. The body is the simplest form of communication, in the sense that even an animal understands you since it's in a position to see you, hear you, and smell you. The body is the point of departure and probably also the point of arrival, after having completed an ellipse, after having also passed through and shaken the body of the spectator.[42]

Theatrical expression in its barest form takes advantage of our ability to respond to the expressive capabilities of other humans through their gesture, movement, and expression. This extends to the personification of objects and animals as well. Making use of these basic ingredients places us in a position to smell, see, and hear the actor, thereby activating our sensory web. If we are attentive to the objects and expressions that generate feelings and emotions, then we might begin to grasp the potential of the senses as extensions to the literal narrative of performance. SRS arranges the components of composition to attract the brain's attention and imbed the experience in the memory. The expressive capabilities of the actor are projected to the attendants who make sense of what is happening according to their own experiences. This reception is through the body. From the perspective of the actor, the presence of attendants is a feedback loop for their expression.[43] SRS intuitively exploits the fact that each new experience encountered creates neuronal pathways that have the potential to transform the brain.

The design of *Tragedia* made efforts to compose the elements and principles of design to affect attendant's embodied processes. Castellucci explains that the sonic vibrations begin before the attendants even reach their seats, and many will be made so uncomfortable that they will want to leave. This sound will have a direct effect because we cannot escape its stimulation because we cannot shut out the vibrations of sound. He continues:

> When everybody is seated a video-projection starts on a white screen that covers the stage space. It should be a projection capable of getting into the brain and playing with the cerebral cortex. We've been trying out a range of very fast sequences of complementary lights such as red–blue, green–red, that might provoke an induced emotion. We need something very optical, something cold, as if an experiment or a test were being carried out on the entire audience.[44]

Moment by moment, each attendant's sensory system will be offered an array of stimuli in hopes that neuronal activity will light up the brain. Traditional conceptions of the aims of performance are a byproduct rather than a goal. He details:

> It's the spectator's encephalon that is interesting here, not his soul (that comes later). I've tried to introduce a few frames of letters of the alphabet, in white, into the very fast colour sequence, anticipating the appearance of the "letters box" later. . . . something fast and 'bad' that might capture the spectator's eye and put his cerebral cortex to a severe test. Something like perceptive tests or brain tricks. I've tried introducing subliminal shapes, drawings of everyday things, but they look too slow (I can't get below 1/25 of a second). This first part needs to be scientifically disturbing and aggressive.[45]

This stimulation is not restricted to sound, color, and movement. Bodies, or automaton proxies, are used as a further layer to make the abstract expression concrete in physical terms. They make use of theatrical mimesis to bombard the attendants with a bewildering array of stimuli. Castellucci hypothesized how they could further aggressively disturb the attendants' sensibilities:

> One further image that could be introduced . . . right after the bombing of the colours, is an epileptic who flings himself about on the floor. I'm thinking of a mannequin, whose spasms are human at first and then become more and more frantic until they seem bestial; although the public mustn't be able to tell for sure that the mannequin is powered by compressed air.[16]

The effects confuse the attendants' sensory systems, leaving them unsure of what they have experienced.

The confluence of sight, hearing, and movement is important because when we remember a theatrical experience, we do not merely remember the words spoken. Joe Kelleher describes his reaction to the stimuli of episode *C#1*:

> The room is darkened, and the sound becomes assaultive, fixated upon the pumping beat of what might be the theatre's own respiratory system. This sound touches us too it seems, intimately, somatically, each of us in our own blood. The repetitive beat is like something knocking for entrance at the door of my sensations, insistent, unforgiving, an experience exacerbated by the projection on screen of a random alphabetic inscriptions which, as the projections accelerate, speed into a strobic blur of blots and splatterings. . . . But this is a language we barely know how to play with yet.[47]

Whereas we can access fleeting sensations for a few moments after experiencing them, what we remember long term is how the performance felt, or the sounds of the battering-ram swinging back and forth in SRS' installation in Avignon. The physical surroundings of performances remain in our minds as much as anything else. Like the students who attended *Gulio Cesare* who were going to have nightmares for a month, they may not have been able to recognize the art references, but there were stimuli that promoted these negative feelings and emotions, and through those perceptions, they understood the horror of the war that ensued after Caesar's death. We can identify some of the images that made us uneasy like the sound of Mark Anthony's tracheotomist inhalation and how it made us squirm, whereas in another we can only get a sense that the vibrations from the aural feedback made us uneasy. All of those sights, smells, and touches shaped our brains and our expectations of the world through embodiment.

It is what the stimuli do to attendants that make up the silent transgressions. Guida describes how the sounds are deliberate:

> A lot of the sounds we've found are sounds that shift the hearing, as if the ears might turn up in the heart, or in the stomach, or outside the body, as if the ears themselves were a body, equipped with movement and gravity. Often it felt as if my body were without ears, until I found them again, here, in this part of my body, or there, or further up or further down. My ears felt like bodies detached from me, responding to the provocations of my voice. I could see them clearly, or rather I felt myself as an ear. My voice was another's voice, and with my voice I could feel, for a moment, the vanishing of sounds that had barely been audible. My voice was a memory of hidden sounds. My voice was water and fire. I've been using the sound of some bones, and it sounds like the skeleton rising up against the flesh.[48]

These stimuli transformed her body-map, changing her for a moment into something other than human. Her transformation allowed her brain to perceive the world in an unfamiliar fashion, thus laying the ground work for her brain to shape new perceptions of the world based on this transformed body image. As one becomes cognizant of SRS' visceral vocabulary, the more one's brain creates neuronal pathways that become excited by these types of non-verbal stimuli. The performances become ingrained in our memories.

The process of transmission and reception works in three steps: 1. the introduction of a representation; 2. the attendant's response to the representation; 3. the blurring of sensation and response. A moment in the Brussels episode, where fake blood is poured from a bottle while a beating takes place, demonstrates the transformation of a staged representation into an embodied experience for attendants. The moment is a form of montage where sounds of beating are intertwined with the action of a beating, and as the rhythms increase and empathetic responses are welling up in the attendants, the fake blood becomes real. We know the blood is a representation of blood, but we respond as if it is real because of its relationship to the action. Guidi reasons:

> Since the bottle enters into direct relation with the audience, because the audience recognize it, it is a very clear message for the audience, look at me opening the bottle, emptying it onto the ground. So, by means of this bottle, I communicate information to the audience. This information has the clarity of immediate communication between the person thinking the thought and the audience who see this thought. What happens?[49]

At first, the action is straightforward: Here is a character calmly pouring red liquid on the stage while another character is beaten. Out of context, the image appears obscure; however, as the sounds and rhythms of the beating impinge upon the attention of the attendants, it transforms into something new. We begin to feel empathetic responses to the characters. She continues:

> The audience follows this path of information. At a certain point, it feels the need to say, during the beating, enough, I don't want to see any more, it upsets me; enough, it's too much. Something happens that moves above and beyond logic, beyond thought, beyond that immediate communication that makes us all peaceful and tranquil and replaces it with an emotional aspect. An emotional aspect takes over. Emotional, rather than sentimental, in the sense that an emotion comes that makes you say, it's too much, enough, it's upsetting. From the first blow, you feel pain in your back, the first blow gives you a sensation of your own bones breaking. What's happening? Where is the idea in this scene? The idea is not in the original communication which was the opening of the bottle, but neither is it in the literal representation of a beating, so where is the idea?[50]

Each part of the scene is intertwined with the attention and reception of the attendants. These theatrical actions are processed by the body and mind of the attendant as if they are real because of our active empathy with the beaten character. Guidi observes:

> It is in the fact that the public, at the end of all this, says, have mercy, the theatre has taken me in. In the sense that there is this optic of the theatre and my body, my mind has not been able to react to this image with the same cool and lucidity with which I said look, let us open the bottle, let's empty it on the floor. I am sliding, I've fallen into representation, but not by a logical route which was the logic of opening the bottle. I have crashed emotionally into a representation that has neither narrative nor logical context. [51]

These conventional theatrical devices lead us to actively blur fiction and reality and become engrossed in sensation. Literal actions become more than the sum of their parts because of the embodied nature of their processing and reception by the attentive attendant.

To blur our experience of the everyday with the experience of mimesis challenges our assumptions of the ways in which we interpret theatrical experience. It becomes a fusion of active attentiveness and rational contemplation. Michael Taussig confronted this in his description of the world as a nervous system. He explains a physiological frame with which to know the world:

> But what sort of sense is constitutive of this everydayness? Surely this sense includes much that is not sense so much as sensuousness, an embodied and somewhat automatic "knowledge" that functions like peripheral vision, not studied contemplation, a knowledge that is imageric and sensate rather than ideational; as such it not only challenges practically all critical practice, across the board, of academic disciplines but is a knowledge that lies as much in the objects and spaces of observation as in the body and mind of the observer. What's more, this sense has an activist, contructivist bent; not so much contemplative as it is caught in *media res* working on, making anew, amalgamating, acting and reacting. [52]

If we sense the world in an active way, our knowledge can be seen as embodied and defying mere logical expression. Our body receives sensory data as if casting a net out in the water, trolling for significant data. As it focuses on stimuli, it begins to perceive and form predications about the world according to our preconscious assumptions about the world. Paying attention to what makes us respond can enrich our experience of the world and, in turn, enrich our experience of mimetic representation. To attend the theatre is to offer oneself as a vessel in which creation may ferment. The knowledge that performance can instill is dynamic because it is embodied. To participate is to be attentive. Castellucci asserts creation's inevitability:

There is nothing you need beyond the pleasure of being there. It confirms your own decision about going to the theatre. And, when you leave the theatre, there is a superstructure that continues to grow, and that burns you, like a fire, and whose logic is this: you burn me, and I cannot *not* burn. This fire cannot be calmed, as if it had touched something outside of my reason, outside of my conception. There is no consolation of any sort. I have understood nothing, except that this is the situation in which I find myself. This, I believe, is the future of theatre.[53]

Our presence is generative and ensures that theatrical expression will carry on because once it is experienced it lives within our memories.

SRS' adaptation of Louis-Ferdinand Céline's *Voyage au bout de la nuit* (1932) is another example of the multiple sensorial tracks that the company employs to evoke expression. Céline's novel is a semi-autobiographical picaresque that follows its protagonist across continents from job to job through WWI and its aftermath, and satirizes, among other things, scientific research and the medical profession. Experimental in form, it is written as natural speech making use of vernacular language, excesses of hyperbole, and ellipses. Timothy Scheie describes SRS' adaptation as a concerto of music and images in six movements. Its first section is performed by four performers that "whispered, clucked, groaned, and shrieked fragments of Céline's text in tightly orchestrated rhythms, weaving the words into abstract tonalities and percussive noise."[54] Sounds created a mood to augment the images that were presented. The two-dimensional qualities of Celine's work were brought into three-dimensions to be experienced by the proximal attendants. Images were collaged with sound and moved through space in the form of objects and actors' bodies that moved across the stage. Scheie describes the contrast between the "restrained tension of the opening" and a deluge of video images whose significant noise became a "barrage of noise and light."[55] This sequence of stimuli consisting of text, noise, image, and effect encapsulated Celine's narrative structures. Narrative prose was made manifest through theatrical means to give form to linguistic games. The performance drove attendants to distraction. Rather than describe images by way of language, the performance design played upon the attendant's sensations. Scheie notes its effect: "The net result was a dizzying assault on both mind and senses that kept the spectators in a constant state of discomfiture and confusion."[56] He felt that this was a faithful adaptation that captured the distinctive stylistic elements through scenographic means, thus capturing "the chaotic horror of modern society, but also the bewildered realization that life on earth doggedly continues nonetheless."[57] This style made apparent SRS' interpretation of the novel and its subsequent reception. Attendants had to wade through the confusion and discomfort to make sense of the novel, the adaptation, and their own conscious interpretation of what they witnessed. As reviews show, multiple narratives were available and supplied critics with plausible interpretations.

However, what happens when it doesn't burn us? In other words, what happens when attendants resist willing complicity with the production and rebel? One recurring question with the reception of the avant-garde concerns the willingness of the attendants to participate. What happens when the instigations of the performers are rejected or framed not as experience? Scheie emphasizes that most admonished the production: "Harsh on both eyes and ears, semiotically dense to the point of opacity, it was less a nightmare than a tiresome test of endurance."[58] Attendants booed and fled rather than remain for the duration. If attendants refuse to be attentive to the experience, then what remains of the event? When it comes down to it, the ways in which we receive, process, and interpret stimuli are shaped by the complicity of the perceiver. Alva Noë suggests that action potential is just a potential that depends on the receiver's active involvement with cultivating the stimuli into a meaningful action.[59]

As cultural views of cognition state,

> It is common knowledge that different individuals see the same thing in different ways. Each selects, emphasizes, and values different components of an experience. When a continuous stream of stimulation is broken into discrete events, it is not uncommon for two individuals watching the same series of events to disagree as to whether some particular event even occurred.[60]

However, that intrinsic truth does not negate the fact that the two individuals experienced the same stimuli. How each of us engages the stimuli gives us our own perspective, as well as allows for a broad range of interpretations from a given set of stimuli. To provoke sensuously is to speak to attendants intimately, appealing to our senses to respond to the triggers that give us the most pleasure, or that seem the most relevant to us. Take, for instance, a demonstration by researchers where groups were shown videos of athletes passing balls. They were told to count the number of passes that the athletes make. In completing the task, most of the participants did not see a large figure dressed as an ape frolicking in the center of the picture. The action of counting balls directed them to disregard distractions and their attention filtered out the ape, which they did not expect to see. A performance can misdirect our attention, as it did with the magic show, so that we will not perceive. Artists direct our attention so that they may achieve a result. How we interpret that result is dependent upon our own personal experiences of the world, as well as our own willingness to participate in the experience.

Scientific research is far from consistent in findings. There are arguments between the different branches of research, suggesting often contradictory conclusions based on similar material. If we solely rely on stimuli and our responses, we cannot account for those who resist taking the journey with the performances. Bruce Wexler explains:

> Observation of everyday life events and laboratory experiments make it clear that perceptual mechanisms operate in such a way as to select and value sensory input that is consonant with already existing internal structures, thus increasing the degree to which the external world is experienced as consistent with the internal one. Other studies have demonstrated a motivated component in actions that increase this consonance. People experience familiar stimuli as more pleasurable than unfamiliar ones, and experience conflict between their actions and their beliefs as unpleasant.[61]

We are resistant to new experiences, therefore we often select details that reassert our view of the world despite evidence to the contrary. When a company such as SRS provokes us, resistance can trigger adverse reactions that do not jibe with the form and structure of the event. That does not deny that the event can be understood in a coherent way, but rather it emphasizes the necessity of the attendant's willing active perception of the event.

Another experiment tested whether we could be influenced to have a positive affective preference to something based on familiarity. Researchers planted unfamiliar Turkish words in university newspapers to show that repeated exposure will lead to a preference to some object. Wexler describes:

> The words appeared daily for several weeks without explanation. Over time, some of the words were printed only once, others twice, and the rest 5, 10, or 25 times. Words presented frequently in one newspaper were presented infrequently in the other. Afterwards, students . . . were asked . . . to indicate which words they liked better . . . the students preferred the words that had appeared in the paper most frequently, despite not knowing what the words meant or why they were in the paper.[62]

If stimuli are presented enough times, even if we resist, the stimuli will become familiar. As provoking techniques become commonplace, we accept them and become an expected facet of reality.

In effect, we train what we are attentive to and the ways that we understand the resulting information. We discriminate between stimuli to find the most pleasurable and concordant effects. When our expectations are disrupted, we are unsettled. As Wexler describes:

> The world presents an immensely rich and varied stream of stimulation (information) to the individual. Internal neural structures are created that correspond to those aspects of environmental stimulation that are most commonly experienced by a particular individual. These

structures then limit, shape, and focus perception on the aspects of the information stream that are most like themselves. This increases the sense of correspondence between the external world and the internal one, and progressively limits the power of sensory stimulation to change the structures. Concordance between external stimulation and the internal structure is experienced as pleasurable, and individuals preferentially place themselves in situations in which the incoming stimulation is likely to be in agreement with their internal structure. When discordant information is encountered, that information is ignored, discredited, re-interpreted, or forgotten.[63]

We choose our entertainments with the expectation that they will reassert our world view. We are complicit in the amount of involvement that we can have with a given theatrical event. To a hostile attendant, SRS is obscure and boring; to another, a masterwork; and to another, an example of whatever analytic tool that might be in fashion.

Jim Williams breaks down the different triggers of sensory stimulation used in *Hey Girl!'s* (2008) performance design. There are few set pieces onstage. A table, column and windows were supplemented with video projections. He describes SRS' use of montage, tableaux, and aural cues as:

> Artaudian vibrating, pulsating, and, at times, ear-splitting electronic sounds and music. . . . [where] visual and aural scenes culminated as sensory evocations of a young woman's conformity and nonconformity to cultural and societal norms, explorations of struggles between power and oppression, as well as the suppression of individuality.[64]

He goes further and applies a feminist lens after classifying the sensory barrage he experienced. Williams' description made sense of the images, substances, and montages by providing a narrative of the actions. When she was born, she emerged "from a wet, reddish plastic goo substance on top of a long rectangular table. Breathing in heavy rhythmic pants and bursts, [She] struggled to break free of the wet slime as she lifted herself off the table, laboring to maintain balance."[65] Citing breathing, textures, fabrics, actions, and movements as made manifest by the actress, Williams was able to construct an iconic persona, noting her actions that indicated an examination of gender, such as applying lipstick and kneeling before a broadsword, because of the context in which he was attentive to the action. In another setting, this might be a burlesque show or a horror movie. What enabled Williams to read into this action in this particular way were his cultural and political views of the representations of female gender. His preferences for a gendered reading focused his attention on the detail of the performance that supported his view. Had another attendant been there to judge, the same stimuli may have been read differently as parody, as cliché, or as pornography. How he felt and made sense of the event shows as much about him as it does the potential expression that SRS designed. Though they may have guided an attentive attendant to this reading, the stimuli hit their mark differently with each attendant according to his or her own social and cultural background, and familiarity with the practices and traditions of the avant-garde.

At first blush, SRS is unlike your average West End play. However, it makes use of text, image, actors, and sound in rather mundane ways to create a world of make-believe. Mario Jacques articulates the assumptions that most hold about the theatrical element that most captures the attendant's attention. He speculates:

> The actor, who is undoubtedly the focus of the spectator's attraction, acts within a universe of extremely complex elements. These include elements of a visual nature, such as the stage setting and of performance and all types of visual elements which relate to the performance; and elements of an audio nature, including music sheets, or noises reproducing realistic or atmospheric sounds, which make up what is generally described as the performance soundtrack; or sounds that, while not included in the original plan, wrap themselves around the performance and occasionally interfere with it, whether they come from the audience or outside the theatre itself. . . . The actor himself is also a universe of meaningful elements, both audio, through words, sounds and noises produced, and visual through the way the actor's body occupies the space, through his gestures, and facial expressions (which are bound to express his emotions). But the meaningful elements that the actor expresses do not have the same material nature as the other elements. A recorded sound may be maintained, so too may a lighting effect, a stage setting, a phrase, a body.[66]

The material aspects of performance remain, whereas the fleeting moment-to-moment evocations of the actor's glance and the attendants' responses dissipate. It is important to note that even the most fantastic images and virtual experiences can be perceived as real even though they are imaginary. Nicholas Ridout argues that "this tendency to see the 'real' in the work of Socìetas Raffaello Sanzio is in fact an effect of the success of their theatrical pretending."[67] Theatrical pretend still evokes within the attendant strange and unfamiliar experiences that are perceived as if they are real. We are willing to accept that they are plausible extensions of our experience of the world. This cathartic engagement allows us to be transported into an alternate reality from our own. For a few hours, we merge with the fantasies of the artists. It does not matter whether we are walking through an installation, listening to music, or watching a play, we wholeheartedly engage in make-believe, which stimulates our bodies and brains. Theatre, performance, and art merge into potential realities within which we can get lost. I am not advocating naturalistic performance, but rather that, in the creation of make-believe, we harness the mind's propensity to seek out sensorial stimulation to make the theatrical or performative event more engaging.

We are fascinated with human bodies. As James Elkins argues, we are constantly searching out human presences and see bodies even when there are none.[68] The body onstage is our fascination; while we experience them in real time, they can also be acts of fiction. Whereas avant-garde performance can be off-putting, at its heart it makes familiar techniques strange to challenge us to break free from our expected comfort zone and try and experience the world from a different perspective to see what it reveals. SRS mixed the real and the artificial in deliberate ways. Ridout describes his attendance of *Giulio Cesare* as feeling

> like an encounter with something absolutely alien, unlike any theatre I had ever witnessed before. The obvious explanation for this might be offered in terms of the real, live horse, the emaciated bodies of the two women playing Brutus and Cassius, the visceral impact of an actor playing Mark Antony without a larynx, the sheer volume of the wrestler in the role of Cicero, not to mention the extraordinary experience of being shown another person's vocal cords. The overwhelming sense of an encounter with something strange and powerful would be attributed to the impact of all this 'real' stuff.[69]

Ridout goes on to explain that none of what he experienced was, in fact, real. Each example was displayed in a complex system of representation. The event's success lay in its effectiveness at triggering our sensory system to perceive the elements it encountered as real. The event encouraged our willing suspension of skepticism in favor of responding viscerally to the semblance of a body. On a neuronal level, our empathetic responses were firing, we read light and shadow as movement, and we considered it in the context of experiences that we needed to monitor.

Ridout argues for considering the "real" before we neglect the true potential of the power of make-believe. His attentiveness to SRS' theatricality is a testament to the mastery of their performance design. He analyzes its effects:

> The tendency in critical responses to the work to emphasise the "real" as opposed to the pretend is testimony to the success of the pretending. The theatre is working; it is making us take its make-believe for real. The intensity of the encounter was produced by the fact that I had never seen anyone else taking the imitation game so seriously. It was as though no other theatre had considered that it might be possible to make representations that might be taken for the real thing; as though no one else believed that the theatre might be a kind of magic.[70]

Successful theatre has the potential to play with and trick our perception. It is our active complicity with this process that gives theatre its power. We willingly give ourselves over to play and be tricked, thus exercising our ability to remain flexible in our responses to the world. When we stop allowing ourselves to interact with art in this way, it becomes powerless and we become inflexible, unable to appreciate the magic of theatre.

Noë posits that

> What governs the character of our experience—what makes experience the kind of experience it is—is not the neural activity in our brains on its own; it is, rather, our ongoing dynamic relation to objects, a relation that, as in this case, clearly depends on our neural responsiveness to changes in our relation to things.[71]

By monitoring our relationship to the action on stage, we are able to slip into a state of play and respond to the stimulation of the theatrical event. Our dynamic relationship to the art object is central to its effectiveness. We are able lose ourselves in a fiction and experience it as if it was real because our brains make it possible. It is one of the things that separate us from other animals. If we allow it to change us, it can. But how much of our experiences of theatre really stay with us?

FLEETING FRAGMENTS OF SHARED EXPERIENCE

At its heart, live performance, though fleeting, is the moment-to-moment shared experience between the performers and the attendant. The artist introduces unfamiliar thoughts and sensations into the attendant's sensory system by shaping a provoking event. An attendant's reception of the stimuli presented transforms the material into perceptions and in turn they are shaped and articulated by conscious thoughts. These unfamiliar stimuli trigger the attendant to react and adapt to the new information. Artists are able to shape these responses by transgressing habitual expectations, thereby stretching the brain's capacity to understand. The body responds by adapting to situation and making it possible to readily deal with similar stresses in the future. Processes of adaptation are common in biological responses to the world. Whether lifting a weight or practicing a dance step, the stimulation triggers the body to adapt and change to handle changing stimuli. Whereas it is difficult to chart the stimuli that have induced adaptation, in the healthy brain, the muscle memories, or in the case of performance, the attendant's conscious memories, are remnants of the triggers. We are like archives, preserving fragments of data that will be adapted to cope with future encounters, if needed. These fragments are hard to pin down, and as a result, the remnants, byproducts, and acts of memory produced by performance and live art are problematic to the cultural historian. Whereas the genre of production makes use of strategies derived from visual art, music, dance, and theatre, these works resist traditional historiographic techniques because there is no durable art object to hinge our interpretations upon, only fleeting fragments that seem to be concrete. This structural dissolution is a conscious strategy that resists the exigencies of comodification and analysis. The resulting traces of the events are neither evidence nor theory, but rather collections of fragments that commingle with the rhetoric of each attendant and most often are appropriated for theoretical, conceptual, or artistic products. Thereby, the preservation or description of a time-based artistic creation becomes a process of continual adaptation after the life of the event.

The project of live art documentation is a process wherein production and reception are configured to historicize the avant-garde and impel others to transgress the boundaries of rigid genre, and is a parallel to the processes by which the body makes use of the data it perceives. Archives are places or vessels designed as tools to facilitate the retrieval of fragments. It is the archivist's system of preservation that is like our biological systems. Though the archival building is constant, the archives can be shuffled and used in unexpected ways if the need arises. Their contents may be nothing but scraps of paper until someone comes in and begins to put them into a formula or a system of thought. Without material such as plays traditionally claimed as theatrical remnants, we lose our ability to systematically analyze and recreate with the confidence of scholarly traditions. Matthew Goulish describes the inadequacies of the archive as an accurate record of live art:

> We may think of this problem as a kind of illness characterized by one symptom: Swiss cheese. It forms whenever we try to say something with the material the 20th century has bequeathed us: we find files missing, pages missing, words missing, memories missing, or holes in our ability to listen.[72]

We suffer from an inability to document performance in a comprehensive way. All we get is another product, another day, another utterance changed forever by the constant flow of the river of time. As residue builds on the banks, it changes the path of the river. The act of preservation is an impure process. By its nature it is incomplete. Increasingly, the holes are filled in through the mediation of a third party that is removed from the creation process and from the primary experience.

It is the machine of the theorist's mind that shuffles the data until he finds a frame in which to make rational the material. As Michael Kobialka theorizes,

> I would like to shift the discussion regarding the historical archive from evaluating its position or function vis-à-vis academic research towards perceiving the archive as a medium of thinking, or as the general system of the formation and transformation of statements as Foucault would

have it. That is to say, the archive as a historiographic practice should not be defined as a place (de Certeau's "place" as opposed to "space") housing a text of what was uttered, but as a moment of enunciation of the taking place of the formation and transformation of statements.[73]

The activation of the formation and transformation is instigated by the chemical processes of the attendant's mind. Categorization, memory making, and activation come from the data's interaction with, and relationship to, its moment of explication, which in turn allows a fragment of a performance to become a part of a new whole. Archival material comes to life as part of the articulation and enunciation of its existence in some other state.

An archive's contents are a potential story. It does not matter how insignificant the object; live art and performance art are notoriously fleeting, leaving little to trace. Its performance is inscribed upon the body of the performer or in small art objects—emerging from the lived experience of the moment. Nothing besides the moment is the event. Its instant destruction is inevitable; its effect and how it affects other people is more important. The fragments of the attendant's memory—a photograph, a review, or description of the event—are corpses that stimulate the transmission of an idea into the future. Although the fragments are preserved in files, they remain a potential trigger.

One afternoon, I came upon a book of photographs depicting a crypt in Palermo, Sicily, that I have vivid memories of visiting as a child. I remember the rows of priests whose clothed corpses still had hair and eyes; and I remember especially little baby Maria with her rosy cheeks, though she has been dead for a century. These bodies have lingered in my memory for thirty years. Besides the photographs, the book contains a peculiar essay written as a first person account of tending the dead, apparently from the mouth of a caretaker whom we learn has been interred there himself for fifty years. He describes being in the crypt, what the space has been, and what it has been to the people who have visited. He tells us stories of the people/corpses that inhabit the space. He tells of the Talkers (visitors who hear the dead speak).

As the caretaker hopes,

> Every morning I tell this story, I know it by heart, line after line. I tell it over hoping that some day a real Talker will be born, able to listen to what a dead person really has to say. A Talker—a patient one—who will be capable to distinguishing his voice from mine; who will take a chair and sit next to me with pen and paper in his hand. I have many things to say—death has taught me a lot.[74]

Like the corpses of the crypt in Palermo, the cadavers of performance have potential tales to tell if only someone with the ability to hear can listen. The work only is preserved in the form of fragments that will be adapted as they reconfigure into new thoughts spreading from attendant to attendant in airports and hotel lobbies across the world. More people will experience the effects of the artwork than the actual event. Aware that this instant decay is caused by the fleeting quality of performance and leaves little to commodify, its transformative quality is embraced by the practitioner; for we are all mini-archives, all mini-typewriters spitting out memories, creating our own view of art, history, and preservation. What and how we preserve changes it forever. As the caretaker describes, the skin of the corpses in his care have petrified and cracked, their clothes have rotted. They are but mere shells of the bodies that walked, talked, and sweated. But to some—the Talkers—these are stories floating in the air waiting to be heard:

> Shall I tell my story? Shall I tell something that has been haunting me since I first set foot down here? But how to weave a tale that lacks a plot and is merely a trace, nothing but an absence of time? Albeit that time has deeply impressed its mark here, inscribing it on these clothes and memories of these dear deceased who died in the past centuries.[75]

These relics of our past speak to us, telling us what we want to hear. They excite our imagination. But is not the point to forget the details and move forward into the future, changed? Like the details of Barthes' mother's life—are not we meant to forget the details?[76] Why should we remember all the bright ideas and trials and tribulations everyone else has experienced—would we not lose the delusion of our own uniqueness?

Take, for example, these catacombs where the bodies of the nobility line the walls of a crypt arranged by century, gender, and age. They are more like reliquary removed from the homes in churches and preserved in a museum basement than bodies interred in the church vault. How can we describe this living installation of death? What are the stories that these dead tell? It is rather apt to think of the crypt as a metaphor for thinking about the documentation process of live art, of archiving, and critiquing the activity. A grave or a sepulcher is a place where bodies have been preserved with their costumes—a place that suggests stories—but are irreclaimable. The stories of the lives of each body died with the body. They are vessels of the past, closed to us, but forever unknowable because we do not have their memories to give substance to the stories that they suggest. These relics are the way in which the dead live with us, rotting and full of holes.

I have mixed feelings about archives. I have used them, I have drawn from them. I have traveled thousands of miles to pour through them in large chunks of time. I dive into a swimming pool of material and take away fragments and perceptions, pouring them into my container to see what it becomes. Thousands of fragments separated from the whole of performance, pieced together to create some new creature. This creature spawns. New adaptations emerge triggering the original creation to spawn as ideas, explanations, or ideals. Remembrance is an adaptation. This adaptation metamorphoses into written work. I prefer to think of myself as an individual perceiver of the fragments of creation; that within, these fragments take root and grow into something else—words, theory, memory, speculation. I like basking in the bits, digging up fragments of memory and putting together a conception of a puzzle.

Tim Etchells describes the impulse to preserve and its effect upon the reception of the original work:

> That documentation of live events is an attempt at capture, a dragging down of the ephemeral into the fossilizing mud of all that is fixed and fixing. That documentation commodifies—again, shaping into static and saleable object-form an art-practice which resists the market. That giving way to documents (and analysis) artists are losing hold of their work—that the voices of academia posit readings over which artists have no control, readings which claim a single authority and readings which distance viewers from the work itself.[77]

Any attempt to capture the work changes it into something else—a new generation that differs from the original. Each attempt distances the world from the event. It perverts any potential experience of the work itself. In a way it destroys the work—yet any act of creation is an act of transformation. The stimulus adapts to the world around it. Each chemical reaction is forever modified. Etchells attempts to capture his work to control the dissemination of its interpretation. He would rather capture the spirit or thought process of the creation of the work than try to reproduce or explain the work itself.

Etchells explains the inadequateness of his printed playscripts in understanding what the performances were like:

> These texts are ghosts. They were made in the midst of clumsy and long performance-making processes—in the midst of group rehearsal and improvisation, soundtrack-making, "choreography," argument and set-building. They were not made for other people to "do" them, and they were never really meant to stand alone. I haven't tried to make a "play" from what was not. The words on the page don't try to hard to invoke the past of performance time; no complex stage directions, or long pedantic notes. Instead I've tried to leave the texts alone as the ghosts they are, in a desert of white paper or white sand. These ghost texts are clues. . . . And not to be trusted [78]

Prose description allows the artist to continue to control, to some extent, the dissemination of the ways in which the preservation of the art objects occurs. For example, beyond Etchell's books, Forced Entertainment keeps a range of material housed at their theatre and offers a range of goods for sale.[79] Their website lists typescripts, lists of works on the company, videos, CD-ROMs, pictures, and press clipping—all fragments and remnants of a publicity machine and a creative process. It gives us a range of material to collect and consider, and guides us in the ways in which to capture their performances rather than explaining their work. They use their ghost texts to demonstrate the process of each work's conception. Instead of letting others read the work through the lens of a scholar, Etchells prepares a more direct access to the material as mediated through this written guidance.

Take, for instance, *Speak Bitterness* (1994), a series of confessions to be spoken out during performance—and performances ran up to six hours. The actors, wearing black suits, were positioned behind large fold-out tables, and read from confessions written out on paper strewn on the table and floor. They made eye contact with the audience and whispered, read, and shouted their confessions, which ranged from admission of petty infidelity to egregious hate crimes. Its printed text consists of nine single-spaced pages of prose, production photos by Hugo Glendinning, and a brief description of the context of creation, rules of improvisation, and its performance.[80] Nothing more. Its trace elements do not capture the energy of performance, the attendants' complicity, and the minute interactions of the actors or the tempo of performance. It is a Swiss cheese version of the event; however, its triggers stimulate my experience of that performance and inform the thought processes that have shaped my thinking since then.

These fragments are hints designed to stimulate, not recreate. They cannot be trusted because they are meant to disseminate not pronounce meaning. How would it serve us to hear Richard Foremen systematically explain each line of his play or fill in the details of the still shots presented in press photographs? Rather, what is offered is a hint of the form that suggests the content and experience of the events. Essays that become works capturing the form and spirit of the experience through the constraints of prose are similar to the way a photographer finds the heart of the subject within the constraints of still images, which make up the form of his medium. These are fragments of memory (essay/photos) contaminated by the form and structure of the preserving vessel (media/reception).

Preservation occurs when the remnants of performance are transposed into the form of different media. Each new essay, photo, or piece of artwork brings to life the idea in a new form or strain that cannot be destroyed by time. Like the annoying tick that you picked up as a child by mimicking dad, who may have mimicked his great grandfather, it passed through them to you. It cannot be bought or sold. It exists only as the manifestation of behavior over time, a carrying of the voices of the dead changed by each new manifestation. It lives on through history, often hidden from sight. Because we cannot get close to the original contagion of performance, we are looking for the carriers—but it is the process of mutation that is most interesting, those moments of combustion. Biologically speaking, we are not going to find the ur-performance, its first instance. By its nature, it was destroyed at its genesis—meant to transform into limitless mutation. The nature of the manifestation and how it is allowed to spread is what seems worth looking at.

What is most fascinating is the way in which the carrier unknowingly picks up an image and stores it—its recombination forever reshaping his networks of memory—only to be retrieved and revealed years later in some innocuous way. For example, in *Image and Eye*, Erving Gombrich relates a story of the way in which, a month after seeing abstract paintings by Lawrence Gowing, he caught a glimpse of his checkerboard floor through the bottom of a glass and noticed the resulting distortions in pattern.[81] Though he had seen the pattern through the glass hundreds of times before, he had never taken note until after he took an interest in Gowing's abstracted designs; artwork had transformed his perception of the world. In other words, by experiencing the artwork, he saw the world differently; the artwork still existed, but Gombrich's experience of the artwork became something new. Recreating the work or capturing its essence was not the point, but rather how the work triggered him to make new observations and reflect them in a new work.

Another tactic of using the performance remnant to spawn new work can be seen by the use of the trace elements as the material for the creation of a new work that may reflect the content of the original. Franko B's *Red Cross* is an original piece of art—it came with a catalogue of photos documenting his performances.[82] It is the result of a process that Franko commonly employs. He takes his blood-soaked cloth from beneath his feet during the performance and cuts it up, thereby transforming it into new works. It is a trace of the old, yet something entirely new at the same time. It has moved beyond its first manifestation as a fragment of a performance into a second piece of art, and we cannot forget that it was once just a piece of cloth chosen as a piece of a performance sign. It remains the same, yet the process it has undergone retains the traces of the past, as it is influenced by each new formal manifestation. Its iconic red cross echoes the motif of tattoos on Franko's body, the context of performance, blood, medicine, and a range of other associations made during performance. The artwork is a direct result of the performance, as its production relies on the process of the making of the material, but is also distant from the performance because its resonances are drawn from the form, composition, and process of a different medium. It has transformed into a separate work that is evocative of the past performance, but stands on its own.

In a similar way, some of Nicholas Sinclair's pictures depicting Franko's performance pieces were taken during performance and others were staged to evoke the mood of the performance. These set-shots are designed to evoke the content of the performance though the medium of photographic representation. Each stimulates memories of being attendant to his performances. The work seems adequate—filling in forgotten details—yet are these details really the same as those we experienced during the duration of the performance? Those sensations have lived inside our brain cells for months and years. Now to be stirred up by the sensation of viewing images—have we built immunity to the stimulation? Will our cells respond to a new dose in the same chemical way—or have they already been changed as a result of the first exposure to his performances?

The most interesting part of archival material is that moment of definition and articulation that results from exposure to the traces of performance; that moment where it is what it is and then becomes something else. As we experience the work, the stimuli of performance are collected, categorized, organized, and built into a web of associations between our new and stored memories. The moments of experience and analysis build new threads of thought. It is a living memory contained within our experience, which is our own personal archive. The archive is a mammoth mind (video, photographs, drawings, texts, newspaper reviews, press announcements, theoretical essays, art objects, documentaries, and critical essays) connected by file cabinets, card catalogues, video banks, computers, and the archivist. It may serve to evoke or stimulate the mind to create anew via the pathways and structures of thought that it offers.

Does it matter how I interpret *Mama I can't sing*? Elsewhere, I argue that it is a commentary on the shackles that technology has put on us, thereby isolating us from community.[83] Yet a disability scholar commented that braces and other medical equipment are liberating for someone who could not stand without them. These are opposite readings of the same stimuli; one carries a message of isolation and disaffection, the other one of hope and moving forward. Each reading is colored by the analysts' thoughts, which were seeded by a fragment from the fleeting images seen during a performance. Neither encapsulates the event or performance as a whole, but each is a derivative of stimuli filtered by perception. No object exists in its own form; it is merely a stepping-stone to a new object, performance, or critique.

The objects of performance plant reference points for the memory to retrieve experiences. As an attempt to instigate a movement forward, the life of Guillermo Gómez-Peña and Roberto Sifuentes' *Temple of Confessions* (1995–6) became a series of art objects.[84] The installation, web-exchange, documentary, and book were a multi-staged piece of performance art. It consisted of a live museum installation, an exhibit, a documentary book, a documentary radio program, and a website. The work never existed in its totality in one place. It grew. It was the event, the response of the attendants in recordings, postcards, emails, and web postings. It was never one thing. In an effort to capture the spirit of what it was, Gómez-Peña and Sifuentes came up with a documentary program, which was a collage of description, spoof, and audience response. The material was shaped into an autonomous art object. The remnants of performance were reprocessed into a new work. Its genesis, performance, and transformation are a model of the archive process. In turn, this documentary has been used as a

National Public Radio broadcast, as a teaching tool, as evidence for theoretical discussion, and as an example of Hispanic-American art history. Its resonance was not, and could not be, contained by the documentation of the event; rather, it created a mountain of refuse that was used as fertilizer for future creations.

Fragments in and of themselves are meaningless. Only by piecing them together can we begin to form a picture of what a performance may have been. Then we can ask ourselves to what use that image formation may be. The creation of history is a manipulation of fragments. Those who control how the works are configured are those who control their meaning. Is it not the nature of time-based performance art a resistance to object making that serves to instigate cultural metamorphosis? The act of preserving, describing, and contextualizing the work reconfigures it as well. Does this reconfiguration matter if the aim of using performance is not contingent upon objective authenticity or even fixed meaning? Why should it matter how material is preserved? Can we rather consider how the fragments, byproducts, and acts of memory stimulate or instigate thought, theory, or art making? Material evidence is a means to trigger memory—the actual event and its remnants are a structure to shape a deeply phenomenological methodology of experience, memory, and conceptualization/theorization.

Returning to the crypt and the lives of those I imagine had contact with my ancestors in Sicily, the fragments connect us to the past and allow us to trace who we are and what we make back to the imagined sources. The caretaker reminds us that we can take pride in our existence because we never know what effect we will have:

> Of all the pictures taken by tourists, photographers, Talkers, students and curious people, none has ever reached here, and if they knew, if these famous Sicilian ladies and gentleman knew, they who never left the island, if they knew their images had traveled high and low . . . if they knew they had landed in America, in Australia, in Japan, I am sure that they would act and stand proud within the narrow space that each niche grants them.[85]

Notes

NOTES TO CHAPTER 1

1. Michael S. Gazzaniga, *Human: The Science Behind What Makes Us Unique* (New York: Ecco, 2008).
2. Bruce McConachie and H. Elizabeth Hart, eds., *Performance and Cognition: Theatre Studies and the Cognitive Turn* (London: Routledge, 2006); Ronda Blair, *The Actor, Image, and Action: Acting and Cognitive Neuroscience* (London: Routledge, 2008); and Bruce McConachie, *Engaging Audiences: A Cognitive Approach to Spectating in the Theatre* (London: Palgrave Macmillan, 2008).
3. Jackson Beatty, *The Human Brain: Essentials of Behavioural Neuroscience* (London: Sage Publications, 2001), 36–42.
4. Catherine Parker Anthony and Gary A. Thibodeau, *Textbook of Anatomy & Physiology* (St. Louis: Mosby, 1983), 328–346.
5. Ibid.
6. Arlette Steri, "Perception" in *Dictionary of Cognitive Science: Neuroscience, Psychology, Artificial Intelligence, Linguistics, and Philosophy*, ed. Oliver Houde (New York: Psychology Press, 2004), 274.
7. Norman Doidge, *The Brain that Changes Itself: Stories of Personal Triumph from the Frontiers of Brain Science* (New York: Penguin Books, 2007), 303.
8. Steri, "Perception," 274.
9. Antonio Damasio, *The Feeling of What Happens: Body and Emotion in the Making of Consciousness* (New York: Harcourt, 1999), 11.
10. Ibid., 53.
11. Ibid., 54.
12. Bernard J. Baars, *In the Theatre of Consciousness* (Oxford: Oxford University Press, 1997), 64.
13. Ibid., 43.
14. Ibid., 45.
15. Ibid., 107.
16. Gazzaniga, *Human*, 367.
17. Doidge, *Brain that Changes*, 211–212. (Emphasis in original).
18. Gazzaniga, *Human*, 365.
19. Baars, *Theatre of Consciousness*, 103. (Emphasis in original).
20. Benedict Carey, "For the Brain, Remembering is like Reliving," *New York Times*, September 4, 2008. http://www.nytimes.com/2008/09/05/science/05brain.html
21. V.S. Ramachandran and Sandra Blakeslee, *Phantoms in the Brain: Probing the Mysteries of the Human Mind* (New York: Quill, 1998), 60.

22. Ibid., 61.
23. Doidge, *Brain that Changes*, 207.
24. Gazzaniga, *Human*, 64.
25. Ibid., 102.
26. Ibid., 168–169.
27. Ibid., 169–170.
28. Ibid., 171.
29. Ibid., 181.
30. Ibid., 189.
31. Ibid.
32. George Mandler, "Remembering," in *Oxford Guide to the Mind*, ed. Geoffrey Underwood (Oxford: Oxford University Press, 2001), 32.
33. Gazzaniga, *Human*, 186.
34. Ibid., 199.
35. Ibid.
36. Doidge, *Brain that Changes*, 304.
37. Mandler, "Remembering," 32.
38. Ibid., 30.
39. Baars, *Theatre of Consciousness*, 43.
40. Joe Winston, *Burning Man Festival*, DVD (Ow.MyEye Productions, 2001).
41. Molly Steenson, "What is Burning Man?" http://www.burningman.com/whatisburningman/about_burningman/experience.html
42. Violet Blue, "Burning Man and Safer Sex: Free your Mind, but Watch out for Crabs," *San Francisco Gate*, August 23, 2007. http://www.sfgate.com/cgi-bin/article.cgi?f=/g/a/2007/08/23/violetblue.DTL
43. Michelle Bienias, "Burning Man Festival, One Man's Experience," *VRMAG*, April/May 2003. http://www.vrmag.org/issue11/BURNING_MAN_FESTIVAL_ONE_MAN_S_EXPERIENCE.html
44. Ibid.
45. Ibid.
46. Steenson, "What is Burning Man?"
47. Bienias, "Burning Man Festival."
48. A. Leo Nash, *Burning Man: Art in the Desert* (New York: Abrams, 2007), 6.
49. David Pescovitz, "Mark Pauline's Machine Mayhem," *Make* 7 (2006): 28–35.
50. Cinthea Fiss, Complaint Letter, SRL Press Book, 10.
51. Gary Morris, "Ai, Robot! Survival Research Laboratories: 10 Years of Robotic Mayhem on DVD," *Bright Lights Film Journal* 45 (2004). http://www.brightlightsfilm.com/45/srl.htm
52. Geeta Dayal, "The End of the World as we Know it?" *Associated Press*, August 19, 2006. http://hamptonroads.com/node/141661
53. David Garver, "Violent Theatricality: Displayed Enactments of Aggression and Pain," *Theatre Journal* 47 (1995): 57.
54. Ibid.
55. Doidge, *Brain that Changes*, 297.
56. Ibid., 288.
57. Damasio, *The Feeling*, 284.
58. Doidge, *Brain that Changes*, 208. (Emphasis in original).

NOTES TO CHAPTER 2

1. For overview of visual cognition theories, see Pierre Jacob and Marc Jeannerod, *Ways of Seeing: The Scope and Limits of Visual Cognition* (Oxford: Oxford University Press, 2003).

2. Stewart H.C. Hendry, Steven S. Hsiao, and M. Christian Brown, "Fundamentals of Sensory Systems," in *Fundamental Neuroscience*, eds. Michael J. Zigmond et al. (San Diego: Academic Press, 1999), 659.
3. Beatty, *Human Brain*, 137–162.
4. Ibid.
5. Alva Noë, *Action in Perception* (Cambridge, MA: MIT Press, 2004).
6. Geoffrey Montgomery, "Breaking the Code," in *Seeing, Hearing, and Smelling the World: New Findings Help Scientists Make Sense of our Senses*, ed. Maya Pines (Chevy Chase, MD: Howard Hughes Medical Institute, 1995), 22.
7. Max Keller, *Light Fantastic* (Munich: Prestel, 1999), 7.
8. Manfred Wagner, "The Nature of Light in the Theatre," in Keller, *Light Fantastic*, 228.
9. Pamela Howard, *What is Scenography?* (London: Routledge, 2002).
10. Dieter Dorn, "Making Light," in Keller, *Light Fantastic*, 10.
11. Ibid., 11.
12. Wagner, "Light in the Theatre," 227.
13. Jonah Lehrer, *Proust was a Neuroscientist* (New York: Houghton Mifflin, 2007), 119.
14. Ibid., 104–105.
15. Richard Hudson, quoted in Howard's *What is Scenography?*, xvi.
16. Keller, *Light Fantastic*, 25.
17. Wassily Kandinsky, *Concerning the Spiritual in Art* (New York: Dover, 1977), 20.
18. Ibid., 41.
19. Keller, *Light Fantastic*, 38.
20. Kandinsky, *Concerning the Spiritual*, 38.
21. Keller, *Light Fantastic*, 27.
22. Jan Butterfield, *The Art of Light and Space* (New York: Abbevile Press, 1993).
23. Ibid., 10.
24. Gustav Kuhn and Michael F. Land, "There's More to Magic than Meets the Eye," *Current Biology* 16, no. 22 (2006): 950–951.
25. Ibid.
26. Mark Changizi, quoted in Jeanna Bryner, "Key to All Optical Illusions Discovered," *Live Science*, June 2, 2008. http://www.Livescience.com
27. Bryner, "Optical Illusions."
28. See Chapter 3.
29. Changizi, "Optical Illusions."
30. Bryner, quoted in Bryner, "Optical Illusions."
31. Geoffrey Montgomery, "How we see things that Move," in Pine, *Seeing, Hearing, and Smelling*, 26.
32. Ibid., 27.
33. Ibid., 28.
34. Dorn, "Making Light—a forward," 11.
35. Ibid., 48.
36. Sven Nykvist, Bernardo Bertolucci, Marcello Mastoianni, and the Association of European Cinematographers, *Making Pictures: A Century of European Cinematography* (New York: Harry N. Abrams, 2003).
37. David Bradby and David Williams, "Robert Wilson," in *Director's Theatre* (London: Macmillan, 1988), 233.
38. Thomas Frick, "A Conversation with Robert Wilson," *Art New England* (June 1985): 20.
39. Taduesz Kantor, *A Journey Through Other Spaces*, ed. Michael Kobialka (Berkeley: University of California Press, 1993), 209.

40. Robert Stearns, "Before the Deafman Glanced," in *Robert Wilson*, by Franco Quadri, Franco Bertoni, and Robert Stearns (New York: Rizzoli, 1998), 207.
41. Kantor, *A Journey*, 213.
42. Robert Jones, "Listen to the Pictures," *New York News*, November 21, 1976.
43. Arthur Holmberg, *The Theatre of Robert Wilson* (Cambridge: Cambridge University Press, 1996), 122.
44. Robert Enright, "A Clean, Well-lighted Grace: An Interview with Robert Wilson," *Border Crossings: A Magazine of the Arts* 13 (1994): 20.
45. Philip Glass, *Opera on the Beach* (New York: Faber and Faber, 1989), 33.
46. Robert Storr, *Tony Smith: Architect, Painter, Sculptor* (New York: MOMA, 1998).
47. Stefan Brecht, *The Theatre of Visions: Robert Wilson* (London: Methuen, 1994), 420.
48. Gascon Bachelard, *The Poetics of Space* (Boston: Beacon Press, 1994), 4.
49. Bill Simmer, "Robert Wilson and Therapy," *The Drama Review* 20 (1976): 99–110.
50. Robert Wilson, "Lohegrin Drawings," http://robertwilson.com/studio/lohengrin/lohengrin1.htm
51. Kantor, *A Journey*, 240.
52. Susan Letzler Cole, "Robert Wilson Directs *The Golden Windows* and *Hamletmachine*," in *Director's in Rehearsal: A Hidden World* (London: Routledge, 1992), 152.
53. Edward Hall, *The Silent Language* (New York: Doubleday, 1990).
54. In different cultures there are unwritten comfort distances at which people stand next to each other without invading personal space. See Hall, *The Silent Language*.
55. D.H. Hubel and M.S. Livingstone, "Segregation of Form, Color, and Stereopsis in Primate Arca," *Journal of Neuroscience* 18, no. 7 (1987): 3378–3415.
56. Holmberg, *Theatre of Robert Wilson*, 165.
57. Wagner, "Light in the Theatre," 227.
58. Ibid.
59. Ibid., 50.
60. DIA held a two-part exhibition of Irwin's work in 1998–99, showing two site-specific installations, *Prologue: x183* and *Excursus: Homage to the Square*.
61. Howard, *What is Scenography?*
62. Joan Acocella, "A Silvered World" in eds, Jeffrey Escoffier and Matthew Lore, *Mark Morris' l'allegro, il penseroso ed il moderato: A Celebration* (New York: Marlowe & Company, 2001), 16.
63. "James F. Ingalls on the Lighting Design," in Escoffier and Lore, *Mark Morris*, 153.
64. Hubel and Livingstone, "Segregation of Form."
65. Keller, *Light Fantastic*, 169.
66. Veronique Vial, *'O': Cirque du Soleil at Bellagio* (New York: Power House Books, 2001).
67. Pope Benedict XVI, quoted in Cardinal Joseph Ratzinger, *The Spirit of the Liturgy*, trans. John Saward (San Francisco: Ignatius Press, 2000).

NOTES TO CHAPTER 3

1. Tiffany Field, *Touch* (Cambridge, MA: MIT Press, 2003), 39.
2. Recent studies that are important to understanding the role of touch in culture are Mark Paterson, *The Senses of Touch: Haptics, Affects and*

Technology (Oxford: Berg, 2007); Caroline A. Jones, ed., *Sensorium: Embodied Experience, Technology, and Contemporary Art* (Cambridge, MA: MIT Press, 2006); Constance Classen, ed., *The Book of Touch* (Oxford: Berg, 2005); Gabriel Josipovich, *Touch* (New Haven, CT: Yale University Press, 1996).

3. *X-Men* is a fictional comic book created by Stan Lee and Jack Kirby in 1963. *X-Men*, directed by Bryan Singer (Twentieth-Century Fox, 2000).
4. Field, *Touch*, 57.
5. Marina Abramović, *Marina Abramović: Artist Body Performances, 1969–1998* (Milan: Charta Editions, 1998), 175.
6. Roger Cholewiak and Amy Collins, "Sensory and Physiological Bases of Touch," in *The Psychology of Touch*, eds. Morton Heller and William Schiff (Hillsdale, NJ: Lawrence Erlbaum, 2001), 23.
7. Janet Weisenberger, "Cutaneous Perception," in *Blackwell Handbook of Perception*, eds. E. Bruce Goldstein, Glyn Humphreys, Margaret Shiffrar, and William Yost (London: Wiley-Blackwell, 2001), 548.
8. Gabriel Robles-De-La-Torre, "The Importance of the Sense of Touch in Virtual and Real Environments," *IEEE MultiMedia* (July–September 2006): 24–30.
9. Ainsley Iggo, "Touch," in Underwood, *Guide to the Mind*, 40.
10. Field, *Touch*, 75.
11. Ibid., 77.
12. Cholewiak and Collins, "Physiological Bases," 23.
13. Ibid., 24.
14. Ibid., 54.
15. Weisenberger, "Cutaneous Perception," 536.
16. Performed at Robodock 2007, NDSM Wharf, Amsterdam, Sept. 19–22, 2007.
17. Cholewiak and Collins, "Physiological Bases," 36.
18. Iggo, "Touch," 92.
19. Richard O'Brien, "Touch-a, Touch-a, Touch Me," in *The Rocky Horror Picture Show*, directed by Jim Sharman (Twentieth-Century Fox, 1975).
20. *Marina Abramović*, 175.
21. Ashley Montagu, *Touching: The Human Significance of the Skin* (New York: Harper & Row, 1986), 204–205.
22. Field, *Touch*, 77.
23. Abramović, *Marina Abramović*, 150.
24. Cholewiak and Collins, "Physiological Bases," 29.
25. *Time*, "New Plays: *Dionysus in '69*," June 28, 1968. http://www.time.com/time/magazine/article/0,9171,841343,00.html
26. Henry C. Lacey, *To Raise, Destroy and Create: The Poetry, Drama and Function of Imamu Amiri Baraka*, (Albany, NY: Whitston, 1981), 153.
27. Harry Elam, "Social Urgency, Audience Participation, and the Performance of *Slave Ship* by Amiri Baraka," in *Crucibles of Crisis: Performing Social Change*, ed. Janelle Reinelt (Ann Arbor: University of Michigan Press, 1996), 15–16.
28. Iggo, "Touch," 93.
29. Ibid.
30. Weisenberger, "Cutaneous Perception," 536.
31. At PSI#7 in Mainz, Germany (2001).
32. *In the Realm of the Senses*, directed by Nagisa Oshima, (Argos Films, 1976).
33. Wikia Entertainment, "The Star Trek Experience." http://memory-alpha.org/en/wiki/Star_Trek:_The_Experience

34. Mitch Mandell, "A Visit to Star Trek the Experience at the Las Vegas Hilton," *Fabulous Travel*, August 6, 2007. http://www.fabuloustravel.com/usa/startrek/startrek.html
35. "Star Trek: The Experience," www.vegas4visitors.com/attractions/detail/startrek.html
36. Edward de Bono, "Lateral Thinking," in *Oxford Guide to the Mind*, 225.
37. Underwood, *Guide to the Mind*, 3.
38. Stephen Di Benedetto, "Guiding Somatic Responses within Performative Structures: Contemporary Live Art and Sensorial Perception" in *Senses in Performance*, eds. Banes and Lepeki, 130–132.
39. Weisenberger, "Cutaneous Perception," 536.
40. Ibid.
41. Rudolf Arnheim, *Visual Thinking* (Berkeley: University of California Press, 1969), 19.

NOTES TO CHAPTER 4

1. Constance Classen, David Howes, and Anthony Synott, *Aroma: The Cultural History of Smell* (London: Routledge, 1994), 1.
2. Oliver Sacks, *The Man Who Mistook His Wife for A Hat* (London: Duckworth, 1987), 159. (Emphasis in the original).
3. John C. Leffingwell, "Olfaction—Update #5," *Leffingwell Reports* 2, no. 1 (May 2002): 1. http://www.leffingwell.com/olfaction.htm (emphasis mine).
4. K. Ackerl, M. Atzmueller, and K. Grammer, "The Scent of Fear," *Neuroendocrinology Letters* 23, no. 2 (2002): 79–84.
5. Denise Chen and Jeanette Haviland-Jones, "Rapid Mood Change and Human Odors," *Physiology & Behaviour* 68 no. 1–2 (1999): 241–250.
6. Wang, L., V.E. Walker, H. Sardi, C. Fraser, and T.J.C. Jacob, "The Correlation Between Physiological and Psychological Responses to Odour Stimulation in Human Subjects," *Clinical Neurophysiology* 113 (2002): 542–551.
7. Classen, Howes, and Synott, *Aroma*, 3.
8. R.W. Moncrieff, *The Chemical Senses* (London: Leonard Hill, 1967), 381–382.
9. J.E. Amoore, "The Stereochemical Specificities of Human Olfactory Receptors," *Perfumery & Essential Oil Record* 43(1952): 321–330.
10. J.T. Davies and F.H. Taylor, "The Role of Absorption and Molecular Morphology in Olfaction: The Calculation of Olfactory Thresholds," *Biology Bulletin* 117 (1959): 222–238.
11. G.M. Dyson, "The Scientific Basis of Odour," *Journal of the Society of Chemical Industry* 57 (1938): 647–651.
12. Luca Turin, "A Spectroscopic Mechanism for Primary Olfactory Reception," *Chemical Senses* 21 (1996): 773–791.
13. G. Ohloff, *Scent and Fragrances* (Berlin: Springer-Verlag, 1994), 6.
14. H. Zhao, L. Ivic, J.M. Otaki, M. Hashimoto, K. Mikoshiba, and S. Firestein, "Functional Expression of a Mammalian Odorant Receptor," *Science* 279 (1998): 237–241.
15. B. Malnic, J. Hirono, T. Sato, and LB. Buck, "Combinatorial Receptor Codes for Odors," *Cell* 96, no. 5 (March 1999): 713–723. http://www.hhmi.org/news/buck.htm
16. Leffingwell, "Olfaction," 5.
17. K. Stern and M.K. McClintock, "Regulation of Ovulation by Human Pheromones," *Nature* 392, no. 6672 (1998): 177–179.
18. P.F. Bone and P.S. Ellen, "Scents in the Marketplace: Explaining a Function of Olfaction," *Journal of Retailing* 75, no. 2 (1999): 243–262.

19. Stephen Di Benedetto, "Sensing Bodies: A Phenomenological Approach to the Performance Sensorium," *Performance Research* 8, no. 2 (June 2003): 100–108.
20. Sissel Tolaas, quoted in Sarah Cowan, "MIT's 'Sensorium' Brings Sixth Dimension to Five Senses," *Tufts Daily*, November 2, 2006. http://www.tuftsdaily.com/2.5516/mit-s-sensorium-brings-sixth-dimension-to-five-senses-1.593276
21. Ibid.
22. Ibid.
23. Ibid.
24. Ibid.
25. C. Miles and R. Jenkins, "Recency and Suffix Effects with Immediate Recall of Olfactory Stimuli," *Memory* 8, no. 3 (2000): 195–205.
26. S. Chu and J.J. Downes, "Long Live Proust: The Odour-cued Autobiographical Memory Bump," *Cognition* 75, no. 2 (2000): B41–B50.
27. W.J. Freeman, "The Physiology of Perception," *Scientific American* 264, no. 2 (1991): 78–85.
28. David Roberts, ed., *Signals and Perception: The Fundamentals of Human Sensation* (London: Open University Press and Palgrave Macmillan, 2002).
29. Joan Beadle, "*Cure*: A Darkly Humorous Look at Life on the Edge," *BMJ* 321, no. 7274 (2000): 1476.
30. "Smell-O-Vision," University of Florida Special Collections. www.uflib.ufl.edu/SPEC/belknap/exhibit2002/smell.htm
31. Martin Smith and Patrick Kiger, "The Lingering Reek of Smell-O-Vision," *West Los Angeles Times*, February 5, 2006, 26.
32. Randall Fitzgerald, "Responses to Smell-O-Vision is Back," in Nuke, Blog, April 24, 2006. http://www.frikafrax.com/mnuke/blog2/2006/04/24/smell-o-vision-is-back/
33. From Earl message boards, "*My Name is Earl*, May 3, 2007."
34. Greg Garcia, "Get A Real Job," *My Name is Earl*, Season 2, NBC, April 3, 2007.
35. Liesl Schillinger, "Odorama," *New York Times*, February 23, 2003.
36. Aroma Composer, "Prototype: Aroma Diffusion System," www.aromacomposer.org/index.html
37. Nuke, "Smell-O-Vision is Back," Blog, April 23, 2006. http://www.frikafrax.com/mnuke/blog2/category/media-entertainment/
38. Fitzgerald, "Responses to Smell-O-Vision."
39. Matthew Reason, "Writing the Olfactory in the Live Performance Review," *Performance Research* 8, no. 3 (2003): 79.
40. Lyn Gardner, "Ghost Ward," *The Guardian*, April 4, 2001. http://www.guardian.co.uk/culture/2001/may/04/artsfeatures1
41. Classen, Howes, and Synott, *Aroma*, 2.
42. Ibid., 3.
43. Mary Fleischer, "Incense & Decadents: Symbolist Theatre's Use of Scent" in *The Senses in Performance*, eds. Sally Banes and Andre Lepeki (London: Routledge, 2007), 105.
44. Ibid., 107–108.
45. Kristen Shepherd-Barr, "*Mise en scent*: The Theatre d'Art's *Cantiques* and the Use of Smell as a Theatrical Device," *Theatre Research International* 24, no. 2 (Summer 1999): 152.
46. Ibid.
47. Claude Schumacher, ed., *Naturalism and Symbolism in European Theatre, 1850–1918* (Cambridge: Cambridge University Press, 1996), 18.
48. Classen, Howes, and Synott, *Aroma*, 2.
49. Shepherd-Barr, "*Mise en scent*," 154.

50. Classen, Howes, and Synott, *Aroma*, 2.
51. Shepherd-Barr, *"Mise en scent,"* 157.
52. Ibid.
53. Lauran Neergaard, "You're led by your Nose—and that's Good," *Miami Herald*, March 28, 2008, 5A.
54. Pines, "The Mystery of Smell," in *Seeing, Hearing and Smelling*, 49.
55. Jeremy Caplan, "Scents and Sensibility," *Time*, October 16, 2006. http:// www.time.com/time/magazine/article/0,9171,1543956,00.html
56. Fabulous Beast Dance Theatre, Program for *Fragile* performed at the Project, Dublin, Ireland June 26, 2001.
57. Michael Keegan-Dolan, "Fabulous Beast," email correspondence to author, 2001.
58. Susan Mary Abbott, "Taste: The Neglected Nutritional Factor," Journal of the American Dietetic Association 97, no. 10 (October 1997): S205–S207.
59. Moncrieff, *Chemical Senses.*
60. Ben Brantley, "No Wonder He's Cranky; He's Covered in Condiments," *New York Times*, September 23, 2007. http://theater2.nytimes.com/2007/09/25/ theater/reviews/25bran.html?n=Top/Reference/Times%20Topics/People/M/ Moliere
61. The Taste Science Laboratory, Division of Nutritional Sciences, Cornell University "Taste Science," www.tastescience.com
62. Taste Science Laboratory, "Taste Science."
63. Barbara Hodgson, *The Sensualist* (San Francisco: Chronicle Books, 2001), 65.
64. Beverly J. Cowart and Nancy E. Rawson, "Olfaction," in eds. Goldstein et al., *Handbook of Perception*, 568.
65. Hodgson, *The Sensualist*, 289–290.
66. Taste Science Laboratory, "Taste Science."
67. Denise E. Cole, "Edible Performance: Feasting and Festivity in Early Tudor Entertainment" in *Senses in Performance*, eds. Banes and Lepeki, 92. (Emphasis in original).
68. Ibid., 101. (Emphasis in original).
69. Jennifer Reingold, "Weird Science," *Fast Company* (May 2006): 42.
70. Ibid.,48.
71. Ibid., 47.
72. Rosemary Weatherston, Performance Review of Nao Bustamante and Coco Fusco's *Stuff*, *Theatre Journal* (December 1997): 516–518.
73. Olivia Lory Kay, "Review of *Stuff*," August 16, 1997. http://www.physics-room.org.nz/2cents/stuff.htm
74. Nao Bustamante and Coco Fusco, Program for STUFF, performed at the ICA, London, November 1996.
75. Di Benedetto "Guiding Somatic Responses," 124–137.
76. *Le Campenent*, Program, performed at the Industrial Palace, Prague, Czech Republic, June 27, 1999, 4.
77. Patrick Süskind, *Perfume: The Story of a Murderer*, trans. John E. Woods (New York: Vintage International, 2001).
78. Ibid., 44.
79. Ibid., 33–34.
80. Ibid., 34.

NOTES TO CHAPTER 5

1. Brian Moore, "Hearing," in Underwood, *Guide to the Mind*, 10.
2. Diane Ackerman, *A Natural History of the Senses* (London: Phoenix, 2000), 177.

3. Jeff Goldberg, "The Quivering Bundles that Let us Hear," in Pines, *Seeing, Hearing, and Smelling*, 36.
4. Beatty, *Human Brian*, 183–193; Aage R. Moller, *Auditory Physiology* (New York: Academic Press, 1983); and Society for Neuroscince, *Brain Facts: A Primer on the Brain and Nervous System* (Washington, DC: Society for Neuroscience, 2002).
5. Goldberg, "The Quivering Bundles," in Pines, *Seeing, Hearing, and Smelling*, 36.
6. Peter W. Alberti, "The Anatomy and Physiology of the Ear and Hearing," in *Occupational Exposure to Noise: Evaluation, Prevention and Control*, eds. Berenice Goelzer, Colin H. Hansen and Gustav A. Sehrndt (Bremerhaven: World Health Organization, 2001). http://www.who.int/occupational_health/publications/occupnoise/en/index.html
7. Jim Drobnick, "Listening Awry," in *Aural Cultures*, ed. Jim Drobnick (Toronto: YYZBOOKS & Walter Phillips Gallery Editions, 2004), 11.
8. Luigi Russolo, *The Art of Noise*, trans. Robert Filliou (New York: Something Else Press, 1967), 7.
9. Douglas Kahn, *Noise, Water, Meat: A History of Sound in the Arts* (Cambridge, MA: MIT Press, 1999), 22
10. John Cage, "The Future of Music: Credo," in *Silence: Lectures and Writings* (Middletown, CT: Wesleyan University Press, 1961), 3.
11. Georgina Kleege, "Voices in my Head," in Drobnick, *Aural Cultures*, 99.
12. Stephen Connor, *Dumb Speak* (Oxford: Oxford University Press, 2000).
13. Kleege, "Voices in my Head," 102.
14. Richard Leppert, "The Social Discipline of Listening," in Drobnick, *Aural Cultures*, 20.
15. Ibid., 21.
16. Daniel J. Levitin, *This is Your Brain on Music: The Science of a Human Obsession* (New York: Plume, 2007).
17. Lehrer, *Proust Was a Neuroscientist*, 133.
18. Ibid., 141.
19. Ibid.
20. Andra McCartney, "Soundscape Works, Listening, and the Touch of Sound," in Drobnick, *Aural Cultures*, 179.
21. Matthew Goulish, *39 Microlectures: In Proximity to Performance* (London: Routledge, 2000), 24.
22. Jonathan Sterne, *The Audible Past: Cultural Origins of Sound Reproduction* (Durham: Duke University Press, 2003), 11.
23. Michael Zwerun, "A Lethal Measurement," in *John Cage*, ed. Richard Konstelanetz (New York: Oraeger, 1970), 166.
24. Bernd Schulz, *Resonanzen: Aspekte der Klangkunst = Resonances: Aspects of Sound Art* (Heidelberg: Kehrer, 2002), 15.
25. Kahn, *Noise*, 165.
26. Ibid., 158.
27. Ibid.
28. Robert Bean, "Polyphonic Aurality and John Cage," in Drobnick, *Aural Cultures*, 130. (Emphasis in the original).
29. Allen B. Ruch, *Joyce—Music John Cage's "Roaratorio."* http://www.themodernword.com/joyce/music/cage_roaratorio.html
30. Bean "Polyphonic Aurality," 127. (Emphasis in original.)
31. Ibid., 134. (Emphasis in original.)
32. Anna Kisselgoff, "Dance: 'Roaratorio' at Next Wave," *New York Times*, October 8, 1986. http://www.nytimes.com/1986/10/08/arts/dance-roaratorio-at-next-wave.html

33. Christof Mignoe, "Flatus Vocis: Somatic Winds," in Drobnick, *Aural Cultures*, 84.
34. Jean Nohain and F. Caradec, *Le Petomane: 1857–1945* (New York: Dorset Press, 1993), 37–38.
35. Paul Spinrad, *The RE/Search Guide to Bodily Fluids* (San Francisco: RE/Search Publications, 1994).
36. Kahn, *Noise*, 27.
37. Nohain and Caradec, *Le Petomane*, 72–73.
38. Gabor Csepregi, "On Sound Atmospheres," in Drobnick, *Aural Cultures*, 170.
39. Ibid,, 172.
40. Ibid.
41. Ibid., 171.
42. Schulz, *Resonances*, 17.
43. Ibid., 15.
44. Susan Hiller, "Susan Hiller with Mary Horlock," in Drobnick, *Aural Cultures*, 138.
45. Ibid.
46. Csepregi, "On Sound Atmospheres," 170.
47. Kahn, *Noise*, 11.
48. Russolo, *The Art of Noise*, 6. Emphasis in original.
49. Ibid., 7.
50. Kahn, *Noise*, 20.
51. Ibid., 31.
52. Cowan, "Sensorium."
53. Charles Stankievech, "From Stethoscopes to Headphones: An Acoustic Spatialization of Subjectivity," *Leonardo Music Journal* 17 (2007): 57.
54. Ibid.
55. Ibid.
56. EMPAC, "Press Release for Dumb Type *Voyage*." http://www.empac.rpi.edu/events/opening/gala/dumbtype.html
57. Alison Croggon, "MIAF: Voyage Festival diary #4," October 20, 2006. http://theatrenotes.blogspot.com/2006/10/miaf-voyage.html
58. Ibid.
59. Ackerman, *A Natural History*, 178.
60. Di Benedetto, "Stumbling in the Dark: Robert Wilson's *H.G.*," *New Theatre Quarterly* 17, no. 3 (August 2001): 280–281.
61. Ibid., 281.
62. *Hartford Courant*, "Concert Plays Part in Brain Research," April 9, 2006.
63. Ackerman, *A Natural History*, 217.
64. Drobnick, "Listening Awry," 10.
65. Kathleen Forde, *What Sound Does A Color Make?* (New York: Independent Curators International, 2005), 16.
66. Ibid., 19.
67. Kimberly W. Benston, *Baraka: The Renegade and the Mask* (New Haven, CT: Yale University Press 1976), 251.
68. Elam, "Social Urgency," 16–17.
69. Ibid.
70. Andra McCartney, "Soundscape Works," 185.
71. Kunsthaus-Bregenz, "KUB Press Rlease Janet Cardiff & George Bures Miller," May 2008. http://www.kunsthaus-bregenz.at/presse_cariff_miller/PresseinformationE.pdf
72. Jenifer Fisher, "Speeches of Display: Museum Audioguides by Artists," in Drobnick, *Aural Cultures*, 57.

73. Gregory Williams, "The Voice of Authority," *PAJ* 59 (1998): 62–63.
74. Ibid.
75. Fisher, "Speeches of Display," 59.
76. Public Art Fund, "Press Release, Janet Cardiff: *Her Long Black Hair.*" http://www.publicartfund.org/pafweb/projects/04/cardiff_J_release_04.pdf
77. Williams, "The Voice of Authority," 62.
78. Paige McGinley, "Eavesdropping, Surveillance, and Sound," *PAJ* 82 (2006): 52.
79. Ibid.
80. Kunsthaus-Bregenz, "KUB Press Release."
81. Cowan, "Sensorium."
82. Kunsthaus-Bregenz, "KUB Press Release."
83. Fisher, "Speeches of Display," 60.
84. Drobnick, "Listening Awry," 11.
85. Csepregi, "On Sound Atmospheres," 172.
86. Ibid., 173.
87. Stephen Di Benedetto, "Sensing Bodies: A Phenomenological Approach to the Performance Sensorium," *Performance Research* 8, no. 2 (June 2003): 105.
88. Csepregi, "On Sound Atmospheres," 174.

NOTES TO CHAPTER 6

1. Steven Pinker, *How The Mind Works* (Penguin Press, 1997).
2. Peter Carruthers, *Phenomenal Consciousness: A Naturalistic Theory* (Cambridge: Cambridge University Press, 2000), 4.
3. Fisher, "Speeches of Display," 52.
4. Linda M. Bartoshuk, "Taste, Smell and Pleasure" in *The Hedonics of Taste*, ed. Robert C. Bolles (Hillsdale, NJ: L. Erlbaum Associates, 1991), 19.
5. Teresa Thomas, "The Medium and the Message: Eyes and Ears Understand Differently, Carnegie Mellon Scientists Report in the Journal *Human Brain Mapping*," *Eurek Alert!*.http://eurekalert.org/pub_releases/2001–08/cmu-tma081401.php
6. Doidge, *Brain that Changes*, 308.
7. Ibid., 275.
8. Ibid., 214.
9. Anne Bogart, *And Then, You Act: Making Art in an Unpredictable World* (London: Routledge, 2007), 52.
10. Ibid.
11. J. John Lennon and Malcolm Foley, *Dark Tourism: The Attraction of Death and Disaster* (Cengage Learning Business Press, 2000).
12. Seth Mydans, "Visit the Vietcong's World: Americans Welcome," *New York Times*, July 7, 1999. http://www.nytimes.com/1999/07/07/world/cu-chi-journal-visit-the-vietcong-s-world-americans-welcome.html
13. Ioan Grillo, "In Mexico, a Theme Park for Border Crossers," *Time*, November 11, 2008. http://www.time.com/time/world/article/0,8599,1858151,00.html
14. Ibid.
15. Ibid.
16. Coco Fusco, "The Other History of Intercultural Performance," *TDR* 38, no. 1 (1994): 145.
17. Diana Taylor, "A Savage Performance: Guillermo Gómez-Peña and Coco Fusco's *Couple in the Cage*," *TDR* 42, no. 2 (1998): 166.

18. Fusco, "The Other History," 154.
19. Ibid., 162.
20. Ibid., 157.
21. Antonin Artaud, *The Theatre and its Double*, trans. Mary Caroline Richards (New York: Grove, 1958), 86.
22. Lydia Lunch, *Paradoxia: A Predator's Diary* (London: Creation Books, 1997), 60–61.
23. Gray Watson, "Franko B: Interview," June 13, 2000. http://www.ainexus.com/franko/interview.htm
24. Anthony Julius, *Transgressions* (London: Thames & Hudson, 2002), 102.
25. Ibid., 107.
26. Richard Huelsenbeck, ed., *Dada Almanach*, trans. Malcolm Green (London: Atlas Press, 1998), 105.
27. G. Ribemont-Dessaignes, "To the Public," in Huelsenbeck, *Dada Almanach*, 105.
28. Julius, *Transgressions*, 113.
29. Artaud, *Theatre and its Double*, 31.
30. Stephen Di Benedetto, "The Body as Fluid Dramaturgy: Live Art, Corporeality and Perception," *Journal of Dramatic Theory and Criticism* 16, no. 2 (2002): 12.
31. Stuart Morgan, "The Illustrated Man: Franko B," in *Franko B*, eds. Lois Kaiden, Stuart Morgan, and Nicholas Sinclair (London: Blackdog, 1998), 10.
32. Artaud, *Theatre and its Double*, 74.
33. Louis Aragon, quoted in Maurice Nadeau, *The History of Surrealism*, trans. Richard Howard (New York: Pelican 1973), 53.
34. Dorita Hanna and Olav Harslof, "Introduction: Performative Expressions Across Disciplines," in *Performance Design*, eds. Dorita Hanna and Olav Harslof (Copenhagen: Museum Tusculanum Press, 2008), 13.
35. Ibid., 18–19.
36. Daniel Sacs, review of "Festival D'Avignon, France 4–26 July 2008," *Theatre Journal* 61, no. 1 (2009): 117.
37. Romeo Castellucci, "On the Earth's Stage," in *The Theatre of Societas Raffaello Sanzio*, eds. Claudia Castellucci et al. (London: Routledge, 2007), 33.
38. Valentia Valentini and Bonnie Marranca, "The Universal: The Simplest Place Possible," *PAJ* 77 (2004): 17–18.
39. Chiara Guidi et al., "A Conversation about the Future," in Castellucci et al., *Societas*, 258.
40. Chiara Guidi et al., "A Conversation about Dramaturgy, contd.," in Castellucci et al., *Societas*, 214.
41. Chiara Guidi, "S. #08," in Castellucci et al., *Societas*, 148.
42. Valentini and Marranca, "The Universal," 20.
43. See Rhonda Blair for theories of cognitive science and the relevance to actors.
44. R. Castellucci and C. Castellucci, "C.#1, Cesena," in Castellucci et al., *Societas*, 36.
45. Ibid., 36–37.
46. Ibid., 37.
47. Ibid., 44–45.
48. Guidi, "Laboratory," in Castellucci et al., *Societas*, 26–27.
49. Guidi et al., "Conversation about Dramaturgy," 218.
50. Ibid.
51. Ibid., 218–219.
52. Michael Taussig, *The Nervous System* (New York: Routledge, 1992), 141–142.

53. Guidi et al., "A Conversation about the Future," in Castelluci et al., *Socìetas*, 259.
54. Timothy Scheie, review of *Voyage au bout de la nuit*, Concerto after Louis-Ferdinand Céline by Socìetas Raffaello Sanzio, Avignon, July 16, 1999, *Theatre Journal* 52, no. 1 (2000): 128.
55. Ibid.
56. Ibid., 129.
57. Ibid.
58. Ibid.
59. Alva Noë, *Out of Our Heads: Why you are not your Brain, and Other Lessons from the Biology of Consciousness* (New York: Hill and Wang, 2009).
60. Bruce E. Wexler, *Brain and Culture: Neurobiology, Ideology, and Social Change* (Cambridge MA: MIT Press, 2006), 145.
61. Ibid., 155.
62. Ibid., 158.
63. Ibid., 169.
64. Jim Williams, review of *HEY GIRL!* by Romeo Castellucci and Socìetas Raffaello Sanzio, Walker Art Center, Minneapolis, February 15, 2008, *Theatre Journal* 60, no. 4, (2008): 667.
65. Ibid.
66. Mario Jacques, "Can Theatre Be 'Museable'?" in *Guide: Museu National do Teatro*, ed. Instituto Português de Museus (Lisbon: Instituto Português de Museus, 2006), 23.
67. Nicholas Ridout, "Make-believe: Socìetas Raffaello Sanzio do Theatre," in *Contemporary Theatres in Europe*, eds. Joe Kelleher and Nicholas Ridout (London: Routledge, 2006), 177.
68. James Elkins, *Pictures of the Body: Pain and Metamorphosis* (Stanford, CA: Stanford University Press, 1999).
69. Ridout, "Make-believe," 177.
70. Ibid.
71. Noë, *Out of Our Heads*, 59.
72. Mathew Goulish, "Unwinding Kindergarten," *Performance Research* 7, no. 4 (2002): 96.
73. Michal Kobialka, "Historical Archives, Events and Facts: History Writing as Fragmentary Performance," *Performance Research* 7, no. 4 (December 2002): 7.
74. Laura Facchi, "The Living Dead," in *The Living Dead: Inside the Palermo Crypt*, by Marco Lanza and Laura Facchi (London: Westone, 2000), 22.
75. Ibid., 1.
76. Roland Barthes, *Camera Lucida: Reflections on Photography*, trans. Richard Howard (New York: Hill and Wang, 1981).
77. Tim Etchells, "On Documentation and Performance," in *Certain Fragments*, by Tim Etchells (London: Routledge, 2001), 71.
78. Etchells, "Performance Texts," in *Certain Fragments*, 133.
79. Forced Entertainment, "Company Website," www.forced.co.uk
80. Etchells, "Speak Bitterness," in *Certain Fragments*, 177–190.
81. E. H. Gombrich, *Image and the Eye: Further Studies in the Psychology of Pictorial Representation* (Oxford: Phaidon, 1982), 33–34.
82. Kaiden, Morgan, and Sinclair, *Franko B.*
83. Di Benedetto, "Fluid Dramaturgy," 4–15.
84. Guillermo Gómez-Peña, *Temple of Confessions: Mexican Beasts and Living Santos* (New York: Powerhouse Books, 1996).
85. Facchi, *Living Dead*, 17.

Bibliography

Abbott, Susan Mary. "Taste: The Neglected Nutritional Factor." Journal of the American Dietetic Association 97, no. 10 (October 1997): S205–S207.

Abramović, Marina. *Marina Abramović: Artist Body Performances, 1969–1998.* Milan: Charta Editions, 1998.

Ackerl, K., M. Atzmueller, and K. Grammer. "The Scent of Fear." *Neuroendocrinology Letters* 23, no. 2 (2002): 79–84.

Ackerman, Diane. *A Natural History of the Senses.* London: Phoenix, 2000.

Amoore, J.E. "The Stereochemical Specificities of Human Olfactory Receptors." *Perfumery & Essential Oil Record* 43(1952): 321–330.

Anthony, Catherine Parker, and Gary A. Thibodeau. *Textbook of Anatomy & Physiology.* St. Louis: Mosby, 1983.

Arnheim, Rudolf. *Visual Thinking.* Berkeley: University of California Press, 1969.

Aroma Composer. "Prototype: Aroma Diffusion System." www.aromacomposer. org/index.html

Artaud, Antonin. *The Theatre and its Double.* Translated by Mary Caroline Richards. New York: Grove, 1958.

Baars, Bernard J. *In the Theatre of Consciousness* (Oxford: Oxford University Press, 1997).

Bachelard, Gascon. *The Poetics of Space.* Boston: Beacon Press, 1994.

Banes, Sally and Andre Lepeki, eds. *The Senses in Performance.* London: Routledge, 2007.

Barthes, Roland. *Camera Lucida: Reflections on Photography.* Translated by Richard Howard. New York: Hill and Wang, 1981.

Beadle, Joan. "*Cure*: A Darkly Humorous Look at Life on the Edge." *BMJ* 321, no. 7274 (2000): 1476.

Beatty, Jackson. *The Human Brain: Essentials of Behavioural Neuroscience.* London: Sage Publications, 2001.

Benston, Kimberly W. *Baraka: The Renegade and the Mask.* New Haven, CT: Yale University Press 1976.

Bienias, Michelle. "Burning Man Festival, One Man's Experience." *VRMAG*, April/ May 2003. http://www.vrmag.org/issue11/BURNING_MAN_FESTIVAL_ONE_ MAN_S_EXPERIENCE.html

Blair, Ronda. *The Actor, Image, and Action: Acting and Cognitive Neuroscience.* London: Routledge, 2008.

Blue, Violet. "Burning Man and Safer Sex, Free your Mind, but Watch out for Crabs." *San Francisco Gate.* August 23, 2007. http://www.sfgate.com/cgibin/ article.cgi?f=/g/a/2007/08/23/violetblue.DTL

Bogart, Anne. *And Then, You Act: Making Art in an Unpredictable World.* London: Routledge, 2007.

Bolles, Robert C., ed. *The Hedonics of Taste*. Hillsdale, NJ: L. Erlbaum Associates, 1991.

Bone, P.F. and P.S. Ellen. "Scents in the Marketplace: Explaining a Function of Olfaction." *Journal of Retailing* 75, no. 2 (1999): 243–262.

Bradby, David and David Williams. *Director's Theatre*. London: Macmillan, 1988.

Brantley, Ben. "No Wonder He's Cranky; He's Covered in Condiments." *New York Times*, September 23, 2007. http://theater2.nytimes.com/2007/09/25/theater/reviews/25bran.html?n=Top/Reference/Times%20Topics/People/M/Moliere

Brecht, Stefan. *The Theatre of Visions: Robert Wilson*. London: Methuen, 1994.

Bryner, Jeanna. "Key to All Optical Illusions Discovered." *Live Science*, June 2, 2008. http://www.livescience.com

Bustamante, Nao and Coco Fusco. Program for Stuff. Performed at the ICA, London, November 1996.

Butterfield, Jan. *The Art of Light and Space*. New York: Abbevile Press, 1993.

Cage, John. *Silence: Lectures and Writings*. Middletown, CT: Wesleyan University Press, 1961.

Le Campenent. Program. Performed at the Industrial Palace, Prague, Czech Republic, June 27, 1999.

Caplan, Jeremy. "Scents and Sensibility." *Time*, October 16, 2006. http://www.time.com/time/magazine/article/0,9171,1543956,00.html

Carey, Benedict. "For the Brain, Remembering is like Reliving." *New York Times*, September 4, 2008. http://www.nytimes.com/2008/09/05/science/05brain.html

Carruthers, Peter. *Phenomenal Consciousness: A Naturalistic Theory*. Cambridge: Cambridge University Press, 2000.

Castellucci, Claudia, Romeo Castellucci, Chiara Guidi, Joe Kelleher, and Nicholas Ridout. *The Theatre of Socìetas Raffaello Sanzio*. London: Routledge, 2007.

Chen, Denise, and Jeanette Haviland-Jones. "Rapid Mood Change and Human Odors." *Physiology & Behavior* 68, no. 1–2 (1999): 241–250.

Chu, S., and J.J. Downes. "Long Live Proust: the Odour-cued Autobiographical Memory Bump." *Cognition* 75, no. 2 (2000): B41–B50.

Classen, Constance, ed., *The Book of Touch*. Oxford: Berg, 2005.

Classen, Constance, David Howes, and Anthony Synott. *Aroma: The Cultural History of Smell*. London: Routledge, 1994.

Cole, Susan Letzler. *Directors in Rehearsal: A Hidden World*. London: Routledge, 1992.

"Concert Plays Part in Brain Research." *Hartford Courant*, April 9, 2006.

Connor, Stephen. *Dumb Speak*. Oxford: Oxford University Press, 2000.

Cowan, Sarah. "MIT's 'Sensorium' Brings Sixth Dimension to Five Senses." *Tufts Daily*, November 2, 2006. http://www.tuftsdaily.com/2.5516/mit-s-sensorium-brings-sixth-dimension-to-five-senses-1.593276

Croggon, Alison. "MIAF: Voyage Festival diary #4," October 20, 2006. http://theatrenotes.blogspot.com/2006/10/miaf-voyage.html

Damasio, Antonio. *The Feeling of What Happens: Body and Emotion in the Making of Consciousness*. New York: Harcourt, 1999.

Davies, J.T., and F.H. Taylor. "The Role of Absorption and Molecular Morphology in Olfaction: The Calculation of Olfactory Thresholds." *Biology Bulletin* 117 (1959): 222–238.

Dayal, Geeta. "The End of the World as we Know it?" *Associated Press*. August 19, 2006. http://hamptonroads.com/node/141661

Di Benedetto, Stephen. "Sensing Bodies: A Phenomenological Approach to the Performance Sensorium." *Performance Research* 8, no. 2 (June 2003): 100–108.

———. "The Body as Fluid Dramaturgy: Live Art, Corporeality and Perception." *Journal of Dramatic Theory and Criticism* 16, no. 2 (2002): 4–15.

———. "Stumbling in the Dark: Robert Wilson's *H.G.*" *New Theatre Quarterly* 17, no. 3 (August 2001): 273–284.

Doidge, Norman. *The Brain that Changes Itself: Stories of Personal Triumph from the Frontiers of Brain Science*. New York: Penguin Books, 2007.

Drobnick, Jim, ed. *Aural Cultures*. Toronto: YYZBOOKS & Walter Phillips Gallery Editions, 2004.

Dyson, G.M. "The Scientific Basis of Odour." *Journal of the Society of Chemical Industry* 57 (1938): 647–651.

EMPAC. "Press Release for Dumb Type *Voyage*." http://www.empac.rpi.edu/events/opening/gala/dumbtype.html

Escoffier, Jeffrey, and Matthew Lore, eds. *Mark Morris' l'allegro, il penseroso ed il moderato: A Celebration*. New York: Marlowe & Company, 2001.

Elkins, James. *Pictures of the Body: Pain and Metamorphosis*. Stanford, CA: Stanford University Press, 1999.

Enright, Robert. "A Clean, Well-lighted Grace: An Interview with Robert Wilson." *Border Crossings: A Magazine of the Arts* 13 (1994): 14–22.

Etchells, Tim. *Certain Fragments*. London: Routledge, 2001.

Fabulous Beast Dance Theatre. Program for *Fragile*. Performed at the Project, Dublin, Ireland June 26, 2001.

Freeman, W.J. "The Physiology of Perception." *Scientific American* 264, no. 2 (1991): 78–85.

Frick, Thomas. "A Conversation with Robert Wilson." *Art New England* (June 1985): 4–20.

Field, Tiffany. *Touch*. Cambridge, MA: MIT Press, 2003.

Fiss, Cinthea. Complaint Letter. San Francisco: SRL Press Book, July 13, 1989.

Forced Entertainment, "Company Website." www.forced.co.uk.

Forde, Kathleen. *What Sound Does A Color Make?* New York: Independent Curators International, 2005.

Fusco, Coco. "The Other History of Intercultural Performance." *TDR* 38, no. 1 (1994): 143–167.

Garcia, Greg. "Get A Real Job," *My Name is Earl*. Season 2, NBC, May 3, 2007.

Gardner, Lyn. "Ghost Ward," *The Guardian*. May 4, 2001.

Garver, David. "Violent Theatricality: Displayed Enactments of Aggression and Pain." *Theatre Journal* 47, no. 1 (March 1995): 43–64.

Gazzaniga, Michael S. *Human: The Science Behind What Makes Us Unique*. New York: Ecco, 2008.

Glass, Philip. *Opera on the Beach*. New York: Faber and Faber, 1989.

Goelzer, Berenice, Colin H. Hansen, and Gustav A. Sehrndt, eds. *Occupational Exposure to Noise: Evaluation, Prevention and Control*. Bremerhaven: World Health Organization, 2001. http://www.who.int/occupational_health/publications/occupnoise/en/index.html

Goldstein, E. Bruce, Glyn Humphreys, Margaret Shiffrar, and William Yost, eds. *Blackwell Handbook of Perception*. London: Wiley-Blackwell, 2001.

Gombrich, E. H. *Image and the Eye: Further Studies in the Psychology of Pictorial Representation*. Oxford: Phaidon, 1982.

Gómez-Peña, Guillermo. *Temple of Confessions: Mexican Beasts and Living Santos*. New York: Powerhouse Books, 1996.

Goulish, Mathew, "Unwinding Kindergarten," *Performance Research* 7, no. 4 (2002): 92–107.

———. *39 Microlectures: In Proximity to Performance*. London: Routledge, 2000.

Grillo, Ioan. "In Mexico, a Theme Park for Border Crossers." *Time*, November 11, 2008. http://www.time.com/time/world/article/0,8599,1858151,00.html

Hall, Edward. *The Silent Language*. New York: Doubleday, 1990.

Hanna, Dorita, and Olav Harslof, eds. *Performance Design*. Copenhagen: Museum Tusculanum Press, 2008.

Heller, Morton A., and William Schiff, eds. *The Psychology of Touch*. Hillsdale, NJ: Lawrence Erlbaum, 1991.

Hodgson, Barbara. *The Sensualist*. San Francisco: Chronicle Books, 2001.

Holmberg, Arthur. *The Theatre of Robert Wilson*. Cambridge: Cambridge University Press, 1996.

Houde, Oliver, ed. *Dictionary of Cognitive Science: Neuroscience, Psychology, Artificial Intelligence, Linguistics, and Philosophy* New York: Psychology Press, 2004.

Howard, Pamela. *What is Scenography?* London: Routledge, 2002.

Hubel, D.H., and M.S. Livingstone. "Segregation of Form, Color, and Stereopsis in Primate Area." *Journal of Neuroscience* 18, no. 7 (1987): 3378–3415.

Huelsenbeck, Richard, ed. *Dada Almanach*. Translated by Malcolm Green. London: Atlas Press, 1998.

Instituto Português de Museus. *Guide: Museu National do Teatro*. Lisbon: Instituto Português de Museus, 2006.

Jacob, Pierre, and Marc Jeannerod. *Ways of Seeing: The Scope and Limits of Visual Cognition*. Oxford: Oxford University Press, 2003.

Jones, Caroline A., ed. *Sensorium: Embodied Experience, Technology, and Contemporary Art*. Cambridge, MA: MIT Press, 2006.

Jones, Robert. "Listen to the Pictures." *New York News*, November 21, 1976.

Josipovich, Gabriel. *Touch*. New Haven, CT: Yale University Press, 1996.

Julius, Anthony. *Transgressions*. London: Thames & Hudson, 2002.

Kahn, Douglas. *Noise, Water, Meat: A History of Sound in the Arts*. Cambridge, MA: MIT Press, 1999.

Kaiden, Lois, Stuart Morgan, and Nicholas Sinclair. *Franko B*. London: Blackdog, 1998.

Kandinsky, Wassily. *Concerning the Spiritual in Art*. New York: Dover, 1977.

Kantor, Taduesz. *A Journey Through Other Spaces*. Edited by Michael Kobialka. Berkeley: University of California Press, 1993.

Kay, Olivia Lory. "Review of Stuff," August 16, 1997. http://www.physicsroom. org.nz/2cents/stuff.htm

Keegan-Dolan, Michael. "Fabulous Beast." Email correspondence to author, 2001.

Kelleher, Joe, and Nicholas Ridout, eds. *Contemporary Theatres in Europe*. London: Routledge, 2006.

Keller, Max. *Light Fantastic*. Munich: Prestel, 1999.

Kisselgoff, Anna. "Dance: *Roaratorio* at Next Wave." *New York Times*, October 8, 1986. http://www.nytimes.com/1986/10/08/arts/dance-roaratorio-at-next-wave. html

Kobialka, Michal. "Historical Archives, Events and Facts: History Writing as Fragmentary Performance." *Performance Research* 7, no. 4 (December 2002): 3–11.

Konstelanetz, Richard, ed. *John Cage*. New York: Oraeger, 1970.

Kuhn, Gustav, and Michael F. Land. "There's More to Magic than Meets the Eye." *Current Biology* 16, no. 22 (2006): 950–951.

Kunsthaus-Bregenz. "KUB 05.08 Press release Janet Cardiff & George Bures Miller." http://www.kunsthaus-bregenz.at/presse_cariff_miller/PresseinformationE.pdf

Lacey, Henry C. *To Raise, Destroy and Create: The Poetry, Drama and Function of Imamu Amiri Baraka*. Albany, NY: Whitston, 1981.

Lanza, Marco, and Laura Facchi. *The Living Dead: Inside the Palermo Crypt*. London: Westone, 2000.

Leffingwell, John C. "Olfaction—Update #5." *Leffingwell Reports* 2, no. 1 (May 2002): 1–5. http://www.leffingwell.com/olfaction.htm

Lehrer, Jonah. *Proust was a Neuroscientist*. New York: Houghton Mifflin, 2007.

Lennon, J. John, and Malcolm Foley. *Dark Tourism: The Attraction of Death and Disaster*. London: Continuum, 2000.

Levitin, Daniel J. *This is Your Brain on Music: The Science of a Human Obsession*. New York: Plume, 2007.

Lunch, Lydia. *Paradoxia: A Predator's Diary*. London: Creation Books, 1997.

Macmillan, Malcolm. *An Odd Kind of Fame: Stories of Phineas Gage*. Cambridge, MA: MIT Press, 2002.

Malnic, B., J. Hirono, T. Sato, and L.B. Buck. "Combinatorial Receptor Codes for Odors." *Cell* 96, no. 5 (March 1999): 713–723. http://www.hhmi.org/news/buck.htm

Mandell, Mitch. "A Visit to Star Trek: The Experience at the Las Vegas Hilton." *Fabulous Travel*, August 6, 2007. http://www.fabuloustravel.com/usa/startrek/startrek.html

McConachie, Bruce. *Engaging Audiences: A Cognitive Approach to Spectating in the Theatre*. London: Palgrave Macmillan, 2008.

McConachie, Bruce, and H. Elizabeth Hart, eds. *Performance and Cognition: Theatre Studies and the Cognitive Turn*. London: Routledge, 2006.

McGinley, Paige. "Eavesdropping, Surveillance, and Sound." *PAJ* 82, 28, no.1 (2006): 52–57.

Miles, C., and R. Jenkins. "Recency and Suffix Effects with Immediate Recall of Olfactory Stimuli." *Memory* 8, no. 3 (2000): 195–205.

Moller, Aage R. *Auditory Physiology*. New York: Academic Press, 1983.

Moncrieff, R.W. *The Chemical Senses*. London: Leonard Hill, 1967.

Montagu, Ashley. *Touching: The Human Significance of the Skin*. New York: Harper & Row, 1986.

Morris, Gary. "Ai, Robot! Survival Research Laboratories: 10 Years of Robotic Mayhem on DVD." *Bright Lights Film Journal* 45 (2004). http://www.brightlightsfilm.com/45/srl.htm

Mydans, Seth. "Visit the Vietcong's World: Americans Welcome." *New York Times*, July 7, 1999. http://www.nytimes.com/1999/07/07/world/cu-chi-journal-visit-the-vietcong-s-world-americans-welcome.html

Nadeau, Maurice. *The History of Surrealism*. Translated by Richard Howard. New York: Pelican 1973.

Nash, A. Leo. *Burning Man: Art in the Desert*. New York: Abrams, 2007.

Neergaard, Lauran. "You're Led by your Nose—and that's Good." *Miami Herald*, March 24, 2008.

"New Plays: *Dionysus in '69*," *Time*, June 28, 1968. http://www.time.com/time/magazine/article/0,9171,841343,00.html

Noë, Alva. *Action in Perception*. Cambridge, MA: MIT Press, 2004.

———. *Out of Our Heads: Why you Are not your Brain, and Other Lessons from the Biology of Consciousness*. New York: Hill and Wang, 2009.

Nohain, Jean, and F. Caradec. *Le Petomane: 1857–1945*. New York: Dorset Press, 1993.

Nuke. "Smell-O-Vision is Back." Blog. http://www.frikafrax.com/mnuke/blog2/category/media-entertainment/

Nykvist, Sven, Bernardo Bertolucci, Marcello Mastoianni, and the Association of European Cinematographers. *Making Pictures: A Century of European Cinematography*. New York: Harry N. Abrams, 2003.

O'Brien, Richard. *The Rocky Horror Picture Show*. Directed by Jim Sharman. Twentieth Century-Fox, 1975.

Ohloff, G. *Scent and Fragrances*. Berlin: Springer-Verlag, 1994.

Paterson, Mark. *The Senses of Touch: Haptics, Affects and Technology*. Oxford: Berg, 2007.

Pescovitz, David. "Mark Pauline's Machine Mayham." *Make* 7 (2006): 28–35.

Pines, Maya, ed. *Seeing, Hearing, and Smelling the World: New Findings Help Scientists Make Sense of our Senses*. Chevy Chase, MD: Howard Hughes Medical Institute, 1995.

Pinker, Steven. *How the Mind Works*. New York: Penguin Press, 1997.

Public Art Fund. "Press Release, Janet Cardiff: *Her Long Black Hair*." http://www.publicartfund.org/pafweb/projects/04/cardiff_J_release_04.pdf

Quadri, Franco, Franco Bertoni, and Robert Stearns. *Robert Wilson*. New York: Rizzoli, 1998.

Ramachandran, V.S., and Sandra Blakeslee. *Phantoms in the Brain: Probing the Mysteries of the Human Mind*. New York: Quill, 1998.

Ratzinger, Joseph. *The Spirit of the Liturgy*. Translated by John Saward. San Francisco: Ignatius Press, 2000.

In the Realm of the Senses. Directed by Nagisa Oshima. Argos Films, 1976.

Reason, Matthew. "Writing the Olfactory in the Live Performance Review." *Performance Research* 8, no. 3 (2003): 73–84.

Reinelt, Janelle. *Crucibles of Crisis: Performing Social Change*. Ann Arbor: University of Michigan Press, 1996.

Reingold, Jennifer. "Weird Science." *Fast Company* (May 2006): 40–49.

Roberts, David, ed. *Signals and Perception: The Fundamentals of Human Sensation*. London: Palgrave Macmillan, 2002.

Robles-De-La-Torre, Gabriel. "The Importance of the Sense of Touch in Virtual and Real Environments." *IEEE MultiMedia* (July–September 2006): 24–30.

Ruch, Allen B. "Joyce—Music John Cage's *Roaratorio.*" http://www.themodernword.com/joyce/music/cage_roaratorio.html

Russolo, Luigi. *The Art of Noise*. Translated by Robert Filliou. New York: Something Else Press, 1967.

Sacks, Oliver. *The Man Who Mistook His Wife for A Hat*. London: Duckworth, 1987.

Sacs, Daniel. Review of "Festival D'Avignon, France 4–26 July 2008." *Theatre Journal* 61, no. 1 (2009): 117.

Scheie, Timothy. Review of *Voyage au bout de la nuit*, Concerto after Louis-Ferdinand Céline by Socìetas Raffaello Sanzio, Avignon (July 16, 1999). *Theatre Journal* 52, no. 1(2000): 128–129.

Schillinger, Liesl. "Odorama." *New York Times*, February 23, 2003.

Schulz, Bernd. *Resonanzen: Aspekte der Klangkunst = Resonances: Aspects of Sound Art*. Heidelberg: Kehrer, 2002.

Schumacher, Claude, ed. *Naturalism and Symbolism in European Theatre, 1850–1918*. Cambridge: Cambridge University Press, 1996.

Shepherd-Barr, Kristen. "*Mise en scent*: The Theatre d'Art's Cantiques and the Use of Smell as a Theatrical Device." *Theatre Research International* 24, no. 2 (Summer 1999): 152–159.

Simmer, Bill. "Robert Wilson and Therapy." *The Drama Review* 20 (1976): 99–110.

"Smell-O-Vision." University of Florida Special Collections. www.uflib.ufl.edu/SPEC/belknap/exhibit2002/smell.htm

Smith, Martin, and Patrick Kiger. "The Lingering Reek of Smell-O-Vision." *West Los Angeles Times*, February 5, 2006.

Society for Neuroscience. *Brain Facts: A Primer on the Brain and Nervous System*. Washington, DC: Society for Neuroscience, 2002.

Spinrad, Paul. *The RE/Search Guide to Bodily Fluids*. San Francisco: RE/Search Publications, 1994.

Stankievech, Charles. "From Stethoscopes to Headphones: An Acoustic Spatialization of Subjectivity." *Leonardo Music Journal* 17 (2007): 55–59.

"Star Trek: The Experience," www.vegas4visitors.com/attractions/detail/startrek.html

Steenson, Molly. "What is Burning Man?" http://www.burningman.com/whatis-burningman/about_burningman/experience.html

Sterne, Jonathan. *The Audible Past: Cultural Origins of Sound Reproduction.* Durham, NC: Duke University Press, 2003.

Stern, K., and M.K. McClintock. "Regulation of Ovulation by Human Phero-mones." *Nature* 392, no. 6672 (1998): 177–179.

Storr, Robert. *Tony Smith: Architect, Painter, Sculptor.* New York: MOMA, 1998.

Süskind, Patrick. *Perfume: The Story of a Murderer.* Translated by John E. Woods. New York: Vintage International, 2001.

The Taste Science Laboratory, Division of Nutritional Sciences, Cornell University. "Taste Science." www.tastescience.com

Taussig, Michael. *The Nervous System.* New York: Routledge, 1992.

Taylor, Diana. "A Savage Performance: Guillermo Gómez-Peña and Coco Fusco's *Couple in the Cage.*" *TDR* 42, no. 2 (1998): 160–175.

Thomas, Teresa. "The Medium and the message: Eyes and Ears Understand Differ-ently, Carnegie Mellon Scientists Report in the *Journal Human Brain Mapping.*" *EurekAlert!* http://eurekalert.org/pub_releases/2001–08/cmu-tma081401.php

Turin, Luca. "A Spectroscopic Mechanism for Primary Olfactory Reception." *Chemical Senses* 21 (1996): 773–791.

Underwood, Geoffrey, ed. *Oxford Guide to the Mind.* Oxford: Oxford University Press, 2001.

Valentini, Valentia, and Bonnie Marranca. "The Universal: The Simplest Place Pos-sible." *PAJ* 77 (2004): 16–25.

Vial, Veronique. '*O*': *Cirque du Soleil at Bellagio.* New York: Power House Books, 2001.

Wang, L., V.E. Walker, H. Sardi, C. Fraser, and T.J.C. Jacob. "The Correlation between Physiological and Psychological Responses to Odour Stimulation in Human Subjects." *Clinical Neurophysiology* 113 (2002): 542–551.

Watson, Gray. "Franko B: Interview." June 13, 2000. http://www.ainexus.com/franko/interview.htm

Weatherston, Rosemary. Performance Review of Nao Bustamante and Coco Fus-co's *Stuff. Theatre Journal* (December 1997): 516–518.

Wexler, Bruce E. *Brain and Culture: Nuerobiology, Ideology, and Social Change.* Cambridge MA: MIT Press, 2006.

Wikia Entertainment. "The Star Trek Experience." http://www.memoryalpha.org/en/wiki/Star_Trek:_The_Experience

Williams, Gregory. "The Voice of Authority." *PAJ* 59, 20, no. 2 (1998): 62–67.

Williams, Jim. Review of *HEY GIRL!* by Romeo Castellucci and Socìetas Raffa-ello Sanzio. *Theatre Journal* 60, no. 4 (2008): 667.

Wilson, Robert. "Lohengrin Drawings." http://robertwilson.com/studio/lohen-grin/lohengrin1.htm

Winston, Joe. *Burning Man Festival.* DVD. Ow.MyEye Productions, 2001.

X-Men. Directed by Bryan Singer. Twentieth-Century Fox, 2000.

Zhao, H., L. Ivic, J.M. Otaki, M. Hashimoto, K. Mikoshiba, and S. Firestein. "Functional Expression of a Mammalian Odorant Receptor." *Science* 279 (1998): 237–241.

Zigmond, Michael J., Floyd E. Bloom, Story C. Landis, James L. Roberts, and Larry R. Squire, eds. *Fundamental Neuroscience.* San Diego: Academic Press, 1999.

Index